China's Normative Power in Cyberspace

The book delves into China's extension of its influence over global digital standards and governance.

The author introduces the concept of normative power adapted for the digital domain and constructs a multi-level theory of normative diffusion, disaggregating mechanisms operating at bilateral, regional and international levels. The book examines bilateral dynamics through eight cases: Vietnam, Chile, Malaysia, Zambia, Egypt, Kazakhstan, the Philippines and Laos. At the regional level, it analyses how China navigates and shapes regional digital orders through the SCO, RCEP, BRICS and ASEAN. Regarding the international arena, the book traces China's strategies across two decades of engagement with the UN system and the ITU. In addition, it outlines its implications for digital governance and the future of global digital ordering. The book argues that Chinese normative power in cyberspace is real but bounded, and it operates not as unilateral export but as a relational push-and-pull between Beijing and recipient states that actively seek, filter, adapt and resist what China offers.

This book will appeal to academics and students studying international law, comparative politics, cybersecurity and China studies.

Maria Adele Carrai is Associate Professor from the Department of Politics and International Relations and the Oxford School of Global and Area Studies (OSGA) at the University of Oxford and a Fellow of St Cross College. She previously served as Assistant Professor of Global China Studies at NYU Shanghai and taught as an adjunct at NYU School of Law. She has been Associate at the Harvard University Asia Center since 2021 and Adjunct Associate Research Scholar at Columbia University's Weatherhead East Asian Institute since 2019.

China's Normative Power in Cyberspace

The Contested Making of Global Digital Governance

Maria Adele Carrai

Routledge
Taylor & Francis Group
LONDON AND NEW YORK

First published 2027
by Routledge
4 Park Square, Milton Park, Abingdon, Oxon OX14 4RN

and by Routledge
605 Third Avenue, New York, NY 10158

Routledge is an imprint of the Taylor & Francis Group, an informa business

British Library Cataloguing in Publication Data
A catalogue record for this book is available from the British Library

Library of Congress Cataloging in Publication Data

Names: Carrai, Maria Adele author
Title: China's normative power in cyberspace : the contested making of global digital governance / Maria Adele Carrai.
Description: Abingdon, Oxon [UK] ; New York, NY : Routledge, 2026. | Includes bibliographical references and index.
Identifiers: LCCN 2026027653 (print) | LCCN 2026027654 (ebook) | ISBN 9781041140566 hardback | ISBN 9781041406082 paperback | ISBN 9781042023738 ebook
Subjects: LCSH: Digital media–Law and legislation–China | Internet–Law and legislation–China | Computer networks–Law and legislation–China | Digital media–Law and legislation | Internet–Law and legislation
Classification: LCC KNQ3512.5 .C37 2026 (print) | LCC KNQ3512.5 (ebook)
LC record available at https://lccn.loc.gov/2026027653
LC ebook record available at https://lccn.loc.gov/2026027654

ISBN: 978-1-041-14056-6 (hbk)
ISBN: 978-1-041-40608-2 (pbk)
ISBN: 978-1-042-02373-8 (ebk)

DOI: 10.4324/9781042023738

Typeset in Times New Roman
by Deanta Global Publishing Services, Chennai, India

Contents

List of figures *vi*
List of tables *vii*

Introduction 1

1 What Is ‘Chinese’ about China’s Digital Norms? 16

2 How China’s Digital Norms Circulate: A Multi-Level Theory of Digital Normative Power 40

3 Mechanisms in Practice: Mapping Chinese Normative Power across Bilateral Cases 69

4 Normative Power at the Regional Level: Mechanisms, Institutions and the Diffusion of China’s Digital Governance Norms 109

5 The International Arena: Contestation, Coalition and the Normative Transformation of Global Digital Governance 131

Conclusion 171

Appendix *181*
Index *194*

Figures

2.1 Push and pull mechanisms at the bilateral level 48
2.2 Push and pull mechanisms at the regional level 53
2.3 Push and pull dynamics at the international level 56

Tables

1.1 Comparing China, the EU and the US on Digital Governance 22
1.2 China's Foundational Data Governance Laws – Comparative Overview 24
3.1 Lexical similarity scores against China's three foundational laws (selected cases) 73
3.2 Mechanism intensity and lexical signal across all three Chinese reference instruments 100

Introduction

In 2018, Vietnam enacted a cybersecurity law that bore unmistakable resemblance to China's own 2017 Cybersecurity Law, mandating data localisation, imposing surveillance obligations on platforms and centralising state authority over digital infrastructure (Bui and Lee, 2022; Law on Cyber Security, 2018; Jones Day, 2018). A Chinese training seminar for Vietnamese public security officials in April 2017, held closely to when China's Cybersecurity Law took effect, was followed within a year by the submission of a Vietnamese draft law closely modelled on it (Freedom House, 2018; The Vietnamese, 2024). The architects of that law, including former Minister of Public Security and then-President Tran Dai Quang, had publicly embraced the language of 'cyber sovereignty' and treated Xi Jinping's speeches on internet governance as authoritative (Article 19, 2025). The Diplomat described the outcome bluntly as Vietnam's internet control 'following in China's footsteps' (Sherman, 2019; SCMP, 2019). The story seems to offer a clean instance of what scholars and journalists have begun calling the export of digital authoritarianism: a powerful state diffusing its governance model outward, reshaping the digital orders of weaker states in its own image. Freedom House's 2018 report documented how the seminar directly preceded the passage of Vietnam's law and observed similar sequences in Uganda and Tanzania, where 'restrictive media and cybersecurity laws closely followed Chinese engagement' (Freedom House, 2018; CNAS, 2023). Cambodia has since moved furthest along this path, issuing a 2021 sub-decree authorising a National Internet Gateway widely characterised by outside observers as modelled on China's Great Firewall, though implementation has stalled since 2022. Tanzania's Deputy Minister for Communication publicly praised the firewall model at an event co-sponsored by the Cyberspace Administration of China; Zimbabwe enacted a cybersecurity law in 2021 that critics characterised as Chinese-inspired, following a strategic partnership with the Chinese facial-recognition firm CloudWalk (Al Jazeera, 2024; Article 19, 2024; Freedom House, 2018; CNAS, 2023).

This book argues that the export reading of China's normative influence is incomplete in two important ways. The first is comparative. Vietnam is not the modal case. Across the eight-country corpus examined in this book, dense Chinese engagement and statutory convergence co-occur rarely, and the cases that complicate the picture do so in opposite directions. Chile, distant from Beijing geographically and ideologically, shows substantial textual borrowing without

DOI: 10.4324/9781042023738-1

formal coordination. Malaysia and Zambia show some of the densest Chinese engagement on every supply-side channel and produce statutes that score below the corpus baseline for textual similarity to the Chinese reference instruments. Chinese influence is real, but it is heterogeneous in mechanism, uneven in outcome and substantially shaped by recipient configurations that the metaphor of 'export' obscures. Local governments often actively seek out Chinese technology and governance frameworks to serve purposes they have already defined for themselves, with Chinese firms and officials proving willing partners rather than architects.

The second incompleteness is conceptual. The literature has tended to collapse together two analytically distinct questions. Is the concern that China is reshaping digital governance internationally, through the UN system, the ITU and the negotiation of binding multilateral instruments? Or is it that China is reshaping digital governance regionally and bilaterally, through statute-by-statute legal borrowing, infrastructure-linked technology transfer and direct training of officials in particular states? The two scales of influence operate through different mechanisms, are constrained by different recipient conditions and produce different kinds of evidence. A Chinese-authored treaty article that survives into the text of a UN convention is a different object from a data-localisation provision that recurs across statutes in Belt and Road economies. Nor is scale the only axis along which the literature blurs distinctions. Accounts of Chinese digital influence routinely run together the diffusion of norms with the export of infrastructure, as though the laying of fibre-optic cable and the adoption of sovereignty-first legal vocabulary were a single phenomenon rather than causally related but separable processes. They likewise treat 'cyber' as an undifferentiated domain, when cybersecurity, cybercrime, data governance and internet governance each have their own institutional venues, negotiating dynamics and patterns of alignment, and Chinese influence varies markedly across them. Conflating them produces both overstatement and understatement of what Beijing has actually achieved.

This book's argument is that Chinese normative influence operates simultaneously at three levels, and that the relationship between them is the object requiring explanation. Internationally, through the UN's cybersecurity working groups, the 2024 Convention against Cybercrime and the 2024 Global Digital Compact, China has worked to shift the foundational vocabulary of global internet governance. Regionally, through ASEAN, the Shanghai Cooperation Organisation and BRICS, Chinese preferences enter multilateral arenas where they are filtered through the priorities of groupings that have their own interests. Bilaterally, infrastructure financing, technology exports and training programmes embed Chinese norms in recipient digital architectures, though only in some cases do these inputs translate into convergent legal text. The three levels are analytically distinct, but they reinforce each other. International recognition of sovereignty-first vocabulary makes regional and bilateral invocations easier to defend; the accumulation of bilateral cases makes international claims about the preferences of 'the broader community' more credible at the negotiating table. What looks at any single level like a contingent phenomenon appears, across all three, to be part of something more systematic, a mutually reinforcing ensemble that constitutes a form of normative power, but one whose surface effects are configurational rather than uniform.

1. China as a Cyber Power: Normative Ambition and Material Fact

When Xi Jinping convened the inaugural meeting of the CCP's high-level cyber leading group in February 2014 and called for 'building China into a strong cyber power' (wangluo qiangguo, 网络强国), the phrase registered as aspiration. A decade later, it reads as description. China is already a cyber power, not merely in the sense of having formidable offensive and defensive capabilities, but in that it exercises structural influence over the physical, institutional and normative architecture of global cyberspace simultaneously (Segal, 2018; Bradford, 2023). This requires a prior definitional move. Cyberspace is not simply 'the internet' but a layered system composed of at least three interdependent strata: a physical layer of cables, servers, satellites and devices that carry data; a logical layer of protocols, standards and software that organise how that data travels and is processed; and a content and governance layer of laws, platforms, norms and institutions that shape what can be said, by whom, subject to whose authority (DeNardis, 2014). Each layer offers distinct points of leverage, and China's influence now operates across all three. Control of the physical layer helps reshape what is possible at the normative and standard layers, although the two layers can be separable.

China substantiates its normative ambition with a material digital footprint that would have been unimaginable when Xi made his 2014 speech. It has the world's largest internet user base, over 1.1 billion users as of early 2025, representing roughly 78.6 per cent of the population, supported by some 4.19 million 5G base stations. Huawei had secured an estimated 50 per cent of commercial 5G contracts outside China by the end of 2023 (IPVM, 2024). Chinese firms (HMN Tech, Huawei Marine and others) are significant players in the global submarine cable market, with the SAIL cable connecting Cameroon and Brazil reshaping data traffic flows between Africa and South America. In surveillance and smart-city technology, Hikvision, Dahua and Huawei have deployed integrated systems in over 1,000 cities across more than 100 countries, combining high-definition cameras, facial recognition and centralised data platforms. Notable deployments include systems in Belgrade, Nairobi, Lahore and Quito. China's BeiDou Navigation Satellite System now provides services integral to critical infrastructure in over half the world's countries. TikTok counts over 1.5 billion monthly active users worldwide (DataReportal, 2024); Xiaomi, Oppo and Transsion Group account for nearly 40 per cent of global smartphone market share (Canalys, 2023); and DJI controls an estimated 70 to 80 per cent of the global civilian drone market.

This comprehensive digital footprint, from seabed cables to satellite constellations, surveillance platforms to consumer devices, is frequently grouped under the label Digital Silk Road, conceived as the digital component of the 2013 Belt and Road Initiative. While the term 'Digital Silk Road' features in official rhetoric, Beijing has never promulgated it as a single, codified master plan with its own dedicated institutional framework. Instead, the label serves as an evolving umbrella term for a heterogeneous range of commercial, technological, and diplomatic activities—from seabed cables to satellite constellations—that began largely as market-driven expansions by firms like Huawei and ZTE, before being progressively absorbed into a broader state-strategic agenda (Triolo, in Nouwens, 2023).

The normative dimension of this footprint requires separate theoretical treatment. Chapter 2 develops the concept of normative power in full, drawing on and adapting Manners' (2002) formulation. The core claim, previewed here, is that China's influence in cyberspace is not primarily about compulsion or attraction but about shaping what governance instruments, institutional designs and regulatory vocabularies are treated as normal, workable, and legitimate in the choices of other actors. The governance instruments that constitute China's digital regulatory architecture, including data classification systems, localisation requirements, cybersecurity review mechanisms and platform accountability rules, can be, in their individual components, largely separable from the political context in which they were developed. A government that wants to assert greater control over data flows for domestic reasons can adopt elements of China's governance toolkit without endorsing China's political system. The instruments are modular, and it is that modularity that helps make them portable, and that underlies the push and pull dynamics examined in the rest of the book.

Beijing codified its preferred ordering principles through a cascading series of domestic laws: the Cybersecurity Law (2016, effective 2017), the Data Security Law (2021), and the Personal Information Protection Law (2021) (Creemers, 2017; Liu, 2021). Its International Strategy of Cooperation on Cyberspace (2017) projected these principles outward under the banner of 'cyber sovereignty', first fully articulated at the 2015 World Internet Conference in Wuzhen: 'respecting each country's right to choose its own internet development path, its own internet management model, and its own public policies on the internet' (China MFA, 2017). Chapter 1 maps this architecture in detail.

2. Competing Ordering Models: Beyond the US–China Binary

The significance of China's normative ambition cannot be assessed against a simple bilateral backdrop. Framing global cyber governance as a US–China or West-China contest is analytically reductive. The actual landscape of competing ordering models is more crowded than that, and the terms of competition do not map neatly onto democratic versus authoritarian lines (Pohle and Thiel, 2020; Aaronson and Leblond, 2018). At least four partially overlapping models warrant initial sketching here: the US, Chinese, EU, Russian, and emerging-economy approaches.

The United States has historically championed an open, market-driven internet governed through multistakeholder institutions such as ICANN and the Internet Engineering Task Force, with relatively light-touch state involvement. This approach emerged from the internet's origins in American academic and military circles and from a Silicon Valley libertarian ethos (Turner, 2006; Abbate, 1999), and it was formally articulated in Secretary of State Hillary Clinton's 2010 Internet Freedom speech, which framed an uncensored web as essential for democracy and human rights (Clinton, 2010). Yet the US model is not purely principled. It has also served the commercial interests of American platform companies and the intelligence-gathering interests of American agencies, a tension that Edward Snowden's 2013 revelations made globally visible, weakening US claims to normative leadership among precisely those Global South governments whose support the model needed (Pohle and Thiel, 2020; ECDPM, 2023).

Beijing conceptualises cyberspace as a sovereign domain subject to state control, an extension of the Party-state's territorial and political authority. This cyber sovereignty doctrine has been institutionalised through the layered legislation described above, which together place data, networks and digital infrastructure firmly under the state's regulatory reach. The National Intelligence Law's compulsion clause, which requires Chinese citizens, organisations and companies to support, cooperate with and collaborate in national intelligence work, has generated concern that state demands may extend to Chinese companies operating abroad. The provision creates a legal risk relevant to foreign governments' assessments, but it does not establish that overseas infrastructure automatically gives Chinese authorities access to data.

The European Union has occupied a distinct third position, seeking to build what it calls 'digital sovereignty' through regulation rather than through either market freedom or state control (European Commission, 2020). The General Data Protection Regulation, which applies extraterritorially to any entity processing data of EU residents, has become the most globally consequential data governance instrument of the past decade, a form of regulatory power that Bradford (2020) terms the Brussels Effect: the capacity of the EU's large internal market to pull global standards toward its own requirements. The EU model is rights-centred rather than state-centred; its concern is protecting individuals from both corporate surveillance and government overreach, extended most recently through the Digital Services Act. Yet the EU model is internally contested. European data protection law is framed as the world's most rights-protective regime, but national security remains a reserved competence of the member states under Article 4(2) TEU, and member states rely extensively on national-security exceptions that sit uneasily with EU fundamental rights standards. The Court of Justice of the European Union has repeatedly intervened, invalidating both EU-level adequacy decisions and member-state surveillance regimes as incompatible with the Charter of Fundamental Rights. The EU's rhetorical positioning emphasises distance from the United States, but its operational record, including the EU–US Trade and Technology Council and the 2023 EU–US Data Privacy Framework, shows transatlantic coordination, particularly vis-à-vis China. The EU's 'digital sovereignty' project itself bundles two distinct programmes: an individual-rights agenda embodied in the GDPR and the Digital Services Act, and an industrial and technological autonomy agenda embodied in the Digital Markets Act, the Chips Act and initiatives such as Gaia-X. These do not always point in the same direction, which limits the EU's capacity to project a fully coherent alternative to either the American or the Chinese model (Pohle and Thiel, 2020).

Russia shares with Beijing an insistence on state sovereignty over cyberspace and treats information content, not merely infrastructure, as a security domain subject to state control. The Russian concept of 'information security' (informatsionnaya bezopasnost') explicitly encompasses disinformation, foreign political influence and content deemed threatening to regime stability (McKune and Ahmed, 2018). But Russia's digital economy is far smaller than China's, its firms have no equivalent global reach, and its model is less an export offer than a defensive posture, reinforced by its 2019 sovereign internet law and its consistent blocking of Western human rights language in the UN's GGE and OEWG processes (Freedom House, 2023; Segal, 2018). Russia and China share tactical interests at multilateral venues without sharing a fully coherent joint model. Their interests diverge in key respects, including over Chinese dominance of digital infrastructure in Central Asia (Jancic et al., 2023) and over Russia's preference for confrontational diplomacy in UN forums where China has favoured patient embedding of sovereignty-aligned language. Chapter 5 traces this divergence empirically through the September 2024 Global Digital Compact, where Russia introduced an amendment that China declined to support.

A further tier of complexity is added by the digital middle powers and the Global South more broadly (Pannier, 2023). India occupies a significant and ambiguous position. As a member of the Quad and a democracy with deep ties to the US technology ecosystem, it nominally supports open internet principles; but it has also enacted data localisation requirements, blocked TikTok and hundreds of Chinese apps since 2020, and pursued a Digital India framework that reserves significant state authority over data governance. India participates in both BRICS and the Quad, simultaneously bridging and exploiting these fault lines (IJEDR, 2025). Brazil has championed a distinctive multistakeholder model: the 2014 Marco Civil da Internet is a pioneering rights-based framework, and Brazil has asserted sovereignty claims over its own data infrastructure while hosting the NETmundial governance forum launched in response to the Snowden revelations (Pohle and Thiel, 2020). Indonesia has enacted its own data protection law while remaining formally non-aligned. African states, through the African Union's Malabo Convention on data protection and cybersecurity, have sought a regional framework that asserts collective digital sovereignty without endorsing any single great-power model, though the practical traction of the AU framework remains limited relative to the bilateral digital deals its member states are signing (Jili, 2021; Africa China Reporting Project, 2021).

What this landscape reveals is that the governance competition is not a binary contest between an 'open internet' and a 'closed internet' but a multipolar contest among at least four partially overlapping ordering models (the US market-driven model, the EU rights-centred regulatory model, the Sino-Russian state sovereignty model, and the family of emerging-economy frameworks that combine elements of several while asserting distinctive national interests, ECDPM, 2023; Jancic et al., 2023). As Creemers (2020) observes, what began as a discourse about internet governance has become a discourse about the fundamental organisation of political economy in the digital age, about who controls the flows of data that now underwrite economic value, political power and social life simultaneously. Yet this contest is neither singular nor neatly polarized; it is plural, overlapping, and shaped by multiple competing visions of digital order.

China's normative power operates within and upon this multipolar contest. China is not trying to impose a unified model on an otherwise unified world. It is trying to shift the centre of gravity of an already fragmented normative field, by building coalitions, by embedding its technical standards in global infrastructure, by occupying leadership positions in multilateral bodies and by offering a legitimating vocabulary that resonates with the anti-hegemonic instincts of states that would never describe themselves as sharing Beijing's political values. The success of this strategy cannot be measured by counting the number of states that have adopted Chinese-style model of cyber sovereignty. It must be assessed by examining how far sovereignty-first principles have entered the mainstream of global digital governance, for example by how they have become accepted reference points in treaty law, standards processes, other domestic legislation and regional frameworks.

3. Prevailing Discourses and Their Limits

The dominant strand portrays Beijing as a deliberate revisionist power intent on exporting authoritarian governance and undermining the liberal digital order. Feldstein's (2019) Carnegie survey of AI surveillance exports documents the global spread of Chinese surveillance systems with empirical precision, mapping deployments across over seventy countries and establishing a clear link between Chinese technology transfers and governments with poor human rights records; Polyakova and Meserole (2019) frame China and Russia as complementary vectors of 'digital authoritarianism' whose tools and governance models furnish authoritarian states worldwide with instruments of repression; Walker (2021), writing in Foreign Affairs, argues that China offers not merely inspiration but supplies 'the tools, training, and resources' through which authoritarian leaders insulate themselves from democratic pressure. The empirical record assembled in Chapters 3–5 revises this reading at three specific points. The Kazakhstan case (Chapter 3) shows a recipient state adopting a Chinese-modelled data-localisation rule and applying it against Russian platforms – incompatible with the 'Sino-Russian authoritarian bloc' thesis that organises much of this strand. The Hanoi Convention negotiations (Chapter 5) show China actively dropping the most explicitly authoritarian content of its earlier proposals – the 'false information' clause specifically – to secure consensus, and voting with the no-action motion against the Russian amendment A/79/L.3 at the Summit of the Future. The 79-country coalition that supported the original 2019 cybercrime resolution included democratic developing states whose support reflected representational grievance against Western-led governance institutions, not authoritarian alignment with Beijing. The digital authoritarianism literature is right that Chinese authoritarian governance instruments travel; but they share a tendency to treat diffusion as relatively frictionless, as if Beijing's technologies and norms travel to recipient states much as they leave China's borders. The demand side of the equation, the question of why specific states at specific moments find Chinese templates attractive, useful or merely convenient, receives far less attention than the supply side. The result is a literature better at documenting the fact of Chinese influence than at explaining its uneven distribution and variable effects.

A second strand engages China's normative ambitions more directly. Erie and Streinz (2021) introduce the concept of the Beijing Effect, building on Bradford's (2020) Brussels Effect, to explain China's growing influence over transnational data governance. Rather than describing this influence simply as the export of Chinese rules through market size and economic leverage, they identify a combination of push and pull factors: Chinese firms provide digital infrastructure, participate in standard-setting, and promote particular regulatory practices, while governments in emerging economies may actively embrace data sovereignty and Chinese-supported models of digital development. This is an important conceptual contribution, and this book builds on it. Yet although the Beijing Effect framework recognises recipient-state demand, domestic mediation, and the possibility of resistance or hybridisation, it does not fully develop a systematic comparative account of why these processes produce different outcomes across countries. Why do some states adopt Chinese-style frameworks while others resist or hybridise them? What explains why Vietnam's cybersecurity law closely mirrors China's, while Indonesia's data protection law draws heavily on the GDPR? Why does Cambodia model its National Internet Gateway on China's Great Firewall, while the Philippines retreats from proposed data-localisation measures under industry pressure? The framework identifies several relevant mechanisms, but the conditions of receptivity, the configuration of domestic political coalitions, and the influence of competing norm entrepreneurs remain insufficiently specified. This book therefore extends rather than corrects the Beijing Effect by asking why China's capacity to shape regulatory practice translates into influence unevenly and by mapping the mechanisms through which recipient states align with, adapt, hybridise, or resist Chinese governance preferences.

A related limitation concerns the level of abstraction at which much of the existing scholarship operates. Cheney (2019) argues that Beijing seeks to leverage the Digital Silk Road to reshape the international order by preserving economic openness while promoting a more illiberal political environment, including through the international diffusion of digital authoritarian practices. Hulvey demonstrates that China's sovereignty-centred framing has attracted support within the ITU, including from states and coalitions that have taken up and reformulated elements of Beijing's position, while Segal (2018) and Rito (2024) examine China's broader advocacy of state-centred internet governance through the ITU and the United Nations. Taken together, these studies illuminate both the strategic objectives of Chinese engagement and its capacity to mobilise support in particular multilateral settings (Segal, 2018; Rito, 2024). But by focusing substantially, though not exclusively, on state-level intentions, international framing contests, and institutional outcomes, they risk missing the messy, localised, and often contradictory processes through which norms actually take root—or fail to. Hulvey, in particular, does investigate variation in international support, but her principal empirical outcome remains multilateral alignment and voting rather than downstream domestic implementation. A government may endorse sovereignty-centred language or Chinese-supported positions at the ITU while declining to implement Chinese-style data localisation domestically; it may accept Chinese infrastructure financing while insisting on European-derived privacy protections in consumer or data-protection law. The disjuncture between the formal multilateral record and practical governance outcomes is analytically important, and it is difficult to capture when institutional votes and declared positions are treated as evidence of broader regulatory convergence.

The Digital Silk Road literature also intersects with debates on digital imperialism and digital colonialism (Gajjala and Birzescu, 2011; Madianou, 2019), though in ways that require specification. Gajjala and Birzescu examine how online social and financial networks can reproduce imperial and neoliberal relations through commodified forms of participation, while the broader digital-colonialism literature foregrounds asymmetries generated through platform ownership, data extraction, technological mediation, and dependence on infrastructures controlled largely by corporations based in dominant economies.

The Digital Silk Road's significance is not wholly separate from these commercial dynamics, but it places particular emphasis on state-backed infrastructural and regulatory projection: financing, telecommunications networks, data centres, vendor ecosystems, training programmes, and governance templates that can configure the defaults of digital development in recipient states while their regulatory systems are still evolving.

The colonialism frame captures something real about the power asymmetries involved; however, accounts centred on unilateral external imposition or extraction are less well equipped to explain the purposive agency of recipient-state governments. Their interests in using Chinese infrastructure, technology, and regulatory knowledge to expand administrative capacity, consolidate domestic control, or pursue geopolitical autonomy may be as significant as pressure emanating from Beijing. The Kazakhstan and Egypt cases in Chapter 3 show recipient states using Chinese governance templates to consolidate domestic state authority and manage their own regional positioning, including in relation to competing major powers—a dynamic that complicates, rather than necessarily invalidates, colonialism or dependency interpretations. Colonial relationships have historically involved local intermediaries and elite collaboration; recipient-state agency alone therefore does not disprove a colonialism framework. What these cases challenge more directly is a unidirectional account in which local governments appear only as passive objects of Chinese projection. The recipient state's interest in using Chinese infrastructure for its own governance objectives is often as significant as any pressure emanating from Beijing, and this is empirically demonstrable in the cases the book examines, not merely a theoretical caveat. More broadly, the field has often relied on binary frameworks—democratic versus authoritarian, open versus closed, or Brussels versus Beijing—that capture genuine tensions but obscure the patterned variation that this book's evidentiary apparatus is designed to register. The book's substantive claim is not that these distinctions are meaningless, but that they are insufficient to describe the combinations and intermediate outcomes found in practice. The relevant variation in Chinese normative power cannot be explained solely by the volume of Chinese engagement, the political character of the recipient regime, or the openness of the recipient internet ecosystem. It lies instead in the configuration through which supply-side push—infrastructure, contracts, financing, and training—interacts with recipient-state capacity and domestic political incentives, the H1–H3 mechanisms, and regional counter-mobilisation, including the EU adequacy regime and ASEAN resistance to binding sovereignty commitments. These factors jointly produce—or fail to produce—observable convergence. Chapter 2 develops a configurational framework capable of registering this variation; Chapters 3–5 show what that framework discloses that binary approaches alone cannot.

4. Methodology

The book's empirical claims are advanced through a deliberately plural methodology. These several methods are used because justified by the fact that Chinese normative power operates differently at the bilateral, regional, and international levels, and has itself changed strategy across two decades, so the method must change with the level and with the period under consideration. The unit of analysis at the bilateral level is national legal text and the dyadic relationships in which it is embedded; at the regional level, declarations and binding agreements produced by intergovernmental bodies whose authority over members is independent of any single state's bilateral leverage; at the international level, the cumulative drift of UN-system instruments and Chinese normative submissions over two decades.

Across all three levels, three converging streams of evidence are read together – a quantitative or text-analytic stream, a documentary stream of primary instruments, and a qualitative set of semi-structured interviews – and each chapter applies the streams in proportions appropriate to its level. The bilateral analysis in Chapter 3 measures lexical proximity between the full English-language texts of cyber and data-protection laws across thirty documents from twenty-three jurisdictions, calibrated against China's three foundational instruments (CSL, DSL, PIPL). The procedure uses TF-IDF cosine similarity, with three corpus baselines computed so that scores can be read as outliers, topical convergence or sub-baseline. The technique is tractable at this level because national laws are sufficiently long, structurally comparable and domain-uniform to make computational comparison meaningful, and because vocabulary is the most direct surface trace of legal transplantation. The lexical signal is treated as a starting point that flags cases for case-study analysis, not as a conclusion in itself.

The regional analysis in Chapter 4 examines at regional instruments are diplomatic rather than legislative and produced under negotiation among states whose vocabularies often diverge from China's even when the structural logic does not. Computational similarity would mislead in this terrain because, as the H2 (selective adaptation) mechanism predicts, recipient states regularly translate Chinese-origin principles into their own legal and diplomatic vocabularies, producing texts that share the structural logic without sharing the surface terms. The chapter therefore traces the recurring Chinese normative vocabulary – cyber sovereignty, community of shared future in cyberspace, the security-led framing of cyber security – through SCO declarations, the RCEP Chapter 12 treaty text, BRICS communiqués from Beijing 2022 to Kazan 2024 and ASEAN-China joint statements, looking for structural encodings of the governance logic. The original coding compiled in the course of this research covers five regional statements and cooperation initiatives, six recurring terms tracked across Chinese official communications, and norm-adoption evidence from four recipient contexts.

The international analysis in Chapter 5 is shaped by an additional consideration: China's posture at this level has shifted directionally over the period under study, from defensive resistance (2001–14), to active norm entrepreneurship (2015–19), to what the chapter characterises as revisionism from within (2019–25). The chapter codes the substantive content of UN-level instruments – General Assembly resolutions, GGE and OEWG reports, the 2024 Convention against Cybercrime, the Pact for the Future and the Global Digital Compact, and Chinese-authored submissions and global initiatives – across three substantive dimensions on which the international contest has run: the core governance principle (cyber sovereignty versus multistakeholder), data and information control (state-conditioned versus free flow) and the cybersecurity approach (security primacy versus rights-bounded resilience). The resulting matrix is read across two decades to identify the points at which Chinese-aligned positions move from minority advocacy to majority endorsement to formally embedded treaty language. Voting and sub-coalition analysis on amendments – L.90 and L.92 in the Cybercrime Ad Hoc Committee, A/79/L.3 at the Summit of the Future – supplements the textual coding by registering where the broader coalition that activates a process fragments when substantive content comes to the floor.

Across all three levels the research has been supplemented with the AidData Global Chinese Development Finance Dataset, treaties and MOUs disclosed through Chinese ministerial channels and host-country gazettes, training rosters, procurement and parliamentary records at the bilateral level; the formal outputs of regional organisations at the regional level; and the UN, ITU and Chinese MFA primary record at the international level. Primary instruments carry the weight of the argument; secondary academic synthesis is cited alongside the primary document where the latter is publicly available. The interview corpus of fourteen semi-structured interviews conducted between March 2024 and July 2025 with regional experts on data protection, cybersecurity law and digital infrastructure (documented in Appendix A; interviewees referenced by code) is read across the three streams as triangulation, used to confirm, complicate or contextualise patterns visible in the textual and documentary record.

A fourth method, comparative process tracing, runs through all three chapters and is what binds the streams into case-level conclusions. Within each case, the analysis reconstructs the temporal sequence of identifiable mechanisms – when financing, agreements, training, regional endorsements, or coalition votes occurred relative to the outcome of interest – and assesses whether that sequence is consistent with influence having operated through specific channels rather than through coincidence or generic convergence. The three attribution conditions developed in Chapter 2 – coherence, channel specificity and cumulativity – discipline the claims that result. Only when all three are jointly met does the analysis move from documenting similarity to attributing normative power; cases that meet some but not all are flagged accordingly. The plurality of methods is therefore guided by a shared evidentiary standard: different techniques are used to analyse different objects, while broadly comparable criteria are applied when assessing whether the evidence supports a claim of normative diffusion or influence.

5. Plan of the Book

The book proceeds as follows. Chapter 1 maps the core normative cluster structuring China's domestic digital governance, including cyber sovereignty, data localisation, critical-information-infrastructure protection, the securitisation of data flows, content regulation and mandated algorithmic transparency through state oversight, and examines the internal coherence and tensions of this architecture. The chapter establishes the three criteria by which a governance norm counts as 'Chinese' in the relevant sense (Party-doctrinal centrality, legal-institutional embedding, external promotion) and applies the criteria to identify a portable core of Chinese digital normative power that is at once recognisable and adapted in transit.

Chapter 2 develops the theoretical framework in full. The chapter introduces the concept of normative power adapted for the digital domain; specifies the push–pull framework summarised above; identifies the mechanisms operating at bilateral, regional and international levels; and sets out the three attribution conditions (coherence, channel specificity, cumulativity) that the empirical chapters apply.

Chapter 3 examines bilateral dynamics, tracing push and pull across eight cases (Vietnam, Chile, Malaysia, Zambia, Egypt, Kazakhstan, the Philippines and Laos). The chapter combines the lexical-similarity analysis against all three Chinese reference instruments with project-level documentary evidence and qualitative interviews. It develops six distinct mechanism configurations that together discriminate among the empirical patterns the framework was designed to capture.

Chapter 4 turns to the regional level, analysing how China navigates and shapes regional digital orders through the SCO, RCEP, BRICS and ASEAN. The chapter develops the four R-mechanisms set out in Chapter 2, with particular attention to the contrast between formal institutional anchoring (SCO and RCEP) and declaratory legitimation (BRICS), and to the counter-mobilisation function of European regulatory frameworks within the ASEAN context.

Chapter 5 examines the international arena, tracing China's strategies across two decades of engagement with the UN system and the ITU. The chapter consolidates the 2019–25 trajectory of the UN Convention against Cybercrime as the cleanest case of what Chinese normative power can produce in binding treaty form, examines the Global Digital Compact of September 2024 as an instance of revisionism from within rather than rejection from outside and reconstructs the South–South coalition that has carried Chinese positions from minority advocacy to majority endorsement.

The Conclusion synthesises the findings, assesses the cumulative effect of China's normative engagement across levels and outlines implications for digital governance and the future of global internet ordering. The conclusion looks forward to the next-layer governance contests (artificial intelligence, post-quantum cryptography, immersive computing, synthetic media and content) that the existing institutional architecture is not yet equipped to manage.

The book's ambition is diagnostic before it is prescriptive. The future of cyberspace will not be determined by a simple victory of one ordering model over another. It will emerge from the same relational push and pull processes this book maps, from the strategic calculations of states navigating between competing offers, from the hybrid legal frameworks assembled by legislators working with templates from multiple jurisdictions, from the technical standards embedded in infrastructure by engineers whose choices carry political consequences they cannot always anticipate, and from the multilateral deliberations in which the meaning of 'sovereignty', 'security', and 'development' is continuously renegotiated. What this book attempts to show is that this patchwork is not the failure of a more coherent order. It is the order, and understanding it on those terms is the precondition for any policy or scholarly engagement that hopes to make sense of where digital governance goes next.

References

Aaronson, S. and Leblond, P. (2018) 'Another Digital Divide: The Rise of Data Realms and Its Implications for the WTO', *Journal of International Economic Law*, 21(2), pp. 245–272.

Abbate, J. (1999) *Inventing the Internet*. Cambridge, MA: MIT Press.

Africa China Reporting Project (2021) *Enter the Dragon: The Impact of China's Digital Authoritarianism on Democracy in Africa*. Available at: https://africachinareporting.com/enter-the-dragon-the-impact-of-chinas-digital-authoritarianism-on-democracy-in-africa/

Al Jazeera (2024) 'China Trying to Develop World "Built on Censorship and Surveillance"', *Al Jazeera*, 2 May. Available at: https://www.aljazeera.com/news/2024/5/2/china-trying-to-develop-world-built-on-censorship-and-surveillance

Article 19 (2025) *China: Southeast Asia Visit Raises Alarm Over Digital Repression*, 14 April. https://www.article19.org/resources/china-southeast-asia-visit-raises-alarm-over-digital-repression/

Bradford, A. (2020) *The Brussels Effect: How the European Union Rules the World*. Oxford: Oxford University Press.

Bradford, A. (2023) *Digital Empires: The Global Battle to Regulate Technology*. Oxford: Oxford University Press.

Bui, N. S. and Lee, J.-A. (2022) 'Comparative cybersecurity law in socialist Asia', *Vanderbilt Journal of Transnational Law*, 55(3), pp. 667–740.

Canalys (2023) Global Smartphone Market Share Q4 2023. Available at: https://www.canalys.com

Cheney, C. (2019) 'China's Digital Silk Road: Strategic Technological Competition and Exporting Political Illiberalism', *Council on Foreign Relations*, 26 September.

China MFA (2017) *International Strategy of Cooperation on Cyberspace*. Ministry of Foreign Affairs, People's Republic of China.

Clinton, H. (2010) *Remarks on Internet Freedom*. US Department of State, 21 January.

CNAS (2023) *The Dangers of the Global Spread of China's Digital Authoritarianism.* Congressional Testimony, Center for a New American Security.
Creemers, R. (2017) 'Cyber China: Upgrading Propaganda, Public Opinion Work and Social Management for the Twenty-First Century', *Journal of Contemporary China*, 26(103), pp. 85–100.
Creemers, R. (2020) *China's Cybersecurity and Data Governance. Background Research for Digital Empires*. Oxford: Oxford Internet Institute.
DataReportal (2024) TikTok Global Statistics 2024. Available at: https://datareportal.com
DeNardis, L. (2014) *The Global War for Internet Governance*. New Haven, CT: Yale University Press.
ECDPM (2023) *Global Approaches to Digital Sovereignty: Competing Definitions, Contrasting Policy Approaches*. Discussion Paper 344.
Erie, M. and Streinz, T. (2021) 'The Beijing Effect: China's "Digital Silk Road" as Transnational Data Governance', *NYU Journal of International Law and Politics*, 54, pp. 1–92.
European Commission (2020) *A European Strategy for Data*. COM(2020) 66 Final.
Feldstein, S. (2019) *The Global Expansion of AI Surveillance*. Washington, DC: Carnegie Endowment for International Peace.
Freedom House (2018) *Freedom on the Net 2018: The Rise of Digital Authoritarianism.* Washington, DC: Freedom House.
Freedom House (2023) *Freedom on the Net 2023*. Washington, DC: Freedom House.
Gajjala, R. and Birzescu, A. (2011) 'Digital Imperialism Through Online Social/Financial Networks', *Economic and Political Weekly*, 46(30), pp. 95–102.
Prokopyshyn, O. and Trushkina, N. (2025) 'The Geopolitics of Cybersecurity: A Comparative Analysis of National Strategies for Digital Sovereignty', *Politics and Security*. 'The Geopolitics of Cybersecurity: A Comparative Analysis of National Strategies for Digital Sovereignty', *Politics & Security*, 12(2), pp. 59–71. doi: 10.54658/ps.28153324.2025.12.2.
IPVM (2024) Huawei 5G Global Contracts 2023. Available at: https://ipvm.com
Jancic, D., et al. (2023) 'Strategic Narratives and the Multilateral Governance of Cyberspace: The Cases of the European Union, Russia, and India', *Contemporary Security Policy*, 44(4), pp. 72–109.
Jili, B. (2021) *China in Africa: Exporting Authoritarianism?* Harvard GSAS Communications. Available at: https://gsas.harvard.edu
Jones Day (2018) 'Vietnam Passes Sweeping Cybersecurity Law', *Jones Day Insights*, June.
Law on Cyber Security, No. 24/2018/QH14 (2018) (Viet.). Apolat Legal. https://apolatlegal.com/wp-content/uploads/2024/01/The-Law-on-Cyber-Security-2018.pdf.
Liu, H. (2021) *China's Data Regulations: An Overview*. China Law Translate. Available at: https://www.chinalawtranslate.com
Madianou, M. (2019) 'Technocolonialism: Digital Innovation and Data Practices in the Humanitarian Response to Refugee Crises', *Social Media + Society*, 5(3), pp. 1–13.
Manners, I. (2002) 'Normative Power Europe: A Contradiction in Terms?', *Journal of Common Market Studies*, 40(2), pp. 235–258.
McKune, S. and Ahmed, S. (2018) 'The Contestation and Shaping of Cyber Norms Through China's Internet Sovereignty Agenda', *International Journal of Communication*, 12, pp. 3835–3855.
Pannier, A. (2023) *Digital Middle Powers and the Global Tech Competition*. Paris: IFRI.
Pohle, J. and Thiel, T. (2020) 'Digital Sovereignty', *Internet Policy Review*, 9(4). https://doi.org/10.14763/2020.4.1532
Polyakova, A. and Meserole, C. (2019) *Exporting Digital Authoritarianism: The Russian and Chinese Models*. Washington, DC: Brookings Institution.
Rito, I. (2024) 'China's Cyber Sovereignty and the United Nations', *IIPE Dialogues*, 4(2), pp. 57–73..

SCMP (2019) 'New Year, New Repression: Vietnam Imposes Draconian "China-Like" Cybersecurity Law', *South China Morning Post,* 1 January.
Segal, A. (2018) *China's Alternative Cyber Governance Regime*. Testimony Before the U.S.-China Economic and Security Review Commission, 13 March.
Sherman, J. (2019) 'Vietnam's Internet Control: Following in China's Footsteps?', *The Diplomat*, December.
Triolo, P. (2023) 'The Digital Silk Road', in M. Nouwens (ed.) *China's Digital Ambitions: A Global Strategy*. London: IISS.
Turner, F. (2006) *From Counterculture to Cyberculture*. Chicago, IL: University of Chicago Press.
The Vietnamese (2024) 'Việt Nam and China's Cybersecurity Cooperation: Shared Control and Strategic Caution', *The Vietnamese Magazine*, 15 July.
Walker, C. (2021) 'How China Exports Authoritarianism', *Foreign Affairs*, September/ October.

1 What Is 'Chinese' about China's Digital Norms?

To study the diffusion of China's digital normative power abroad, we first need to be precise about what we mean by 'Chinese' digital norms – and, just as importantly, what we do *not* mean. 'Chinese' should not be read as 'unique', 'original' or 'exclusive to China'. In the digital normative domain, like many others, it is often difficult to disentangle ideas that are presented as Chinese from principles that have emerged through decades of China's socialisation in international institutions, technical standard-setting bodies and global regulatory debates (Acharya, 2004). Many of the concepts that appear in China's digital governance –security, privacy, sovereignty, risk management, accountability, even 'data as a resource' often associated with China – are not China's inventions.[1] They circulate globally and are articulated, with different emphases, across a wide range of jurisdictions. The European Union's GDPR (2016), Brazil's Marco Civil da Internet (2014) and LGPD (2020), India's digital governance programmes and a growing body of 'AI safety' and platform regulation initiatives elsewhere all illustrate that the contemporary landscape is crowded with normative templates. In such an environment, norms do not travel in a linear, one-way flow from a 'norm entrepreneur' to passive recipients. They circulate, hybridise and are repurposed by domestic actors responding to local political economies, state capacities and geopolitical constraints, as will be discussed in the next chapter.

This does not make the category of 'Chinese digital norms' meaningless. It makes it an empirical and conceptual problem that requires criteria. The point of this chapter is therefore not to argue that China's digital norms are wholly distinctive in their individual components, but to identify a *core normative cluster* that

1 The association of 'data as a resource' with China is largely a product of scale and state ambition rather than origin. While the concept was developed in Western management theory and business journalism – from Levitin and Redman's 1998 MIT Sloan Management Review analysis to Clive Humby's 2006 'data is the new oil' metaphor – China became its most visible political adopter. When Beijing formally designated data a 'factor of production' in 2019–20 and subsequently built an entire state-led data economy around that designation (the 'Twenty Data Measures', 2022; the National Data Administration, 2023), it transformed what had been a corporate or rhetorical concept into a pillar of national industrial policy at a scale no Western government matched. The EU and US adopted similar language in strategy papers, but without the same degree of top-down institutional construction. China's visibility on this issue, then, reflects not invention but intensity of implementation.

DOI: 10.4324/9781042023738-2

structures China's approach to digital governance and that is sufficiently coherent – and sufficiently embedded in state practice – to be projected outward. 'Chinese', as used here, is thus a claim about configuration, prioritisation and institutionalisation: how certain principles are assembled into a governing logic, how they are anchored in legal and bureaucratic systems, and how they are promoted internationally as legitimate solutions to shared regulatory challenges. Another important aspect to consider is that China's data governance and cybersecurity regime is increasingly sophisticated, yet – comparatively speaking – still young. Data governance and cyberspace regulation are novel policy domains for most states, and fast-moving technologies, not least AI, are evolving more quickly than legal frameworks can stabilise. Many of China's headline regulations and implementing instruments are less than a decade old, and important questions about interpretation, enforcement, and cross-agency coordination remain unsettled, so we have to be cautious against over-reading coherence or inevitability where policy is still consolidating, contested and adapted through practice.

Against these challenges, this chapter proceeds with a deliberately bounded definition of what counts as 'Chinese enough to travel'. I treat a norm as 'Chinese' in the relevant sense when it meets three criteria. First, it holds Party-doctrinal centrality: it is repeatedly articulated in authoritative Party discourse and linked to overarching political objectives (such as stability, security and regime resilience). Second, it exhibits legal and institutional embedding: it is operationalised through domestic law, regulatory instruments and institutional arrangements that structure administrative behaviour, corporate compliance and enforcement practices. Third, it is subject to external promotion: it is advanced beyond China's borders through diplomatic language, capacity-building and training programmes, technology and infrastructure exports, participation in international standard-setting, or the broader repertoire of China's 'international norm entrepreneurship'. The criteria are designed to avoid two common pitfalls: treating any regulatory tool used in China as inherently 'Chinese', and, conversely, dismissing China's normative influence because its principles overlap with global regulatory vocabularies. What matters is not whether an idea exists elsewhere, but whether China's particular configuration of ideas, institutions and channels of promotion forms a recognisable package – one that can be taken up or adapted abroad, and that retains a sufficient degree of distinctiveness from other models.

This chapter focuses on a cluster of norms that, taken together, mark China's distinctive approach to digital governance – a paradigm fundamentally anchored in the concept of 'cyber sovereignty'. This framework comprises four interrelated elements, while remaining attentive to the fact that these elements are neither uniquely Chinese nor perfectly coherent across all agencies and policy domains. The first is a security-centred conception of digital order – meaning that China's starting point for thinking about the internet and data is not economic freedom or individual rights, but stability and control. Threats to information security are treated as threats to political order, which justifies broad state authority over digital infrastructure and content. The second is a sovereign and jurisdictional framing of data and networks: data generated, stored, or processed within China, particularly where it implicates national security, public interests, critical infrastructure, or designated categories of important data, is treated as falling within an expansive sphere of state regulatory authority. Networks are not seen as a global common but as extensions of national jurisdiction, to be governed accordingly. The third element is an emphasis on state capacity to access, govern and mobilise data – not merely to regulate how data is used by private actors, but to actively harness it as a national resource for economic development, social management, and security purposes. The state does not position itself only as a referee; it is also a participant and beneficiary. The fourth is a compliance architecture – a set of legal and regulatory instruments that bind private companies to public governance objectives. This architecture operates through several mechanisms: licensing, which makes market access conditional on meeting security and governance requirements; risk assessments, which require companies to evaluate and report on the security implications of their data practices before deploying new products or transferring data abroad; localisation requirements, applicable to specified operators and categories of data, keeping them within reach of state authority; and platform accountability mechanisms, which assign legal responsibility to large digital platforms for the content, behaviour, and data flows that occur on their services – effectively turning private companies into arms of public governance. What makes this cluster distinctive is not that any single element is unique to China – many countries require data localisation, conduct security reviews, or hold platforms accountable for content. It is the combination and the underlying logic that sets China apart: each instrument reinforces the others, and all of them flow from the same foundational premise that digital order is a dimension of state sovereignty, not a domain to be left primarily to markets or individual rights.

The chapter proceeds as follows. First, it identifies in cyber sovereignty a core normative cluster and shows how this concept holds Party-doctrinal centrality. Second, it traces the legal and institutional embedding of these norms within China's domestic regulatory architecture. Finally, it examines the mechanisms through which China promotes this normative package externally.

1. The Core Normative Cluster: Cyber Sovereignty as the 'Master Frame'

The core candidate for the normative cluster that structures China's digital governance is cyber sovereignty (网络主权, *wangluo zhuquan*). In its simplest form, cyber sovereignty is the claim that states possess ultimate authority to regulate the internet within their jurisdiction, including the right to determine the rules that govern information flows, digital infrastructure, platforms and data practices, and the right to resist external interference in these choices (Creemers, 2020; Derivry, 2023).

Sovereignty is a cornerstone of China's foreign policy. It was introduced in the late Qing amid Western countries' imperial expansion and unequal treaties, becoming tied to resisting foreign encroachment and rebuilding state authority after humiliation and fragmentation (Carrai, 2019). Cyber sovereignty carries this tradition into the digital realm: the internet is treated as a domain in which China must safeguard political stability, cultural integrity, and technological self-reliance (Xi, 2015). At its core, the state becomes the final arbiter of internet governance within its borders, entitled to select its 'development path', management model, and public internet policies, and entitled to demand non-interference from other states with respect to domestic digital order. The concept treats cyberspace not as a borderless commons governed primarily by transnational norms or private ordering, but as a domain of national jurisdiction in which the Party-state is the principal rule-maker, rule-enforcer and guarantor of security and development.

As Creemers (2020) argues, cyber sovereignty has become the foundational concept through which China's leadership imagines both domestic online governance and its engagement with the outside world, and it is also a major site of contestation with liberal models centred on openness and individual rights. Cyber sovereignty functions as a high-level organising principle that gives coherence to otherwise diverse regulatory domains – content governance, data regulation, cybersecurity, industrial policy and international standard-setting – by anchoring them in a common claim about authority and jurisdiction. It legitimises strong domestic governance capacities (including content control and security policing) as ordinary expressions of sovereignty; it underwrites industrial and technological policies aimed at reducing dependence on foreign infrastructure and firms; and it provides an outward-facing vocabulary for engaging in global debates about cybersecurity, data governance and technical standards without accepting liberal premises about the primacy of individual rights or the desirability of an open, globally uniform internet. Domestically, it stabilises the Party-state's authority over the digital sphere by grounding internet control in the language of legitimate governance rather than censorship or repression. If the internet within China's borders is an extension of Chinese territory, then regulating it – blocking foreign platforms, requiring data localisation, mandating content controls – is simply what any responsible sovereign does, no different in principle from controlling who crosses a physical border or what is broadcast on national airwaves (Creemers, 2020). The framing recasts what outside observers might call restrictions into the ordinary exercise of jurisdiction.

Internationally, cyber sovereignty performs a different but equally important function. It provides China with a coherent and exportable narrative about what legitimate internet governance looks like globally. The core claim is that the principle of non-interference – one of the foundational norms of the post-1945 international order, embedded in the UN Charter and widely respected across the Global South – should apply as much to the digital domain as to physical territory (MFA, 2017). If states have the sovereign right to govern their own affairs without external interference, then it follows, on this logic, that no outside power, institution or platform should be able to dictate how a country manages its own networks, data or digital public sphere. On this framing, Western pressure over censorship or surveillance can be presented less as the defence of universal rights than as a form of digital interventionism – an attempt by powerful states to impose their own governance models on others (Creemers, 2020).

The concept therefore functions as a prescriptive and normative template for how states should behave: respecting each other's digital jurisdictions, refraining from using networks as instruments of foreign influence and conducting internet governance through intergovernmental bodies where sovereign equality applies, rather than through the multistakeholder institutions – led by civil society, technical communities and the private sector – that Western governments have historically favoured (Creemers, 2020). For countries wary of Western dominance in digital infrastructure and norm-setting, this narrative has considerable appeal, which is precisely why China has advanced it through forums like the World Internet Conference and in bilateral digital cooperation agreements across Africa, Asia and Latin America.

Cyber sovereignty was institutionalised through a series of official texts and diplomatic performances that progressively clarified its meaning and elevated its status in China's domestic and external messaging. A compressed chronology highlights three pivotal moments. First, the White Paper (2010) on the Internet in China, offered one of the earliest authoritative and internationally directed formulations of China's internet-sovereignty position. It presented internet development and regulation as a sovereign domain and implicitly insisted on the legitimacy of differentiated national models of governance. Second, in 2012, China advanced cyber sovereignty as the first of its proposed principles for international cooperation at the Budapest Conference on Cyberspace, signalling that the concept was not merely for internal legitimation but would also structure China's international posture (MFA, 2012). Third, the concept was elevated further at the inaugural World Internet Conference (WIC) in Wuzhen in (2014), Near the close of the conference, organisers circulated a draft "Wuzhen Declaration" that included language consistent with China's sovereignty-centred approach to internet governance. The text was distributed late in the proceedings and did not emerge as an agreed conference document after objections from some participants. The episode should therefore not be treated as evidence of international endorsement of cyber sovereignty. Rather, it illustrates Beijing's early ambition to use the World Internet Conference as a platform for presenting, legitimising, and building support for its preferred vision of global internet governance. Still, these moments show how cyber sovereignty became, in Creemers's formulation, a 'mainstay' in documents and statements designed for international consumption: not just an internal governance rationale, but a flexible diplomatic frame through which China could advocate policy space, oppose external criticism and articulate alternative principles for global governance (Creemers, 2020).

Cyber sovereignty provides a narrative for China's growing activism in shaping the global architecture of information governance (de La Bruyère, 2022). This activism is visible along at least three channels that recur throughout the chapter: (i) diplomacy and international discourse (including sovereignty and non-interference language applied to cyberspace); (ii) technical and capacity-building cooperation (training, regulatory exchanges and governance 'solutions' offered through bilateral or multilateral partnerships); and (iii) participation in standard-setting and infrastructure ecosystems that embed governance assumptions into technology.

Here, cyber sovereignty helps China present its approach as a legitimate alternative model – one that foregrounds state authority, security and order – rather than as an exceptional or illicit deviation from global norms.

This outward projection is frequently interpreted mainly through the lens of cyber operations, espionage, and surveillance exports. While these issues matter, they can obscure a broader contest over governance principles and institutional designs. The question is not only whether states engage in cyber surveillance activities – many do – but which governance assumptions become normalised: who has authority over data; whether cross-border flows are presumed permissible or presumptively securitised; whether platforms are framed primarily as private intermediaries or as governance nodes with public obligations; and whether security claims are bounded by rights protections and judicial constraints or governed primarily through administrative discretion. Cyber sovereignty is consequential because it supplies a coherent language for advancing China's preferred answers to these questions while presenting them as an expression of sovereign equality rather than ideological export.

'Sovereignty talk' is no longer exclusive to China. Many states have moved towards stronger claims over data, infrastructure, and platform governance, and concepts such as strategic autonomy and data governance have gained prominence in liberal democracies as well (Pohle and Thiel, 2020). This overlap cautions against treating cyber sovereignty as a simple autocracy–democracy marker (O'Hara and Hall, 2018). The more precise contrast is how sovereignty claims are justified, institutionalised, and constrained. For instance, the European Union, despite earlier criticisms of China's 'cyber sovereignty' (Christakis, 2020) has increasingly moved towards policies that also emphasise the territorialisation and control of data – most visibly through a growing focus on data sovereignty and stronger state-backed mechanisms for governing cross-border data flows.[2] At the same time, the EU continues to frame its approach in liberal-democratic terms, centring individual rights, rule-of-law constraints and regulatory oversight rather than overt political control (Bradford, 2020; Christakis, 2020). The comparison between China, the EU and the United States, for instance, reveals both continuing divergence and emerging overlap. Beijing's cyber sovereignty remains anchored in regime security and state authority over information, whereas Brussels' digital sovereignty is more closely tied to strategic autonomy, market governance, and rights protection. Yet in practice, the gap between a sovereignty-driven approach (China) and the traditionally more open, multistakeholder orientation associated with Western internet governance is becoming more nuanced (Gao, 2022). Western actors – particularly the EU – are not 'adopting' China's model, but certain policy convergences (especially around data localisation pressures, security exceptions, and state responsibility for digital infrastructures) may make parts of China's normative agenda more legible or, at least, less categorically rejected (see Table 1.1).

2 For instance, the European Union (EU) contends that digital sovereignty is imperative to safeguard its market against the dominance of technology giants from the United States and China.

Table 1.1 Comparing China, the EU and the US on digital governance

Area	*China*	*European Union (EU)*	*United States (US)*
Data Governance	Strict data localisation requirements, government control over data, limited data sharing (Data Security Law, 2021; Personal Information Protection Law [PIPL], 2021).	Focus on data protection and individual rights, stricter regulations on data processing compared to the US (General Data Protection Regulation [GDPR]).	No comprehensive, generally applicable federal consumer-data privacy statute (Sector-specific federal statutes and a growing body of state privacy laws, including California's CCPA CCPA, 2018) put emphasis on data security.
Cybersecurity	Sovereignty focus, critical infrastructure protection, active defense (Cybersecurity Law, 2017).	Risk-based approach, focus on essential services, emphasis on cooperation (NIS Directive, 2016).	Focus on critical infrastructure protection, information sharing, public-private partnerships (Cybersecurity and Infrastructure Security Agency [CISA]).
Digital Standards	Independent standards development and promotion of multilateral approach.	Active participation in international standard-setting, promotes interoperability, promotion of multistakeholder approach.	Active participation in international standard-setting, dominance in some areas like internet protocols; promotion of multistakeholder approach.

In other words, liberal regulatory models can accommodate strong state roles while still embedding rule-of-law checks, transparency requirements, and rights-based constraints; China's approach tends to place political security and Party leadership at the centre of the governance rationale, making the scope of permissible regulation broader and the constraints more administrative than judicial. Cyber sovereignty thus serves as a master frame not because it is the only sovereignty claim in cyberspace, but because it organises a distinctive hierarchy of values – state primacy and security first – and ties that hierarchy to a comprehensive governance toolkit.

For the purposes of this chapter, cyber sovereignty bundles China's digital governance into a travel-ready cluster that can be promoted abroad through law, institutions, infrastructure, and discourse. It does so through three interrelated commitments that recur across domestic policy and external engagement. First, assured

Party-state primacy in cyberspace: the state retains ultimate authority over key digital decisions, including content governance, platform obligations and the terms of data access and control (Derivry, 2023). Second, the fusion of security, development, and control: digital modernisation is not treated as separate from political security but as a domain in which governance capacity must integrate economic strategy, social management, and regime resilience (Bandurski, 2017). Third, technological self-reliance paired with standard-setting ambition: reducing dependence on foreign technologies is framed as a sovereignty imperative, while participation in standards and technical governance is treated as a route to shaping the global environment in which China's digital economy and governance preferences can thrive (Xi, 2016). Together, these commitments explain why cyber sovereignty functions as the 'master frame' for China's digital normative power. It offers intellectual coherence to domestic governance, supplies a legitimating vocabulary for a broad compliance architecture, and provides an outward-facing narrative that can be coupled with concrete mechanisms – training, infrastructure, and standards – through which normative influence travels. Subsequent sections build on this foundation by tracing how the frame is operationalised through law and institutions at home, and how it is projected abroad.

2. The Legal Stack (CSL/DSL/PIPL) as Instruments of the Master Frame

China's legal stack – the Cybersecurity Law (CSL), Data Security Law (DSL), and Personal Information Protection Law (PIPL) – provides the first implementation layer through which cyber sovereignty becomes actionable. Read together, these laws translate jurisdictional claims into compliance obligations for firms, platforms, and public institutions. They also make parts of the framework portable: what tends to travel is rarely a full legal system, but a set of modular mechanisms – classification, localisation rules, security assessments, licensing and approvals, cross-border transfer controls and selective extraterritorial hooks – that other states can adapt to their own priorities. Table 1.2 carries the fine-grained provisions; the focus here is on the governing logic and the signature mechanisms most likely to matter for diffusion.

The CSL is best understood as the legal articulation of cyber sovereignty at the level of networks and infrastructure. Its organising premise is that cyberspace is a domain of national security and social order, and therefore must be governed through enforceable duties placed on network operators and key sectors (DigiChina, 2017). This marks a significant divergence from liberal regulatory traditions. In the United States, internet governance has historically been framed around market freedom and multistakeholder participation, with the state intervening primarily to address specific harms rather than to assert general authority over the digital sphere (DeNardis, 2014). In the European Union, the organising premise is the protection of fundamental rights – privacy, dignity, non-discrimination – which function as constraints on state and corporate power (EU, 2016/679; Reding, 2012). China's CSL operates through a different logic: the state claims final authority over

Table 1.2 China's foundational data governance laws – comparative overview

Law	*Cybersecurity Law (CSL)*	*Data Security Law (DSL)*	*Personal Information Protection Law (PIPL)*
Effective Date	1 June 2017	1 September 2021	1 November 2021
Overview	- Focuses on network security, network operators, critical information infrastructure and data collected or generated through network operations. - Covers network construction, operation, maintenance and use within mainland China, with specific provisions on critical information infrastructure and cross-border data issues.	- Covers a wide range of data, including online and offline data storage and processing. - Establishes a classified and graded data protection system, including heightened obligations for 'important data' and stricter protection for 'national core data'. - Establishes a National Security Review system for data activities related to national security.	Covers the collection, processing and protection of personal information both online and offline.
Applies to	- Network operators, critical information infrastructure operators and relevant entities engaged in network construction, operation, maintenance and use within mainland China. - Foreign actors may face liability where they endanger China's critical information infrastructure and cause serious consequences.	Data processing activities within mainland China, including collection, storage, use, processing, transmission, provision and disclosure. Also has extraterritorial provisions where overseas data activities harm China's national security, public interest, or citizens' and organisations' lawful rights and interests.	- Any individual or entity processing personal information in mainland China, and overseas institutions processing data related to Chinese users (e.g. for products/services or behaviour analysis). - Includes state entities.

(*Continued*)

Table 1.2 (Continued)

Law	*Cybersecurity Law (CSL)*	*Data Security Law (DSL)*	*Personal Information Protection Law (PIPL)*
Key Requirements	- Regularly review cybersecurity and data management to ensure critical risks are addressed. - Regularly review protection of private information in the course of collection, use and dissemination. - Carefully monitor data being transmitted out of China or received from overseas. - Establish defined roles with clear responsibility for cybersecurity and data privacy. - Monitor networks in real time and establish incident reporting processes. - Establish and regularly practice crisis/incident response plans.	- Establish data security management systems and organisational responsibilities. - Conduct data security education and training. - Adopt technical and other measures to safeguard data. - Conduct risk monitoring and, for important data processors, periodic risk assessments and reporting. - Comply with classified and graded protection rules and cross-border data transfer controls where applicable.	- Provide clear notices on who collects data, contact details, purpose, processing methods, categories of personal information and retention periods. - Obtain valid consent where consent is the applicable legal basis, including separate consent for sensitive personal information and certain cross-border transfers. - Retain personal information only for the shortest period necessary to achieve the processing purpose. - Delete personal information when consent is withdrawn, the purpose has been fulfilled, the retention period expires or services are terminated. - Before cross-border transfer, satisfy one of the legally prescribed transfer mechanisms, such as CAC security assessment where required, certification, standard contracts and/or other conditions under law.

(*Continued*)

Table 1.2 (Continued)

Law	*Cybersecurity Law (CSL)*	*Data Security Law (DSL)*	*Personal Information Protection Law (PIPL)*
Enforcement Authorities	Cyberspace Administration of China (CAC); Ministry of Industry and Information Technology (MIIT); Ministry of Public Security (MPS) and other relevant departments within their respective responsibilities.	Cyberspace Administration of China (CAC), Ministry of Public Security (MPS), Ministry of State Security (MSS) and other relevant departments within their respective responsibilities.	Cyberspace Administration of China (CAC), together with relevant departments under the State Council and local authorities within their respective responsibilities.
Penalties/Enforcement Measures	Penalties vary by violation and may include substantial corporate and individual fines, confiscation of unlawful gains, rectification orders, suspension of operations, website closure and licence revocation.	Business fines of RMB 1 million to 10 million; individual fines of RMB 10,000 to 2 million; possible business suspension or license revocation.	Fines up to RMB 50 million or 5 per cent of previous year's turnover.

Note: Adapted from https://www.teneo.com/insights/articles/china-cybersecurity-and-data-regulation-what-multinationals-should-know/, with minor modifications for presentation clarity.

cyberspace and operationalises that claim through mandatory compliance, supervision and enforcement, treating cybersecurity as a precondition for economic modernisation as well as political order (Triolo and Webster, 2017; Creemers, 2022).

The CSL's most diffusion-relevant features are those that fuse sovereignty with operational control through replicable administrative templates. It introduces a regulatory ecosystem built around graded protection and operator obligations – security-by-design, internal governance systems, incident response, monitoring, and cooperation duties – that normalise the idea that private digital actors are governance nodes rather than merely market participants. This stands in contrast to the EU model, where private actors bear compliance burdens primarily to protect the rights of individuals, not to serve state governance functions; the GDPR, for instance, imposes obligations on firms in order to limit what both firms *and* governments can do with personal data (Voigt and von dem Bussche, 2017). In China's architecture, by contrast, compliance obligations flow upward toward the state: operators must cooperate with security organs, provide technical assistance and maintain systems that enable state access and oversight – a design that integrates private infrastructure into the public security apparatus rather than insulating individuals from it. The CSL also anchors a sovereignty-inflected approach to critical infrastructure by formalising Critical Information Infrastructure (CII) as a category deserving heightened protection and supervision (Huld, 2021). While many Western governments also designate critical infrastructure sectors, the defining difference lies in what 'protection' entails: while the United States and the European Union also impose mandatory security, risk-management, reporting, and supervisory obligations on critical sectors, China's framework more directly integrates CII protection into a broader system of national-security review, procurement control, data governance, and Party-state supervision. The contrast is therefore not between regulation and non-regulation, but between different institutional purposes, scopes of administrative discretion, and mechanisms of accountability (CISA, 2023; NIS2 Directive, 2022). In China's model, CII status triggers expanded supervisory authority, procurement controls and localisation obligations that give the state direct leverage over the infrastructure itself, not merely over minimum-security standards. This classification is inherently adaptable and therefore widely portable: many states can define CII expansively to justify stronger oversight over telecoms, finance, energy, transport and platform infrastructures (Huld, 2021). Finally, the CSL's cross-border data and infrastructure provisions establish localisation and security review logics that condition cross-border transfers on state-defined requirements rather than presuming them permissible – a posture closer to trade restriction than to the EU transfer regime, under which data may flow to third countries pursuant to an adequacy decision or other prescribed safeguards designed to secure an essentially equivalent level of protection (European Commission, 2023).

The DSL shifts the master frame from networks to data as an object of sovereign governance (Sheng et al., 2021). Its purpose is not limited to privacy or cybersecurity; rather, it treats data simultaneously as an economic resource for innovation and development and as a security object whose mishandling can threaten national security, public interests, and state capacity (DigiChina, 2021). This dual framing – data as asset and data as risk – distinguishes the DSL sharply from both major Western approaches. The EU's data governance framework, developed through the Data Act (2023), the Data Governance Act (2022), and related instruments, also treats data as an economic resource, but the policy objective is to unlock data for market competition and innovation by reducing barriers to access and sharing, with the state acting as facilitator rather than sovereign (European Commission, 2020). The US approach has been even more market-deferential, relying on sector-specific regulation and largely leaving data flows to commercial determination (Bradford, 2023). China's DSL, by contrast, makes data governable through state-established categories, hierarchical risk tiers and cross-border constraints that give administrative bodies final authority over what data may flow, to whom, and under what conditions (DigiChina, 2021). This is the security–development–control triad in legal form: develop the data economy but do so through a state-defined security governance architecture.

The DSL's diffusion-relevant mechanisms are those that allow governments to scale control through classification and risk. Its logic of data categorisation and hierarchical management can be adopted even when other states define the categories differently – the template is the administrative structure itself, not the specific classifications. Its risk-based security assessments and compliance obligations for processors enable states to tighten or loosen governance through implementing rules without rewriting the underlying architecture (DigiChina, 2021). Comparatively, the EU's risk-based approach in the AI Act (2024) and GDPR uses risk tiers similarly, but the purpose is to calibrate protections for individuals, not to calibrate state access to data flows. China's risk architecture runs in the opposite direction: higher-risk data attracts stronger state oversight, not stronger individual protection. The DSL's cross-border governance mechanisms – conditioning outward flows on security assessments, 'important data' designations, and national security invocations – also diverge from the EU's transfer mechanism, which conditions flows on whether destination jurisdictions provide equivalent *rights* protections, not equivalent security subordination (Sheng et al., 2021). This makes the assessment-and-approval model particularly portable for states that want to control outbound data flows on national interest grounds without adopting a rights-based framework.

The PIPL is often read as China's 'GDPR-like' statute, as it also establishes processing principles, transparency obligations, individual rights, rules for sensitive information, and conditions governing cross-border transfers. (Lee, 2021). Yet the analogy should not obscure their different institutional and constitutional settings. The distinction is not simply that the GDPR constrains the state while the PIPL exempts it. The PIPL also imposes specific obligations on state organs processing personal information, including requirements concerning statutory authority, necessity, notice, and the handling of information outside China. The more significant contrast concerns how these obligations are supervised and contested. Under the EU framework, data-protection rules are embedded in a broader system of fundamental rights, independent supervisory authorities, and judicial review. National security, moreover, cannot be treated simply as a narrow GDPR exemption: it remains principally the responsibility of the Member States under Article 4(2) TEU, and the boundaries between national-security activity, EU data-protection law, and law-enforcement regulation remain legally complex (Article 23, GDPR; CJEU, Schrems II, 2020). In China, personal-information protection operates within a Party-state system in which supervisory bodies are not institutionally independent of the political authorities whose conduct they may oversee, while public-security and national-security organs retain broad statutory powers and administrative discretion. (Shi-Kupfer and Ohlberg, 2019; Creemers, 2020). The central difference therefore lies less in the formal existence of privacy duties than in the independence of oversight, the breadth of security authority, and the institutional and judicial avenues through which individuals may challenge state processing (Creemers and Webster, 2020; Lee, 2021).

The PIPL's most diffusion-relevant mechanisms cluster around cross-border transfer governance and jurisdictional reach. It establishes structured pathways for cross-border transfers – security assessments, certifications, standard contractual mechanisms and consent or notice requirements – which reinforce the broader principle that outbound personal data is not simply a commercial flow but a regulated activity subject to state-defined conditions. Its extraterritorial hooks assert applicability to entities outside China when they process the personal information of individuals in China, echoing the GDPR's extraterritorial ambition but embedding that reach within a broader sovereignty-and-security system rather than a rights-protection one (Wang, 2021). The key difference from GDPR extraterritoriality is that the PIPL's reach can be reinforced through market access leverage, administrative supervision, and procurement rules in ways that make compliance with Chinese authority, rather than compliance with Chinese rights standards, the operative demand on foreign actors.

Taken together, the CSL/DSL/PIPL stack operationalises cyber sovereignty by converting a jurisdictional claim into a compliance regime with portable mechanisms – classification, localisation, reviews, approvals and extraterritorial reach (Creemers, 2022). What distinguishes this stack from Western regulatory frameworks is not the individual instruments in isolation – the EU also uses risk assessments, adequacy decisions and transfer conditions; the US also designates critical infrastructure and imposes sector-specific security obligations – but the underlying architecture that connects them. In EU and US systems, these instruments are more frequently fragmented across rights protection, market regulation and national-security regimes and are ordinarily subject to stronger judicial, constitutional or independent-regulatory constraints. In China, they are more systematically integrated into a Party-state framework linking security, development and political control. In China's system, they are designed to extend and enforce what the state can do with, through, and over digital infrastructure, data and the actors that depend on them (Zhang, 2022). The next sections show how this legal stack is reinforced by the operational and institutional layers – regulators, reviews, standards, and capacity-building – and then projected outward through cooperation channels, infrastructure ecosystems and multilateral arenas where these mechanisms can be selectively adopted, contested and hybridised.

3. External Entrepreneurship: What China Is Selling

China's engagement with digital governance beyond its borders is most accurately understood through the lens of norm entrepreneurship – the sustained, strategic effort to advance particular principles and institutional arrangements in international arenas, build coalitions around them, and embed them in the procedures and precedents through which governance problems get defined and resolved (Finnemore and Sikkink, 1998; Flohr et al., 2010). This is not a uniquely Chinese practice, nor is it a covert one: Xi Jinping's ambition for China is for it to become a cyber superpower (*wangluo qiangguo*) (2018). What distinguishes Beijing's approach is its combination of scale and the particular content of the norms being advanced: a cyber sovereignty framework that asserts state jurisdictional primacy over digital infrastructure and data flows, privileges intergovernmental over multistakeholder governance models and treats content regulation and network control as legitimate exercises of sovereign authority rather than as deviations from an open-internet baseline.

The analytical value of the entrepreneurship framing is that it redirects attention away from the question of whether China is 'exporting' a model – which implies a relatively passive recipient and a relatively finished product – toward the question of how China is working to shift the terms of what counts as legitimate governance across multiple arenas simultaneously. Norm entrepreneurship operates through persuasion, framing and institutional positioning rather than through coercion or legal transplantation (Finnemore and Sikkink, 1998; Acharya, 2004). The sections that follow trace this entrepreneurship across its primary channels: bilateral agreements and Digital Silk Road infrastructure, regional trade and security frameworks, and international standard-setting and UN negotiations.

The most direct channel of China's norm projection is bilateral, and its most consequential vehicle is the Digital Silk Road (DSR) – the digital infrastructure dimension of the Belt and Road Initiative. The Digital Silk Road (DSR) functions as an aggregative label for China's overseas digital cooperation, encompassing connectivity, infrastructure, technology, and regulatory exchange. While officially referenced within Belt and Road discourse, it is less a formal program than a discursive umbrella under which a heterogeneous array of state-backed and commercial activities are progressively grouped. Across sub-Saharan Africa, Southeast Asia, Central Asia, and the Pacific, Chinese state-owned enterprises and technology firms have supplied undersea cables, terrestrial fibre networks, data centres, smart-city platforms, cloud infrastructure, and surveillance systems, often through financing and procurement arrangements involving Chinese lenders or vendors. Ecuador developed the ECU-911 public-security system with Chinese technology and financing; Pakistan's Safe City projects in Lahore and Islamabad have used equipment supplied by firms including Huawei and Hikvision; and Ethiopia's telecommunications infrastructure has been developed with substantial involvement from Huawei and ZTE. These cases demonstrate the scale of Chinese commercial and technical participation, but they do not, without further evidence, establish that recipient governments have adopted Chinese legal rules or a Chinese model of digital governance (Gagliardone, 2014; Cheney, 2019; Hillman, 2021).

The governance significance of the so-called DSR infrastructure lies not only in the hardware itself but also in the institutional and technical arrangements that accompany it. Concession agreements, vendor contracts, service arrangements, maintenance dependencies, training and interoperability requirements can embed vendor-specific standards and data-handling practices that shape the recipient state's governance options over time (Erie and Streinz, 2021). This should not be read as an automatic or uniform transfer of Chinese law or policy. The more precise claim is that digital infrastructure can create path dependencies: when a government builds national networks, smart-city systems, or surveillance platforms around a particular technical architecture, it also acquires defaults about who can access data, how systems are maintained, which forms of monitoring are technically easy, and which procedural channels become routine (DeNardis, 2014). These defaults are often installed through procurement, implementation and network commissioning rather than through explicit ideological adoption, which is precisely what can make them difficult to contest after the fact (Ghiasy and Zhou, 2017).

Beyond infrastructure, China has concluded cybersecurity cooperation agreements and digital economy memoranda with a substantial number of states. These arrangements vary in formality and transparency – from the comprehensive 2015 Sino-Russian information-security agreement to cyber and digital cooperation strands associated with the 2021 China–Iran 25-year strategic partnership, to telecoms and CPEC-related arrangements with Pakistan – but they often resonate with sovereignty-first principles and frame mutual non-interference in information environments as a positive diplomatic commitment (Greitens, 2020). Agreements and partnerships with Gulf states, including Saudi Arabia and the UAE, have combined technology cooperation with language that treats content governance and information security as sovereign security functions. In Central Asia, bilateral digital cooperation frameworks with Kazakhstan, Uzbekistan and Tajikistan have created institutional channels through which Chinese regulatory concepts and governance practices can be transmitted through joint training, technical assistance and shared administrative procedures, even in the absence of formal treaty obligations to adopt them (Hoffman, 2019; Greitens, 2020). Taken cumulatively, I argue, these bilateral instruments contribute to a body of state practice and diplomatic precedent that Beijing can invoke as evidence of growing acceptance of sovereignty-first principles. Bilateral agreements that individually appear as pragmatic partnerships accumulate, across many relationships, into something that begins to resemble a norm cluster – not because states have consciously endorsed an ideology, but because the operational logic of the agreements embeds particular assumptions about how digital governance should work.

China has pursued norm projection with equal persistence through regional institutional frameworks, where multilateral endorsement amplifies legitimacy and treaty obligations can convert principles into routinised state practice. The Regional Comprehensive Economic Partnership (RCEP), which entered into force in January 2022 and covers approximately thirty per cent of global GDP (ASEAN Secretariat, 2022), illustrates how sovereignty-accommodating norms can be embedded in trade architecture through exceptions, omissions, and institutional design. RCEP's digital trade provisions adopt elements of the CPTPP/USMCA template and then preserve substantial regulatory space. Articles 12.14 (Location of Computing Facilities) and 12.15 (Cross-Border Transfer of Information by Electronic Means) mirror CPTPP language in prohibiting data localisation and restrictions on cross-border data flows as default rules, but the obligations are qualified by a self-judging 'legitimate public policy' necessity test (Art. 12.14.3(a), including the footnote stating that 'the necessity behind the implementation of such legitimate public policy shall be decided by the implementing Party'), an essential security exception that 'shall not be disputed by other Parties' (Arts. 12.14.3(b) and 12.15.3(b)), and the exclusion of the e-commerce chapter from RCEP's dispute-settlement mechanism (Art. 12.17.3). RCEP also contains no provision on source code or algorithm transfer, in contrast to CPTPP (Art. 14.17) and USMCA (Art. 19.16), preserving regulatory space for the kinds of national controls that China, Vietnam and Indonesia maintain domestically (Burri, 2021; Baldwin and Forslid, 2023). The effect is not to mandate Chinese-style governance across the Indo-Pacific, but to establish that sovereignty-accommodating approaches are a legitimate and unremarkable baseline for regional digital trade architecture – a precedent with significant long-term implications for the normative standard against which future agreements will be measured.

At the sub-regional level, the Shanghai Cooperation Organisation (SCO) has served since the early 2010s as the most doctrinally explicit vehicle for advancing sovereignty-first cybersecurity norms in a multilateral setting. The International Code of Conduct for Information Security, first circulated in 2011 and revised in 2015, was a joint initiative submitted to the UN by China, Russia, Tajikistan and Uzbekistan (with Kazakhstan and Kyrgyzstan added as co-sponsors of the 2015 revision) that frames cyberspace governance squarely in terms of state sovereignty and non-interference, and has been advanced repeatedly in UN contexts as an alternative to Western-backed approaches that emphasised the applicability of existing international law, accountability for state conduct, and—where legally relevant—international humanitarian law (Inkster, 2016; Klimburg, 2017). Within the SCO framework, cybersecurity cooperation is organised around state-to-state information sharing, joint law enforcement on cybercrime and counter-terrorism protocols that treat online content management as a legitimate security function. When SCO member states participate in joint cyber exercises, adopt shared incident response procedures, or harmonise their definitions of cybercrime through SCO frameworks, they absorb operational assumptions about the relationship between state authority and digital governance that track closely with China's domestic model – without the relationship ever being characterised as one of model transfer.

Southeast Asia has emerged as a particularly important regional arena. Driven by domestic imperatives to contain political conflict and manage public spaces without democratising (Gerschewski, 2013; Rodan, 2014; Lim, 2014), several governments in the region have shown interest in digital governance tools that strengthen state capacity over online information environments. China has cultivated bilateral digital partnerships with Cambodia, Laos, and – before the 2021 coup complicated the relationship – Myanmar, supplying surveillance infrastructure, data governance frameworks, and content-moderation systems whose technical and regulatory design may reflect Chinese templates. Cambodia's 2021 National Internet Gateway proposal, which would have routed internet traffic through state-controlled gateways and expanded state capacity for monitoring, blocking and disconnection, was widely compared by critics to Chinese-style internet control. It was later delayed after domestic and international pressure, but its drafting illustrated the attractiveness of sovereignty-centred and administratively centralised models of internet governance for some partner governments (Human Rights Watch, 2021). At the ASEAN level, China has consistently supported digital economy frameworks that emphasise national sovereignty and development while resisting binding commitments on data flows or rights-based safeguards – working with the organisation's consensus-based decision-making in ways that help keep regional digital governance architecture permissive enough to accommodate the sovereignty-first model (Acharya, 2004; Erie and Streinz, 2021). At the global level, China's norm entrepreneurship has operated through two analytically distinct but strategically complementary channels: the United Nations system and international technical standards organisations (Hoffman, 2019). They are complementary because they operate on different timescales and different audiences – the UN shapes the political and legal vocabulary of cyberspace governance, while standards bodies shape its technical architecture – and because advances in one domain can reinforce and legitimise advances in the other (DeNardis, 2014; Erie and Streinz, 2021).

Within the UN, China has worked across multiple forums to shift the terms of the cybersecurity debate toward a state-sovereignty frame. The most significant site of contestation has been the dual-track process of the Group of Governmental Experts (GGE) and the Open-Ended Working Group (OEWG) – the two negotiating bodies through which states have sought to establish norms for responsible state behaviour in cyberspace. China, frequently aligned with Russia and a rotating coalition of developing states, has resisted or sought to narrow some Western efforts to elaborate the application of international law, attribution practices and accountability mechanisms, while foregrounding sovereignty, non-interference and state-led governance (Maurer, 2011; Grigsby, 2017). The OEWG process was strongly supported by China and Russia because it broadened participation in cyber norms negotiations beyond the smaller GGE format and created a forum in which sovereignty-first framing could resonate with a wider group of states, including many with post-colonial sensitivities toward intervention and unequal technological dependence.

Beyond these negotiations, China has worked to expand the institutional mandate of the International Telecommunication Union (ITU) in ways that would concentrate internet governance authority in an intergovernmental body where state sovereignty is the organising principle by design, at the expense of ICANN and the broader multistakeholder model (DeNardis, 2014; Mueller, 2017). China supported the candidacy of Houlin Zhao as ITU Secretary-General across two terms, and Chinese delegations have advanced proposals within ITU Study Groups that have sought to expand the organisation's technical remit into areas – including content delivery, network management, and identity systems – where governance assumptions embedded in technical specifications carry significant political consequence.

The most dramatic illustration of standards politics as norm projection was the 'New IP' proposal, advanced by Huawei and Chinese research institutions within ITU Study Group 13 beginning in 2019. Critics argued that New IP's proposed redesign of internet architecture – especially its emphasis on semantic addressing, intrinsic security, deterministic networking and more controllable network management – could facilitate stronger identification, centralised control, and state-aligned governance of network traffic, even though its proponents presented it as a technical response to emerging network needs (Segal, 2020; Mueller and Yoo, 2024). The proposal met resistance from several Western governments and technical-community actors concerned about its governance implications. The episode is instructive in two respects: it demonstrated that Chinese actors are willing to contest foundational technical architecture, not merely peripheral specifications; and it illustrated the asymmetric difficulty of standards politics, in which advancing a proposal requires institutional access and drafting capacity, while defeating or redirecting it requires sustained political attention from actors who must first translate a technical document into politically legible stakes.

The pattern across these bilateral, regional, and international channels is not one of a single coherent strategy executed from the centre, but of overlapping and mutually reinforcing entrepreneurial activities that progressively shift the normative environment within which digital governance decisions are made. The components with the highest diffusion potential are sovereignty language – non-interference, jurisdictional authority over data and networks, policy space for domestic regulation – and development framing – connectivity, digital modernisation, capacity-building, technology transfer – because both can be embraced by states regardless of regime type or political alignment with Beijing. A government that would reject any characterisation of its digital governance as influenced by China may nonetheless sign a digital cooperation agreement premised on state-to-state coordination, accept infrastructure investment that embeds Chinese technical standards, endorse a regional trade agreement that preserves broad data localisation discretion, or support a UN resolution affirming national jurisdiction over cyberspace. Each decision is individually unremarkable and locally motivated. Cumulatively, they help constitute a governance environment in which sovereignty-first assumptions have become the baseline rather than the contested position.

4. Conclusion: The Portable Core of China's Cyber Sovereignty Model

This chapter has treated China's digital normative power as the outward projection of a governance cluster anchored by cyber sovereignty rather than as the export of a uniquely 'Chinese' set of ideas. The central claim is that China's influence travels through portable modules – jurisdictional language, compliance mechanisms, institutional templates, and technical standards – that can be adopted, adapted and hybridised by recipient states facing their own security, capacity and development pressures. Cyber sovereignty functions as the master frame because it aligns these modules under a single logic: cyberspace is a domain of national jurisdiction in which the state claims final authority to set rules, manage risk and shape the conditions of digital development.

Across the chapter, the analysis has shown how this frame is supported domestically through a primarily legal and regulatory implementation structure. The CSL/DSL/PIPL legal stack converts sovereignty claims into enforceable duties and establishes governance 'gates' around infrastructure, data, and personal information. China's external entrepreneurship – through bilateral agreements, Digital Silk Road infrastructure, regional frameworks, UN negotiations and standards bodies – then packages the frame in the universal language of sovereignty, security and development, while leaving room for selective uptake and plausible deniability about the more coercive implications of control.

The true measure of China's normative power, therefore, lies not in whether countries wholesale 'adopt China's model', but in which specific modules they borrow, and in the mechanisms through which China and target countries push and pull these digital norms. The chapter's argument can be distilled into a portable core of interlocking principles. First, cyber sovereignty asserts jurisdictional primacy: cyberspace is treated as an extension of territorial sovereignty, and the state claims ultimate authority over networks, platforms and data within its borders. Second, governance is organised around a security–development fusion in which modernisation and innovation are pursued through expansive security rationales that justify strong administrative oversight. Third, these elements are packaged externally as 'responsible governance' through sovereignty and development language, technical cooperation and capacity-building, enabling selective adoption even where political objectives differ. These principles do not imply a monolithic export or passive recipients. They describe travel-ready components of a governance model that can be embedded in laws, institutions, infrastructure systems and standards, and then reinterpreted within local political economies. The next step is therefore to trace how these components interact with recipient agency: when they become attractive tools of state-building, when they are resisted by civil society or market actors and when they are reshaped by competing templates in an increasingly crowded global marketplace of digital governance. In the next chapter, I develop a push–pull theoretical framework that specifies the mechanisms through which these dynamics are operationalised.

References

Acharya, A. (2004) 'How Ideas Spread: Whose Norms Matter? Norm Localization and Institutional Change in Asian Regionalism', *International Organization*, 58(2), pp. 239–275. https://doi.org/10.1017/S0020818304582024

ASEAN Secretariat (2022) 'Regional Comprehensive Economic Partnership (RCEP) agreement enters into force', ASEAN Main Portal, 1 January. Available at: https://asean.org/rcep-agreement-enters-into-force/ (accessed: 9 April 2026).

Baldwin, R. and Forslid, R. (2023) Globotics and Development: When Manufacturing Is Jobless and Services Are Tradeable. *World Trade Review*, 22(3–4), 302–311. doi:10.1017/S1474745623000241.

Bandurski, D. (2017) *Xi Jinping's Web of Laws*. Available at: https://medium.com/china-media-project/chinas-web-of-laws-39cfa747019c (accessed: 28 January 2026).

Bradford, A. (2020) *The Brussels Effect: How the European Union Rules the World*. Oxford: Oxford University Press.

Bradford, A. (2023) *Digital Empires: The Global Battle to Regulate Technology*. Oxford: Oxford University Press.

Brazil (2014) *Law No. 12,965 of April 23, 2014 (Marco Civil da Internet)*. English Translation (UNODC). Available at: https://www.unodc.org/cld/uploads/res/document/blz/law-12965-of-2014_html/Law_12965_2014.pdf (accessed: 16 October 2025).

Brazil (2020) *Data Protection Laws in Brazil*. Available at: https://www.dlapiperdataprotection.com/index.html?t=law and c=BR (accessed: 16 October 2025).

Burri, M. (2021) 'Towards a New Treaty on Digital Trade', *Journal of World Trade*, 55(1), pp. 77–100.

California Consumer Privacy Act (CCPA) (2018) *California Consumer Privacy Act*. Available at: https://oag.ca.gov/privacy/ccpa. (accessed: 16 October 2025).

Carrai, M. A. (2019) *Sovereignty in China: A Genealogy of a Concept Since 1840*. Cambridge: Cambridge University Press.

Cheney, C. (2019) 'China's Digital Silk Road: Strategic Technological Competition and Exporting Political Illiberalism', *Issues and Insights*, 19(8), Pacific Forum. Available at: https://pacforum.org/publication/issues-insights-vol-19-wp8-chinas-digital-silk-road-strategic-technological-competition-and-exporting-political-illiberalism (accessed: 9 Apr 2026).

Christakis, T. (2020) 'European Digital Sovereignty': Successfully Navigating Between the 'Washington Consensus' and the 'Beijing Syndrome'. Multidisciplinary Institute on Artificial Intelligence/Grenoble Alpes Data Institute. https://ssrn.com/abstract=3748098

CJEU (2020) Judgment of the Court (Grand Chamber) of 16 July 2020, Data Protection Commissioner v Facebook Ireland Limited and Maximillian Schrems, Case C-311/18, ECLI:EU:C:2020:559. Available at: https://eur-lex.europa.eu/legal-content/EN/TXT/?uri=CELEX:62018CJ0311 (accessed: 8 Apr 2026).

Creemers, R. and Webster, G. (2020) 'Translation: Chinese Scholar Lu Chuanying on the Stakes for New 'Personal Information' and 'Data Security' Laws', DigiChina, Stanford University, 28 May. Available at: https://digichina.stanford.edu/work/a-chinese-scholar-outlines-stakes-for-new-personal-information-and-data-security-laws-translation/ (accessed: 8 Apr 2026).

Creemers, R. (2022) 'China's Emerging Data Protection Framework', *Journal of Cybersecurity*, 8(1). https://doi.org/10.1093/cybsec/tyac011

Creemers, R. J. E. H. (2020) 'China's Conception of Cyber Sovereignty: Rhetoric and Realization', in Broeders D. and Berg B. van den (eds.) *Governing Cyberspace: Behavior, Power, and Diplomacy*. Digital Technologies and Global Politics. Lanham: Bloomsbury Publishing.

Cybersecurity and Infrastructure Security Agency (CISA). 2023. "2023 Year in Review." Washington, DC: US Department of Homeland Security. https://www.cisa.gov/about/2023YIR?utm_source=chatgpt.com

Data Security Law (2021) *Data Security Law of the People's Republic of China*. Available at: http://www.npc.gov.cn/englishnpc/c2759/c23934/202112/t20211209_385109.html

de La Bruyère, Emily. 2022. "A New Type of Geopolitical Power: China's Competitive Strategy for the Digital Revolution." In China's Digital Ambitions: A Global Strategy to Supplant the Liberal Order, edited by Emily de La Bruyère, Doug Strub, and Jonathon Marek. Seattle: National Bureau of Asian Research.

DeNardis, L. (2014) *The Global War for Internet Governance*. New Haven, CT: Yale University Press. https://doi.org/10.2307/j.ctt5vkz4n

Derivry, T. (2023) *[INTERVIEW] "The Chinese Approach to Digital Sovereignty": 4 Questions to Rogier Creemers*. Available at: https://www.sciencespo.fr/public/chaire

-numerique/en/2023/04/05/interview-the-chinese-approach-to-digital-sovereignty/. (accessed: 16 October 2025).

DigiChina (2017) *Translation: Cybersecurity Law of the People's Republic of China (Effective June 1, 2017)*. Available at: https://digichina.stanford.edu/work/translation-cybersecurity-law-of-the-peoples-republic-of-china-effective-june-1-2017/ (accessed: 28 January 2026).

DigiChina (2021) *Translation: Data Security Law of the People's Republic of China (Effective Sept. 1, 2021)*. Available at: https://digichina.stanford.edu/work/translation-data-security-law-of-the-peoples-republic-of-china/ (accessed: 28 January 2026).

Erie, M. S. and Streinz, T. (2021) 'The Beijing Effect: China's Digital Silk Road as Transnational Data Governance', *New York University Journal of International Law and Politics*, 54(1), pp. 1–92.

EU (2016) *General Data Protection Regulation (GDPR)*. Available at: https://eur-lex.europa.eu/eli/reg/2016/679/oj/eng (accessed: 16 October 2025).

European Commission (2020) 'Communication from the Commission: A European Strategy for Data', EUR-Lex, COM(2020) 66 Final, 19 February. Available at: https://eur-lex.europa.eu/legal-content/EN/TXT/?uri=CELEX:52020DC0066 (accessed: 8 Apr 2026).

European Commission (2023) Adequacy Decisions: How the EU Determines If a Non-EU Country Has an Adequate Level of Data Protection. Available at: https://commission.europa.eu/law/law-topic/data-protection/international-dimension-data-protection/adequacy-decisions_en (accessed: 8 Apr 2026).

Finnemore, M. and Sikkink, K. (1998) International Norm Dynamics and Political Change. *International Organization*, 52(4), pp. 887–917. http://www.jstor.org/stable/2601361

Flohr, A., Rieth, L., Schwindenhammer, S. and Wolf, K. D. (2010) *The Role of Business in Global Governance: Corporations as Norm-Entrepreneurs*. Basingstoke: Palgrave Macmillan.

Gagliardone, I. (2014) 'New Media and the Developmental State in Ethiopia', *African Affairs*, 113(451), pp. 279–299.

Gao, X. (2022) 'An Attractive Alternative? China's Approach to Cyber Governance and Its Implications for the Western Model', *The International Spectator*, 57(3), pp. 15–30. https://doi.org/10.1080/03932729.2022.2074710

Gerschewski, J. (2013) The Three Pillars of Stability: Legitimation, Repression, and Co-Optation in Autocratic Regimes. *Democratization*, 20(1), pp. 13–38. https://doi.org/10.1080/13510347.2013.738860

Ghiasy, R. and Zhou, J. (2017) *The Silk Road Economic Belt: Considering Security Implications and EU-China Cooperation Prospects*. Stockholm: Stockholm International Peace Research Institute (SIPRI). Available at: https://www.sipri.org/sites/default/files/The-Silk-Road-Economic-Belt.pdf (accessed: 9 April 2026).

Greitens, S. C. (2020) *Dealing with Demand for China's Global Surveillance Exports, Global China Report*. Washington, DC: Brookings Institution.

Grigsby, A. (2017) The End of Cyber Norms. *Survival*, 59(6), pp. 109–122.

Hillman, J. E. (2021) *The Digital Silk Road: China's Quest to Wire the World and Win the Future*. New York, NY: Harper Business.

Hoffman, S. (2019) *Engineering Global Consent: The Chinese Communist Party's Data-Driven Power Expansion*. Canberra: Australian Strategic Policy Institute (ASPI).

Huld, A. (2021) 'Critical Information Infrastructure in China – New Cybersecurity Regulations', *China Briefing*, 30 August. Available at: https://www.china-briefing.com/news/critical-information-infrastructure-chinas-new-regulations/ (accessed: 28 January 2026).

Human Rights Watch (2021) Cambodia: Internet Censorship, Control Expanded. 18 February. Available at: https://www.hrw.org/news/2021/02/18/cambodia-internet-censorship-control-expanded (accessed: 9 April 2026).

Inkster, N. (2016) *China's Cyber Power*. London: Routledge/The International Institute for Strategic Studies (IISS).

Klimburg, A. (2017) *The Darkening Web: The War for Cyberspace*. New York, NY: Penguin Random House.
Lee, A. (2021) *Personal Data, Global Effects: China's Draft Privacy Law in the International Context*. Available at: https://digichina.stanford.edu/work/personal-data-global-effects-chinas-draft-privacy-law-in-the-international-context/ (accessed: 28 January 2026).
Lim, M. (2014) 'Seeing Spatially: People, Networks and Movements in Digital and Urban Spaces', *International Development Planning Review*, 36(1), pp. 51–72.
Maurer, T. (2011) *Cyber Norm Emergence at the United Nations – An Analysis of the UN's Activities Regarding Cyber-Security* (Discussion Paper 2011-11). Cambridge, MA: Belfer Center for Science and International Affairs, Harvard Kennedy School.
MFA (2012) *Statement at Budapest Conference on Cyber Issues*. Available at: http://www.chinesemission-vienna.at/eng/zgbd/t977627.htm (accessed: 16 October 2025).
MFA (2017) "Wangluo kongjian guoji hezuo zhanlüe (International Strategy of Cooperation on Cyberspace)." Jointly Issued by the Ministry of Foreign Affairs and the Cyberspace Administration of China, 1 March 2017. Translation, accessed April 8, 2026.
Mueller, M. L. (2017) *Will the Internet Fragment? Sovereignty, Globalization and Cyberspace*. Cambridge: Polity Press.
Mueller, A. and Yoo, C. S. (2024) 'Crouching Tiger, Hidden Agenda?: The Emergence of China in the Global Internet Standard-Setting Arena', *Federal Communications Law Journal*, 76, p. 143. Available at: https://ssrn.com/abstract=4528546.
NIS 2 Directive (2022) Directive (EU) 2022/2555 of the European Parliament and of the Council. Available at: https://eur-lex.europa.eu/eli/dir/2022/2555/oj/eng (accessed: 8 Apr 2026).
NIS Directive (2016) *Directive (EU) 2016/1148 of the European Parliament and of the Council*. Available at: https://eur-lex.europa.eu/eli/dir/2016/1148/oj
O'Hara, K. and Hall, W. (2018) *Four Internets: The Geopolitics of Digital Governance*, CIGI Papers No. 206. Waterloo, ON: Centre for International Governance Innovation. Available at: https://www.cigionline.org/publications/four-internets-geopolitics-digital-governance/ (accessed: 28 April 2026).
Personal Information Protection Law (PIPL) (2021) *Personal Information Protection Law of the People's Republic of China*. Available at: http://en.npc.gov.cn.cdurl.cn/2021-12/29/c_694559.htm
Pohle, J. and Thiel, T. (2020) 'Digital sovereignty', *Internet Policy Review*, 9(4). https://doi.org/10.14763/2020.4.1532
Reding, V. (2012) 'The European Data Protection Framework for the Twenty-First Century', *International Data Privacy Law*, 2(3), pp. 119–129. https://doi.org/10.1093/idpl/ips015
Rodan, G. (2014) *Participation Without Democracy: Containing Conflict in Southeast Asia*. Ithaca, NY: Cornell University Press.
Segal, A. (2020) *China's Vision for Cyber Sovereignty and the Global Governance of Cyberspace, in NBR Special Report no. 87*. Seattle, WA: National Bureau of Asian Research.
Sheng, J., Xu, C. and Tao, E. (2021) *China Adopts New Data Security Law*. Available at: https://www.pillsburylaw.com/en/news-and-insights/china-adopts-new-data-security-law.html (accessed: 28 January 2026).
Shi-Kupfer, K. and Ohlberg, M. (2019) China's Digital Rise: Challenges for Europe. MERICS Papers on China No. 7. Mercator Institute for China Studies (MERICS). Available at: https://merics.org/en/report/chinas-digital-rise (accessed: 8 Apr 2026).
Triolo, P. and Webster, G. (2017) 'China's Strategic Thinking on Building Power in Cyberspace', *DigiChina*, 25 September. Available at: https://digichina.stanford.edu/work/chinas-strategic-thinking-on-building-power-in-cyberspace/ (accessed: 16 October 2025).
Voigt, P. and von dem Bussche, A. (2017) The EU General Data Protection Regulation (GDPR): A Practical Guide (1st ed.). Cham: Springer International Publishing. https://doi.org/10.1007/978-3-319-57959-7

Wang, O. (2021) *China Cybersecurity and Data Regulation: What Multinationals Should Know*. Available at: https://www.teneo.com/insights/articles/china-cybersecurity-and-data-regulation-what-multinationals-should-know/ (accessed: 28 January 2026).

WIC (2014) *Wuzhen Declaration.* Available at: https://www.scribd.com/document/247566581/World-Internet-Conference-Draft-Declaration (Accessed 16 October 2025).

Xi, J. (2015) *Speech at the 2nd World Internet Conference Opening Ceremony.* Available at: https://chinacopyrightandmedia.wordpress.com/2015/12/16/speech-at-the-2nd-world-internet-conference-opening-ceremony/ (accessed: 16 October 2025).

Xi, J. (2016) 在网络安全和信息化工作座谈会上的讲话 [Speech at the Work Conference on Cybersecurity and Informatization]. Available at https://archive.ph/8t2Av#selection-717.0-717.18 (accessed: 16 October 2025).

Zhang. (2022) 'China: The Interplay Between the PIPL, DSL, and CSL', DataGuidance, 30 June. Available at: https://www.dataguidance.com/opinion/china-interplay-between-pipl-dsl-and-csl (accessed: 8 Apr 2026).

2 How China's Digital Norms Circulate

A Multi-Level Theory of Digital Normative Power

The previous chapter mapped the architecture of China's digital governance model: cyber sovereignty as its organising ideology, and the CSL–DSL–PIPL legal stack as the regulatory machinery that translates that ideology into enforceable rules. But identifying what a normative model contains is not the same as understanding how it travels. Norms do not shape international order simply by existing, nor simply because they originate from a powerful state. They matter when they move – when they are adopted, adapted, resisted or quietly absorbed by other actors (Acharya, 2004; Merry, 2006; Stone, 2012). This chapter is about that movement. How do norms of digital order cross borders? And what does tracing that movement reveal about the nature and limits of China's normative power in cyberspace? The question is harder than it first appears. Governments across the world are scrambling, often simultaneously, to regulate digital infrastructure, control data flows and rein in platform power. The pressures driving them are frequently similar – security, sovereignty concerns, the political appeal of visible state control over foreign technology – and so, unsurprisingly, are some of the tools they reach for. Convergence, in other words, does not require a single point of origin. States can arrive at similar instruments independently (DiMaggio and Powell, 1983; Drezner, 2005). They can borrow vocabulary without changing practice or change practice without borrowing vocabulary. They can adopt frameworks that superficially resemble China's for reasons that have nothing to do with Beijing (Erie and Streinz, 2021). This is the attribution problem at the heart of the chapter. If similarity alone cannot establish Chinese influence, what can? Establishing that something specifically Chinese is moving requires more than documenting resemblance. It requires clearly specifying what normative power is – through which channels it operates, what incentives it mobilises and what effects it produces at the receiving end – and then demonstrating that the cumulative pattern across bilateral, regional, and multilateral settings is best explained by push-and-pull dynamics between China and the target country, regional organisation or institution.

The argument here is not that China is the sole or even dominant driver of every governance shift that its model resembles. It is that China has, through deliberate and sustained effort, built a set of governance instruments it is actively promoting beyond its borders, and that across enough cases and contexts, the cumulative pattern is attributable to that effort in ways that cannot be fully explained by

DOI: 10.4324/9781042023738-3

coincidence. Understanding how those instruments travel – who takes them up, in what form, for what reasons, and with what modifications – is precisely what licences us to speak of Chinese normative power in cyberspace, rather than merely a Chinese-inflected moment in a broader global turn towards digital sovereignty. This chapter proceeds in three parts. It first examines what normative power means as a theoretical concept and how existing frameworks need to be adapted for the digital domain. It then develops a multi-level theory of how digital norms circulate, distinguishing among bilateral, regional and multilateral channels and the distinct logics operating within each. Finally, it confronts the attribution question directly: what evidentiary standard is required, and what – if anything – justifies attaching a Chinese label to governance norms whose individual components are, in isolation, rarely unique.

1. Normative Power

Any serious engagement with China's influence on global digital governance must begin by being precise about the kind of power at issue. The claim advanced here is that China shapes what becomes normal, legitimate and practically available in others' governance choices in cyberspace regulation, and that this capacity constitutes a distinctive form of power poorly captured by either the coercion or the soft power frameworks dominating international relations scholarship (Jackson, 1975). The conceptual foundation lies in the constructivist tradition's treatment of norms. In the canonical formulation of Finnemore and Sikkink (1998), norms are shared standards of appropriate conduct that acquire force through socialisation and institutionalisation: actors come to follow them not because they are compelled to, but because the norms have become embedded in organisational routines, professional training, legal frameworks and shared assumptions about what governance looks like. Norms that reach this stage of internalisation are no longer experienced as external constraints – they are simply the way things are done. Power, on this view, is exercised not only when actors are forced to do things they would otherwise resist, but also when the range of options they consider, the vocabulary they use to justify choices, and the institutional designs they treat as obvious or technically correct are shaped by norms that originate elsewhere (Barnett and Duvall, 2005).

Soft power ultimately depends on attraction or persuasion at the receiving end, although states may actively cultivate the resources and channels through which attraction is produced. It is in this register that the concept of normative power operates. The foundational formulation comes from Manners (2002), who argued – originally in relation to the European Union – that normative power lies in an actor's ability to define what passes for normal in international life: 'the ability to shape conceptions of 'the normal'' which is, for Manners, 'ultimately the greatest power of all'. Normative power refers here to the capacity to make a governance repertoire appear legitimate, appropriate, and practically usable beyond the setting in which it was developed. Material inducement, infrastructural dependence, or conditionality are not themselves normative power. They become relevant only when they alter what recipients treat as an appropriate or normal way of governing beyond the immediate transaction. Normative power is also analytically distinct from soft power in Nye's (1990) sense. Soft power ultimately depends on attraction or persuasion at the receiving end, although states may actively cultivate the resources and channels through which attraction is produced. Normative power, as used here, does not require admiration or emulation. Recipient states and institutions may instead come to regard particular instruments, institutional designs, and regulatory vocabularies as workable and legitimate through promotion, professional socialisation, institutional incentives, or repeated use. The recipient's uptake and the conditions shaping it are therefore as important as the promoter's intentions. Normative power is not simply the spread of ideas but the stabilisation of a governance repertoire: a set of principles and instruments that becomes administratively workable, institutionally reproduced, and treated as a plausible or default response to a governance problem (Erie and Streinz, 2021). The test is not merely whether officials acknowledge Chinese influence, but whether a recognisable repertoire can be traced through identifiable channels and whether recipient-side conditions explain why it took hold where and when it did.

The Mannersian concept of normative power was developed in relation to the European Union's distinctive mode of international engagement – one characterised by explicit conditionality, legal harmonisation and dense institutional infrastructure for projecting regulatory standards outward, primarily toward states seeking closer integration (Schimmelfennig and Sedelmeier, 2004; Börzel and Risse, 2012). This context shaped the concept in ways that do not travel straightforwardly to other actors, and particularly not to China, and even less from China to the developing world.

Several bodies of work have expanded the analysis of norm diffusion beyond its Eurocentric origins in ways that are directly relevant here (Checkel, 2005; Steinhilper, 2015). Acharya (2004) challenged the assumption that norm diffusion runs primarily from West to rest and introduced the concept of 'norm localisation' – the process through which local actors reconstruct and adapt external norms to fit their own institutional and cultural contexts, making reception an active and creative process rather than passive adoption. The question is therefore not whether Chinese norms are adopted wholesale but whether Chinese-origin governance instruments become available as building blocks that recipient states assemble in locally inflected ways. Zürn (2018) adds a further dimension by noting that normative authority in a contested international order is increasingly exercised not through consensus but through the selective construction of institutional platforms and coalitions that make certain governance approaches look normal within particular arenas – a dynamic that maps closely onto China's engagement with multilateral digital governance forums. Particularly relevant is the strand of scholarship on 'rest-to-rest' diffusion, which documents how governance models travel among non-Western states through channels that bypass traditional Western-led institutions – bilateral cooperation agreements, regional organisations, South–South technical assistance and infrastructure partnerships (Kang, 2007; Towns, 2012).

Kavalski's (2013) relational account of normative power is an important corrective for the purposes of this chapter. On his account, normative powers do not impose but engage others in shared practices, and the consent of the influenced – partial, conditional, and strategic as it may be – is constitutive rather than incidental to the normative relationship. To the question 'is China imposing its model?', this adds another: 'are other actors orienting themselves toward China's governance repertoire?' Orientation – including resistance, hybridisation and partial adoption – is itself evidence of normative traction, because it means the repertoire is present in the governance field as an option.

This relational insight has a direct structural implication for how the analysis is organised. If normative power is constituted in the interaction between supply and demand, the analysis cannot focus solely on what China does: what standards it promotes, what governance vocabulary it advances and how. It must attend equally to what recipients do: how they demand, filter, adapt, resist and recombine what China offers, and how those recipient-side dynamics shape what normative influence actually produces. This is the analytical logic behind the push–pull framework developed in this chapter's Section 2, which disaggregates both the China-anchored mechanisms through which governance instruments are supplied and the host-country mechanisms through which they are demanded, filtered, and transformed – before examining how these dynamics interact across bilateral, regional, and international levels. Crucially, push and pull do not map onto fixed actors: both Chinese actors and recipients can push and pull simultaneously, and the normative outcome is co-produced in the space between them rather than unilaterally determined by either side.

A central analytical tension has to be addressed in relation to this framework: the separation of normative intent from normative effects. Normative intent refers to what China claims, promotes or seeks to legitimise: the principles articulated in official discourse, the governance vocabulary advanced in bilateral and multilateral settings, the institutional forms and legal devices presented as appropriate responses to digital governance challenges. But intent is not China's alone to declare. Recipient states, regions and international organisations also enter the exchange with their own agendas – seeking infrastructure finance, regulatory templates, technical standards or international legitimisation for governance choices they have already taken or are independently inclined toward (Erie and Streinz, 2021). Their receptivity is not passive: it reflects strategic calculations, bureaucratic interests and prior institutional commitments that shape which elements of a promoted repertoire are adopted, which are rejected and which are adapted beyond recognition (Acharya, 2004). Normative effects, then, refer to what actually changes in recipient settings – law, institutional design, enforcement practice, procurement requirements and routinised compliance behaviour – but those effects are jointly produced by the promoting state's diffusion efforts and the recipient's own purposes in engaging with them. The two dimensions of intent frequently diverge from each other and from observable effects. China may promote a coherent set of governance principles while recipients translate them into locally inflected institutional forms that share the architecture but modify the content – sometimes because the recipient's interests demanded modification, sometimes because local institutional conditions made fidelity impossible. Conversely, effects can occur even when there is no declared alignment on either side, because the circulation of governance instruments may travel through intermediaries – vendors, consultants, technical communities, regional organisations – that obscure the provenance of what is being transmitted and dissolve any clean attribution of intent to a single actor (Ong and Collier, 2005; Peck and Theodore, 2010).

The first error this distinction guards against is the attribution trap: treating any convergence with Chinese governance vocabulary in a foreign legal text as evidence of Chinese normative power. Similar instruments can emerge from entirely independent origins – the Snowden revelations of 2013 were one important catalyst for a surge in data localisation proposals across jurisdictions with very different relationships with China, demonstrating that shared threat perceptions, not Chinese influence, can generate similar governance outcomes (Weyland, 2005; Hill, 2014; Chander and Le, 2015; Pohle and Thiel, 2020). Establishing that something specifically Chinese is moving requires tracing the pathway, not merely documenting the similarity.

The second error is the inverse: treating the absence of explicit Chinese attribution in a recipient's governance choices as evidence that Chinese influence is absent. When governance instruments become sufficiently embedded in international standards and regional frameworks, they cease to be identifiable as Chinese in the minds of the administrators who reproduce them. This is, in a sense, the condition of normative success: a governance repertoire that has to be explicitly labelled retains an element of foreignness, whereas one that has been naturalised is simply how things are done. The analytical task is therefore to trace the genealogy of governance instruments even when the actors reproducing them cannot or do not provide that genealogy themselves.

A further complication – developed fully in the next section – is that Chinese digital governance norms diffuse into a crowded normative environment already populated by European, American and emerging-power governance frameworks, making outcomes almost always hybrid and attribution inherently difficult.

One of the most important features of China's digital governance influence is that it does not depend on recipients sharing China's political values or endorsing its domestic governance arrangements. This is what makes normative power, rather than ideological influence or model export, the appropriate analytical framework.

The governance instruments that constitute China's digital regulatory architecture – data classification systems, localisation requirements, cybersecurity review mechanisms, operator cooperation obligations, content governance frameworks, platform accountability rules – are, in their individual components, largely separable from the political context in which they were developed. A government that wants to assert greater control over data flows for domestic political reasons, or that wants to build state capacity over digital infrastructure for developmental purposes, or that wants to reduce dependence on foreign technology providers for economic or security reasons, can adopt elements of China's governance toolkit without endorsing China's political system, its surveillance practices, or its approach to internet content control (Gunitsky, 2015). The instruments are modular: they can be disaggregated, adapted and recombined in ways that serve locally determined objectives that may differ substantially from China's own.

Technology acquisition alone, however, does not establish adoption of Chinese norms. A normative effect requires additional evidence that associated legal instruments, institutional designs, professional practices, or justificatory vocabularies were transmitted, adapted, and reproduced in the recipient setting. This modularity helps make Chinese-linked technologies and associated governance practices portable across diverse political contexts, and it generates the push and pull dynamics examined next. As Feldstein (2021) has documented in relation to AI surveillance infrastructure, and as Greitens (2020) has shown in relation to 'safe city' technologies, recipients governments that adopt Chinese-linked digital governance instruments are not simply passive consumers of an ideological model. They pursue practical governance objectives such as crime control, political stability, rapid digital modernisation, reduction of technological dependence.

Normative power operates along pathways of institutional availability: where alternative governance repertoires are already entrenched, Chinese-origin instruments face higher barriers to adoption; where governance is being constructed from scratch or reformed under pressure, the availability of a coherent and administratively workable toolkit is itself a significant form of influence. The framework therefore generates the expectation that China's digital governance tends to be stronger in states that share certain structural features – governments prioritising state capacity over individual rights, facing pressures of rapid digital modernisation without established regulatory traditions, sceptical of Western-led governance frameworks or embedded in infrastructure relationships with Chinese providers – than in states with strong pre-existing regulatory traditions, established multistakeholder governance institutions, or deep integration with Western legal and technical standards. Section 2's analysis of pull mechanisms elaborates the specific demand-side conditions that make different recipient states more or less receptive to Chinese-origin governance instruments.

The final analytical question is when the cumulative pattern of governance instrument circulation crosses the threshold at which it is meaningful to speak of Chinese normative power rather than of a more diffuse global trend. The answer proposed here is that the threshold is crossed when three conditions are jointly met – conditions that Section 2's mechanism analysis is designed to establish and that Section 3's method is designed to test.

The first condition is coherence: the instruments that circulate must display a recognisable and sufficiently distinctive governance configuration, rather than a generic combination of sovereignty, security, and regulatory control found in many legal systems. The analysis therefore looks for more specific architectural relationships, such as the integration of cybersecurity with content or public-order objectives, graded data classification linked to national-security review, broad operator cooperation duties, and weak institutional separation between privacy supervision and security authority. Even the appearance of such a configuration is only a clue; it does not establish origin or transmission without process evidence. The second condition is channel specificity: the circulation can be traced through identifiable pathways linking Chinese governance practices to recipient outcomes – bilateral cooperation frameworks, infrastructure partnerships, technical assistance programmes, standards body engagement, regional organisation influence – rather than through diffuse background convergence. Section 2 disaggregates these channels into their constituent mechanisms, distinguishing China-anchored push mechanisms from host-country pull mechanisms and from the regional and international mechanisms that amplify, filter and transform what travels between them. The existence of specific channels does not prove that Chinese influence explains every adoption, but it establishes that the pathway exists and that adoption by states embedded in those channels is more likely than adoption by states that are not.

The third condition is cumulativity: the pattern holds across multiple independently evidenced cases and more than one transmission channel, in ways that cannot be explained by coincidence or by the independent operation of entirely unrelated factors. No single case establishes normative power, and a large number of weakly evidenced cases does not become persuasive through accumulation alone. What matters is the accumulation of cases containing credible process evidence that, taken together, are better explained by the operation of Chinese-origin governance influence than by the alternatives. It is only when all three conditions are met – coherence, channel specificity and cumulativity – that the analysis can move from documenting similarity to attributing the extent of normative power (George and Bennett, 2005; Goertz and Mahoney, 2012; Bennett and Checkel, 2015).

2. The Mechanisms of Normative Power: Push, Pull and Translation across Levels

Most existing accounts of Chinese digital governance influence are supply-side accounts. They focus on what China does – what instruments it promotes, what infrastructure it exports, what positions it advances in multilateral forums – and treat the spread of Chinese-aligned governance norms as a more or less direct function of Chinese agency. This framing is incomplete in two related ways. It understates the degree to which recipient states, regional organisations, and international bodies are active participants in normative circulation rather than passive targets of Chinese projection. And it misrepresents the causal structure of diffusion itself, which is not a unidirectional transmission from promoter to receiver but a relational process in which supply interacts with demand to produce outcomes that neither side fully controls or anticipates. The corrective is to treat normative power as a two-sided phenomenon. Both China and recipient actors can push – projecting, insisting, conditioning, negotiating – and pull – requesting, attracting, selectively borrowing. A government that actively solicits Chinese training programmes, requests infrastructure financing on Chinese terms or endorses Chinese positions in multilateral forums is not a passive object of influence: it is a co-producer of the normative outcome (Gagliardone, 2019; Soulé, 2022). The framework developed here therefore disaggregates both the mechanisms through which governance instruments are supplied and the mechanisms through which they are demanded, filtered, amplified and transformed on the receiving end. These mechanisms operate across three levels of international interaction – bilateral, regional and international – each with its own logic, its own characteristic actors, and its own relationship to the others. The levels are not a simple ladder of scale; they interact recursively, with dynamics at one level shaping and sometimes transforming what is possible at the others. The following three sections examine each level in turn.

2.1 The Bilateral Level

The mechanisms operating at the bilateral level are heterogeneous – infrastructure provision, discursive framing, epistemic socialisation and institutional bargaining – but they share a common analytical feature: they are dyadic, occurring within a relationship in which Chinese actors and a specific counterpart state or institution are the primary parties. What makes the bilateral level analytically distinctive is not only its directness but its asymmetry. Many cases examined here involve asymmetries in market size, financing capacity, technological capability, or bargaining resources, although the form and consequences of those asymmetries vary considerably. (Hu, 2011). That asymmetry structures both the supply and the demand side of normative transfer. On the supply side, it may give Chinese actors leverage to connect financing, training, or market access on governance choices that align with Chinese preferences. On the demand side, it generates genuine demand for off-the-shelf regulatory templates, institutional models, and technical standards among governments that lack the capacity or the time to develop them independently. The bilateral relationship is therefore a meeting point of Chinese projection and recipient-country need, and the governance norms that emerge from it bear the marks of both. Each mechanism described below can be operationalised empirically. The analytical task is not simply to identify the mechanism but to trace its observable imprint – in contracts, laws, procurement records, training rosters and legislative debates – and to assess whether the governance choices that followed reflect Chinese-origin design features rather than convergence that would have occurred regardless. Three China-anchored push mechanisms and three host-anchored pull and resistance mechanisms are identified (see Figure 2.1).

2.2 China-Anchored Push Mechanisms

Infrastructure entanglement and path dependency (C1) is the most visible potential push mechanism, although its normative consequences cannot be inferred from the nationality of the vendor alone. It encompasses the construction and financing of

Figure 2.1 Push and pull mechanisms at the bilateral level.

backbone networks, data centres, surveillance systems, undersea cables and mobile network rollouts – often delivered as integrated packages by Chinese firms operating with state-backed financing. Such projects may create switching costs, maintenance dependencies, training relationships, and technical affordances that make some regulatory and procurement choices easier than others. In particular cases, contractual requirements, system configurations, or associated technical assistance may also facilitate particular approaches to network management, data access, security certification, or interoperability. These effects must be demonstrated at the level of contracts, system design, operating practices, training, or subsequent regulatory decisions; the installation of Chinese equipment does not by itself embed Chinese legal norms (Jasanoff and Kim, 2009; Farrell and Newman, 2019).

Financing itself may generate a distinct and softer form of alignment. In Repnikova's account of Chinese soft power (2022), attraction operates not through the appeal of a political model but through the practical demonstration of responsiveness – China's willingness to provide infrastructure financing without many of the governance and policy conditions commonly associated with Western or multilateral development finance generates goodwill that can translate into diplomatic deference and diplomatic goodwill or openness to Chinese policy experience (Brautigam, 2009). On this reading, recipient governments may align more closely with Chinese governance templates not because infrastructure lock-in constrains their choices but because Chinese financing is experienced as a genuine development partnership, producing voluntary rather than structurally coerced convergence. Tracing these dynamics empirically requires working across several overlapping bodies of evidence. The starting point is establishing the basic fact of Chinese financial presence in each country's digital infrastructure, for which AidData's Global Chinese Development Finance Dataset (Custer et al., 2021) provides an important open-source reconstruction, cross-referenced against MOFCOM project announcements, available policy-bank disclosures, and – where available – host-government budget documents and parliamentary appropriations records. These sources rarely tell the whole story individually; Chinese-side records tend to omit contract terms while host-government records sometimes obscure vendor identity behind procurement categories. Read together, they may permit a reasonable reconstruction of which Chinese firms – Huawei, ZTE, Hikvision, China Telecom and others – hold contracts in which infrastructure domains, and on what financing terms (Tugendhat and Voo, 2021; Agbebi, 2023).

The harder analytical task is assessing what those deployments actually produced in governance terms. The question is not simply whether Chinese infrastructure was installed but whether its installation reshaped the regulatory choices that followed – and here the evidence must be read with some care. The inference is probabilistic rather than deterministic: infrastructure entanglement restructures the opportunity space within which governance decisions are made, making certain regulatory alignments more natural and others more costly, without mandating any particular outcome. What the analysis looks for, in the period following major deployments, is whether decisions on lawful access obligations, data localisation requirements, procurement rules and security certification reflect design choices that are compatible with or constrained by the installed base – and, crucially, whether alignment extends into governance domains where no such technical constraint exists, which would suggest the reputational rather than the structural pathway is doing the work.

Bilateral agreements and standard-alignment clauses (C2) constitute the second mechanism, operating through the formal diplomatic architecture that accompanies infrastructure deployment. Chinese bilateral digital cooperation agreements, technology governance frameworks, and information and communications memoranda may provide a diplomatic or administrative framework alongside infrastructure contracts, and in some documented cases contain governance commitments, procurement preferences, joint standard-development clauses or capacity-building provisions that translate broad political alignment into specific institutional obligations. Their significance is not merely declaratory: they establish reference points that subsequent regulatory and procurement decisions can invoke, and they create the administrative relationships – joint commissions, technical working groups, interministerial exchanges – through which norm diffusion is routinised rather than episodic.

Reconstructing this documentary record requires working across sources that are rarely complete in any single location. Treaty databases, MOFCOM records, host-government gazette publications and parliamentary ratification registers each capture different fragments of the picture, and reading them against one another is often necessary to establish even the basic fact of an agreement's existence, let alone its content. For each instrument identified, the analysis examines what governance commitments it contains and how binding they are in practice; whether it includes procurement preferences or explicit references to Chinese technical standards; and how its signature relates temporally to subsequent regulatory or procurement decisions in the recipient country. That temporal relationship is a necessary but not sufficient basis for inference. Where the content of an agreement explicitly anticipates a subsequent governance choice – where standard-alignment clauses in a cooperation framework are followed by a cybersecurity law whose architecture is structurally compatible with those clauses – the evidentiary chain is meaningfully strengthened. Where alignment appears only after the fact, or in domains the agreement does not address, the inference requires additional support from other channels.

Epistemic socialisation (C3) operates through a different and more diffuse logic. Training programmes, study tours, Huawei ICT Academy[1] university partnerships, Chinese government scholarships administered through the China Scholarship Council and ministry-to-ministry technical exchanges in network management, cybersecurity and data governance do not impose rules directly. What they do is socialise participants into particular vocabularies, problem framings and technical reference ecosystems – a form of influence whose effects may only become visible when alumni move into roles where those frameworks shape institutional design, procurement criteria or regulatory drafting. The mechanism is softer than infrastructure embedding or contractual obligation, but it is not for that reason negligible: professional socialisation shapes what officials treat as the normal and workable approach to a governance problem, and that prior orientation can matter as much as formal instruction when decisions are made under time pressure or resource constraint.

Of the channels through which epistemic socialisation operates, Huawei's ICT Academy is the most tractable for systematic documentation (El Kadi, 2022). Its university partnerships follow a standardised model with publicly announced institutional agreements, publicly described curricula and certification records, making it possible to construct a reasonably complete picture of its reach across the case countries. Other channels are less consistently documented. CSC scholarship records, ministry training participant lists and Confucius Institute programme data are often fragmentary and require reconstruction from parliamentary answers, university press releases, budget documents and, where available, freedom of information requests (Hartig, 2016; Benabdallah, 2020). The evidentiary standard is correspondingly more modest: establishing the existence and approximate scale of these programmes, rather than full participant-level records.

2.3 Host-Anchored Pull and Resistance Mechanisms

Recipient states are not passive objects of Chinese normative projection. They are strategic actors with their own governance priorities, institutional constraints and external relationships, and their responses to Chinese digital engagement are shaped by those factors as much as by Chinese intent. Three host-country mechanisms merit systematic empirical treatment, each leaving a distinct evidential trace and each illuminating a different dimension of how recipient agency shapes normative outcomes.

Hedging and diversification (H1) is the most common response, involving the cultivation of multiple supplier and governance relationships that preserve

1 Homepage of Huawei ICT academy: https://e.huawei.com/en/talent/ict-academy/#/home.

strategic flexibility and reduce dependence on any single external actor. States that deploy Chinese infrastructure in one domain may adopt non-Chinese vendors in others; those that endorse Chinese positions in multilateral forums may simultaneously maintain regulatory frameworks aligned with European or other standards. Hedging is both a pull mechanism – states draw in Chinese infrastructure and financing where it is cost-competitive or strategically useful – and a form of normative resistance, as the cultivation of alternative partnerships retains room for governance manoeuvre that wholesale reliance on Chinese provision would foreclose.

Documenting hedging requires constructing a full vendor landscape across infrastructure domains rather than focusing exclusively on Chinese presence. The relevant sources are procurement registers, contract records, parliamentary budget hearings and regulatory filings, read together to establish not just who won contracts but what alternatives were available and, where the record permits, why particular choices were made. Explicit diversification signals – procurement decisions that passed over Chinese bids, multi-vendor requirements written into legislation or official statements about reducing exposure to single-source dependencies – are analytically more informative than the mere fact of vendor diversity, since they suggest deliberate resistance rather than incidental pluralism. Equally important is whether engagement with alternative partners such as the EU's digital cooperation instruments, USAID's Digital Strategy (USAID, 2020), or the D4D Hub (Expertise France, 2025) extends to governance alignment or remains purely financial. The distinction matters: alternative financing without regulatory reorientation leaves Chinese-origin governance instruments considerable space to consolidate, while genuine normative pluralism – Budapest Convention accession (Council of Europe, 2001), GDPR-aligned data protection reform, participation in Western cybersecurity capacity-building – indicates a more substantive form of resistance whose effects on the overall governance trajectory can be assessed.

Selective adaptation and recombination (H2) captures something more active than resistance: the deliberate filtering, modification and repackaging of Chinese governance instruments according to domestic priorities, legal traditions and external regulatory pressures. The result is governance arrangements that combine Chinese-origin structural logics with non-Chinese legal vocabularies, producing hybrid frameworks in which no single external model is reproduced wholesale and explicit attribution to any source may be entirely absent. This is the mechanism that makes straightforward influence-tracing most difficult, and it is where the analysis must be most methodologically self-conscious.

The work here is primarily legal and architectural rather than quantitative. Comparing a recipient country's data protection statute or cybersecurity framework against Chinese and European reference models at the level of surface vocabulary will often yield misleading results: a law can invoke the GDPR while embedding structural features characteristic of Chinese governance design, and vice versa. The diagnostic questions that matter are architectural: does the law establish hierarchical data classification with state access obligations at each tier? Are cross-border transfers subject to security review rather than adequacy determination? Is cybersecurity defined broadly enough to encompass content regulation or political stability? Are critical information infrastructure designations drawn widely enough to bring commercial platforms under state oversight? These structural choices can persist through multiple rounds of legal revision and relabelling, and identifying them – rather than tracking surface citations – is the core analytical task. The absence of explicit Chinese attribution in a recipient's framework is therefore not evidence of absent influence; it may instead be evidence that the adaptation has been thorough.

Strategic negotiation and institutional bargaining (H3) represents the most direct expression of recipient agency: explicit contestation in which governments use their market size, strategic location, institutional capacity or access to competing offers to push back against Chinese terms and reshape the governance conditions attached to digital cooperation. Where selective adaptation works through domestic filtering after the fact, strategic negotiation operates at the moment of engagement itself – recipient governments reject proposed terms, demand modifications or leverage alternative bids to shift what China is willing to offer.

The evidentiary record for this mechanism is the most dispersed and the most dependent on sources that states and firms have incentives to suppress. Parliamentary debates, public accounts committee reports, audit findings, investigative journalism and – where they have entered the public domain – diplomatic communications are the most productive starting points. Renegotiated contracts, inserted technology-transfer or localisation requirements, and documented uses of competing offers to shift vendor terms all leave traces across these sources, though rarely in a single place. The analytical significance of strategic negotiation extends beyond the individual cases in which it occurs: it establishes the genuine limits of Chinese normative power and demonstrates that those limits are partly endogenous to the recipient's own institutional capacity and strategic position. A country that successfully negotiates vendor choice clauses, data-hosting conditions or regulatory carve-outs is not simply receiving Chinese governance influence in a modified form – it is co-authoring the arrangement that results, and in doing so it modifies what Chinese normative power actually produces within its jurisdiction. That co-authorship is part of what the relational account of normative power, developed in the preceding section, predicts; its presence or absence across the case countries is accordingly one of the central empirical questions the analysis addresses.

3. The Regional Level

The regional level occupies a distinctive analytical position in the diffusion of Chinese digital governance norms. It is an intermediate arena in which governance instruments that originate in bilateral relationships acquire broader legitimacy through regional institutional endorsement – and in which regional organisations function simultaneously as amplifiers, scaling bilateral preferences into frameworks that carry authority over multiple states and as filters, subjecting those preferences to negotiation among actors with divergent interests and often producing

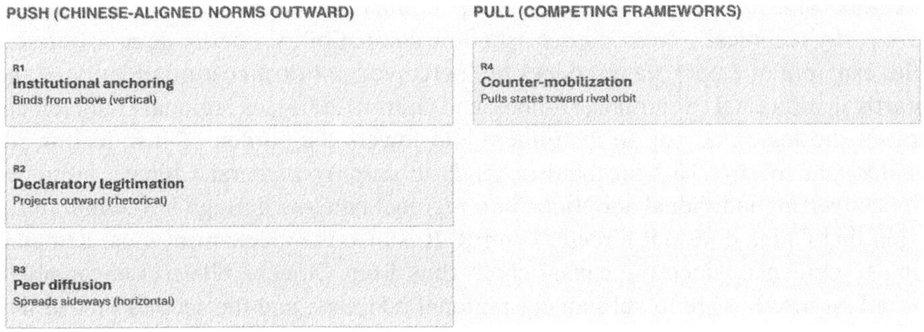

Figure 2.2 Push and pull mechanisms at the regional level.

hybrid outcomes. Four mechanisms are identifiable at this level, each leaving a distinct evidentiary trace (see Figure 2.2).

The first is regional institutional anchoring (R1): the incorporation of Chinese-aligned governance principles or instruments into regional frameworks, including joint declarations, cooperation mechanisms, cybersecurity instruments, and action plans. Such endorsement may give a position authority beyond China's bilateral relationship with any individual state, but Chinese authorship or influence must be demonstrated rather than inferred from compatibility alone. The clearest example is the International Code of Conduct for Information Security, first submitted to the UN by China, Russia, Tajikistan, and Uzbekistan in 2011 and resubmitted in revised form by six SCO member states in 2015 (United Nations General Assembly [UNGA], 2015). It illustrates how positions associated with China and other sovereignty-oriented states can be advanced as a collective initiative. It should not, however, be described as a binding SCO convention or as evidence that every participating state adopted an identical domestic model.

The second mechanism is declaratory legitimation through coalition construction (R2): the use of regional groupings to convert national preferences into positions presented as collectively endorsed. This mechanism does not require recognisably Chinese vocabulary to appear in joint texts, but claims of Chinese influence require evidence of drafting, agenda-setting, or sustained diplomatic sponsorship. Successive BRICS declarations show a growing willingness to affirm sovereign equality and national regulatory authority in digital affairs. Whether this amounts to endorsement of China's more specific doctrine of cyber sovereignty must be established through close textual comparison and evidence of China's role in producing the relevant language; a progression from implicit compatibility to explicit endorsement should not be assumed from general sovereignty language alone (BRICS, 2022; 2024).

The third mechanism is regulatory contagion and peer diffusion (R3): the horizontal spread of governance instruments among states within a region through effects that operate independently of direct Chinese engagement. Once a significant state within a region adopts a Chinese-aligned governance instrument, neighbouring states face pressure to adopt compatible instruments for reasons that are partly technical – cross-border data flow compatibility – partly demonstrative – the example of a peer state reduces the perceived political cost of adoption – and partly institutional (Simmons, Dobbin, and Garrett, 2006), as regional endorsement raises the legitimacy of an instrument and lowers the burden of justification for states that follow. This mechanism tends to amplify bilateral Chinese influence by converting individual adoptions into regional patterns through horizontal diffusion that China does not directly control. It is also the mechanism most demanding to evidence, since the causal chain runs from Chinese bilateral engagement to a first-mover state to subsequent regional adopters, and the second link in that chain – from first-mover adoption to peer diffusion – involves no Chinese actor at all. Tracing it requires documenting both the first adoption and the subsequent pattern, and assessing whether the structural features that travel across the peer group are identifiable as Chinese-origin rather than as independent convergences on similar governance problems and thereby may increase the legal and commercial costs of adopting instruments that conflict with GDPR-style rights, independent supervision, or transfer safeguards.

The fourth mechanism is counter-mobilisation and competitive norm promotion (R4): the organisation, at the regional level, of resistance to Chinese digital governance instruments through alternative institutional frameworks that create strong incentives for incompatible regulatory choices among their members. The EU's adequacy framework is the most analytically consequential counter-mechanism in the cases examined here (Bradford, 2020), because it creates a structural pull toward GDPR-compatible governance among states seeking frictionless data flows with the European market – and thereby may increase the legal and commercial costs of adopting instruments that conflict with GDPR-style rights, independent supervision, or transfer safeguards (Erie and Streinz, 2021; Li and Chen, 2024). Understanding Chinese digital governance influence at the regional level therefore requires attending not only to the mechanisms through which Chinese-aligned norms are promoted and adopted, but to the counter-mechanisms through which competing regional frameworks constrain, redirect and hybridise what Chinese influence actually produces.

The four mechanisms can be understood in terms of who is acting on whom, through which channel and at what level. R1 works vertically downward from a regional organisation to its member states, R2 works outward and upward, from a regional coalition toward the broader international community, R3 works horizontally, from one state to its neighbours, with no Chinese actor involved in the transmission, and R4 is the only mechanism that works against the direction of Chinese influence. R1–R3 are all push mechanisms – they move Chinese-aligned governance norms outward through different vectors (downward through institutions, outward through coalitions, sideways through imitation). R4 is the pull – competing frameworks like the EU's adequacy regime that draw states toward an incompatible regulatory orbit. The actual governance outcome in any given state is the resultant of push and pull acting simultaneously. Tracing these four mechanisms requires working across different bodies of evidence, and the evidentiary standard appropriate to each differs. Regional institutional anchoring is the most documentable: the relevant texts are public, their institutional authority is explicit and the analytical task is to read them for structural features rather than surface vocabulary – the diagnostic questions established in the preceding section apply here as much as at the bilateral level. Declaratory legitimation requires tracking successive iterations of joint statements within the same forum to identify whether structural embeddings harden into explicit endorsements across institutional cycles, as the BRICS case demonstrates (Belli, 2021). Regulatory contagion requires a comparative approach: identifying the structural features present in the first-mover state's governance framework, documenting their appearance in subsequent regional adoptions, and assessing whether the diffusion pattern is consistent with horizontal peer influence or better explained by independent bilateral engagement with China. Counter-mobilisation requires mapping the full normative landscape within which Chinese influence operates – not only where Chinese-aligned instruments appear, but where they are absent or attenuated, and whether that attenuation correlates with the presence of competing regional frameworks with sufficient institutional authority to redirect governance choices.

4. The International Level: Contestation, Legitimation and Structural Position

The international level is where the stakes of normative competition are highest and where China's strategy is most self-conscious and most explicitly articulated. In multilateral forums – the International Telecommunication Union, the United Nations Group of Governmental Experts, the Internet Governance Forum, the World Trade Organization's e-commerce negotiations and others – China has pursued a systematic effort to shift the terms of global debate about digital governance: to legitimise the concept of cyber sovereignty as a recognised principle of international order, to institutionalise governance arrangements that privilege state authority over digital infrastructure and data flows and to challenge the normative consensus, centred on the multistakeholder model and liberal internet norms, that the United States and its allies built in the 1990s and 2000s.

The mechanisms at the international level are different in character from those operating below it. Direct transfer and structured dependence, which are central to the bilateral level, play little role here. What matters at the international level is positional power: the ability to shape agendas, control the drafting of standards and resolutions, build coalitions and frame the terms in which contested questions are debated. China has invested heavily in these positional capacities – increasing its presence in the leadership structures of international organisations, coordinating bloc voting with aligned states and using its market size and infrastructure footprint to give it standing as a standard-setter in technical bodies. The outcomes of this investment are uneven, and the international arena remains one of genuine contestation rather than Chinese dominance. But the effort has produced measurable shifts in what counts as a legitimate position in global digital governance

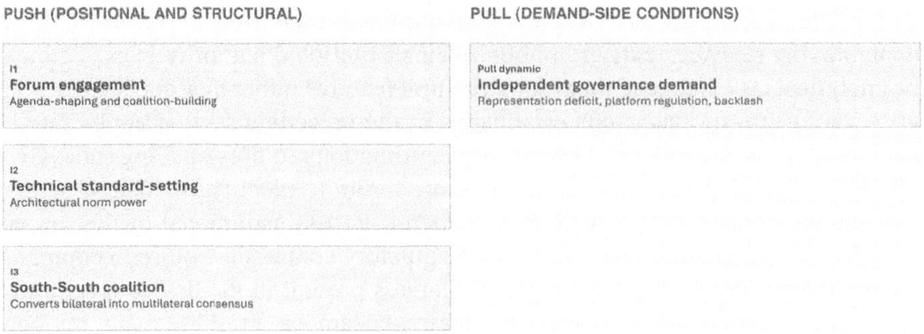

Figure 2.3 Push and pull dynamics at the international level.

debates – shifts that interact, in turn, with what is possible at the bilateral and regional levels (see Figure 2.3).

Three mechanisms are operative at the international level: multilateral forum engagement and institutional positioning (I1), technical standard-setting as structural norm power (I2), and South–South coalition construction (I3). Each produces a distinct kind of normative effect, operates in a distinct institutional arena, and interacts differently with the bilateral and regional mechanisms documented above. But none of the three, individually or collectively, is sufficient to explain why Chinese-aligned governance positions have achieved the international traction they have. That explanation requires a fourth analytical element – the push–pull dynamic at the international level – which is not a mechanism in the same sense as the other three but is instead the structural condition that determines whether the mechanisms produce durable normative effects or merely diplomatic noise. This section introduces all four elements.

I1: Multilateral forum engagement and institutional positioning. The first mechanism is China's systematic engagement with multilateral governance forums as arenas for advancing Chinese-aligned governance principles and contesting Western-dominated governance frameworks. China's multilateral engagement has evolved from a primarily defensive posture aimed at protecting its domestic governance arrangements from external criticism to a more assertive agenda that seeks to establish Chinese-aligned governance principles as the legitimate international baseline (Creemers, 2020). The mechanism through which multilateral forum engagement produces normative effects is not primarily persuasion – China has rarely succeeded in persuading Western states or civil society actors that its governance model is superior. It is instead the construction and consolidation of coalitions among states that share elements of China's sovereignty-centred governance preferences, and the incremental establishment of Chinese-aligned positions as legitimate reference points in governance debates previously dominated by Western multistakeholder frameworks.

I1 encompasses not only direct advocacy within existing forums but also the strategic selection and design of institutional arenas. China has advanced sovereignty-centred positions in UN settings where intergovernmental participation gives developing states formal standing, and it has used parallel venues such as the World Internet Conference to circulate governance vocabulary. (Zeng et al., 2017) The institutional history must nevertheless be stated precisely. The first UN Open-ended Working Group on ICTs in the context of international security was established in 2018 through a Russian-sponsored resolution, while the Ad Hoc Committee charged with negotiating a global cybercrime convention was established through a Russian-led resolution adopted in 2019. China supported and participated actively in both processes, but it should not be described as their sole or original institutional architect. The broader mechanism lies in agenda-shaping, coalition-building, and the sequencing of claims across forums, not in attributing every new intergovernmental process to Beijing. (UNGA, 2015) – (Zeng et al., 2017)

I2: Technical standard-setting as structural norm power. The second mechanism is China's systematic engagement with international technical standards bodies – the ITU, ISO, IEC and the emerging bodies developing standards for AI, quantum communication and next-generation internet architecture. Technical standards can become routes to institutional availability for governance assumptions, in that they establish the baseline architecture within which subsequent governance choices are made: a standard that builds particular access architectures into network equipment, normalises particular identity verification approaches in internet protocols or embeds particular data governance assumptions in cloud service frameworks shapes what is technically feasible and administratively normal for all jurisdictions that adopt the standard or procure systems built around it – regardless of their governance preferences or relationship with China (DeNardis, 2014).

China's engagement with technical standards bodies has been both quantitatively significant – in terms of proposals submitted, leadership positions held, and the size of national delegations – and qualitatively strategic, focused particularly on standards for emerging technologies where the baseline has not yet been set and where early influence can have lasting structural effects. The normative power this generates is distinctive in kind: it is not the power to persuade other states to adopt Chinese governance values, but the power to shape the technical infrastructure within which all states make governance choices, such that certain approaches become more natural, more compatible with deployed infrastructure and more administratively workable than alternatives. This is norm power at the architectural level, and it is particularly consequential because it operates below the threshold of political contestation – technical standards debates are less visible, less politically salient and less accessible to civil society resistance than diplomatic negotiations over governance principles (DeNardis, 2014). I2 interacts with the bilateral-level C1 mechanism (infrastructure entanglement) in a reinforcing loop: ITU-endorsed standards help legitimise the technical approach that Chinese-supplied infrastructure instantiates, and Chinese-supplied infrastructure may shape the practical conditions in which ITU-compatible governance choices become the path of least resistance.

I3: South–South coalition construction. The third mechanism operates through China's positioning as a norm entrepreneur for the Global South (Finnemore and Sikkink, 1998; Chen and Gao, 2024) – advancing governance frameworks that claim to represent the interests of developing states against Western-dominated digital governance institutions, and building coalitions among developing country governments that amplify Chinese positions in multilateral arenas. This mechanism is analytically distinct from bilateral engagement because its primary purpose is not to shape the governance choices of individual partner states but to construct a coalition that shifts the balance of power in international governance debates, making Chinese-aligned positions appear as the majority view in forums where voting or consensus-based decision-making applies.

The normative logic of South–South coalition construction is that it reframes Chinese governance positions – from the preferences of a single state into the collective demands of the global majority – a framing that has significant legitimacy implications in international institutions that nominally operate on sovereign equality. When China can present data sovereignty, state-centred internet governance and conditional cross-border data flows as positions shared by the majority of the world's states, it can become harder for Western governments to dismiss those positions as illegitimate alternatives to the liberal governance model. The coalition thus operates as a legitimating device that helps recast Chinese bilateral influence into apparent multilateral consensus. The effectiveness of I3 depends substantially on the regional mechanisms documented in Section 2.2: the SCO, BRICS and ASEAN-China cooperation frameworks help generate the voting blocs and declaratory positions that China deploys as evidence of broad support in UN and ITU forums.

The push–pull dynamic at the international level. The three mechanisms above describe what China does at the international level. They do not, by themselves, explain why those efforts succeed to the degree they do. A purely supply-side account – China pushes, and norms diffuse – would predict that Chinese normative influence should be strongest where Chinese leverage is greatest. The empirical record documented in Chapter 5 does not support that prediction cleanly. The sovereignty-first governance logic has gained traction in multilateral forums where Chinese material leverage over individual voting decisions is minimal, and among democratic developing states with no significant infrastructure dependence on China. Something beyond Chinese strategic push is operating.

The early development of institutions such as the Budapest Convention, ICANN, and the IETF was heavily shaped by Western states and technical communities, and many developing states have criticised their limited representation. That something is the pull side of the dynamic: the independent demand among a large group of states for governance frameworks that the sovereignty-first model credibly supplies and the Western liberal model has not consistently delivered. Three demand-side conditions are identifiable. The first is the representation deficit in existing governance institutions – the early development of institutions such as the Budapest Convention, ICANN, and the IETF was heavily shaped by Western states and technical communities, and many developing states have criticised their limited representation or unequal influence, and the argument that internet governance should be conducted through UN intergovernmental channels where every state has formal standing resonates independently of any relationship with China (Mueller, 2010). The second is the practical governance challenge of regulating foreign digital platforms – the sovereignty-first framework, which asserts state authority over digital activity within national borders and treats data localisation as a legitimate regulatory tool, speaks directly to operational problems that developing states face and that the liberal governance framework has not resolved. The third is the backlash against perceived Western digital interventionism – the Snowden revelations (Fidler, 2015), GDPR extraterritoriality (Bradford, 2020), and Western platform regulation pressure have weakened the liberal model's claim to represent neutral governance rather than strategic preference, strengthening the appeal of the sovereignty-first alternative among states that have experienced the Western-dominated baseline as externally imposing.

China's strategic contribution is to convert these latent governance demands into institutional reality: into voting coalitions, treaty text and institutional architectures that embed sovereignty-first principles in the operational infrastructure of international governance. Without the push – the coalition-building, the institutional design, the drafting interventions – the demand-side conditions would produce diffuse dissatisfaction rather than coordinated normative outcomes. Without the pull – the genuine governance demand from states whose interests the sovereignty-first framework addresses – Chinese initiative would lack the coalition necessary to pass resolutions and shape negotiating mandates. Neither push nor pull alone explains the outcome; the interaction between them does.

This has a direct implication for the empirical analysis in Chapter 5. Attributing international normative outcomes to Chinese influence requires demonstrating not only that Chinese strategic effort was present (push) but that the demand-side conditions were operative among the states that aligned with Chinese positions (pull), and that the interaction between the two produced outcomes that neither would have generated independently. The push–pull framework is therefore not an alternative to the three mechanisms but their necessary complement: the mechanisms describe how China operates at the international level, and the push–pull dynamic explains why those operations produce the durable normative effects they do.

A final analytical point concerns the normative environment into which Chinese digital governance norms diffuse at the international level. Unlike the bilateral and regional levels, where Chinese-origin governance instruments may arrive in relatively open institutional terrain, the international level is densely populated with established governance frameworks – the Budapest Convention, the multistakeholder model, GDPR-derived data protection standards and the technical standards produced by IETF and W3C processes (Raymond and DeNardis, 2015). Chinese normative influence at the international level therefore operates not in an empty space but in direct competition with entrenched alternatives, and its effects are characteristically partial: the expansion of the range of legitimate governance options to include sovereignty-first instruments, rather than the displacement of the liberal framework altogether. Chapter 5 traces this dynamic empirically across two decades of UN and ITU engagement, documenting both the measurable normative shift that Chinese effort has produced and the limits that organised resistance has imposed on that shift.

5. Method and the Question of Attribution

The bilateral, regional and international levels at which the mechanisms identified in the preceding section operate are not autonomous causal arenas. They are interconnected through recursive feedback loops that amplify, modify and sometimes undermine normative transmission. Bilateral relationships generate the implementation experience – tested governance instruments, documented outcomes, established relationships between Chinese actors and recipient officials – that feeds into what China promotes at regional and international levels. Regional frameworks amplify bilateral governance practices by giving them multilateral institutional endorsement, and feed back into bilateral relationships by creating demand for implementation support among states that have committed to regional governance standards. International standard-setting produces the most structurally consequential feedback: a technical standard adopted at the international level shapes the baseline for all jurisdictions simultaneously, regardless of their regional affiliations or bilateral relationships with China, creating a channel through which Chinese normative influence operates structurally and below the threshold of political visibility.

The central methodological challenge is attribution in a crowded normative environment. Chinese digital governance norms diffuse alongside European data protection frameworks, American cybersecurity standards and the indigenous governance traditions of recipient states. Governance instruments that resemble elements of the Chinese repertoire may have arrived through different channels or developed independently in response to shared threat perceptions. Establishing that something specifically Chinese is moving requires distinguishing Chinese normative influence from background convergence, coincidental similarity and the operation of other norm entrepreneurs (Chen and Gao, 2024). The method proceeds in two stages – textual and structural analysis, then mechanism tracing – but the evidentiary standard and analytical focus differ significantly across levels, and that variation is itself methodologically important. To keep these categories distinct, the empirical chapters classify outcomes as Chinese-origin, Chinese-promoted, Chinese-aligned, Chinese-enabled, or explicitly Chinese-attributed. Compatibility alone establishes only alignment; stronger claims require evidence of promotion, transmission, or genealogy. Case assessments should also distinguish confirmed, probable, compatible-but-unproven, and indeterminate influence.

At the bilateral level, the primary analytical task is textual and structural comparison between China's domestic governance architecture and the governance choices of specific recipient states. This is necessary because bilateral diffusion characteristically operates through indirect channels – default settings in installed infrastructure, governance vocabularies absorbed through training programmes, institutional designs carried by officials who have engaged with Chinese regulatory systems – rather than through visible proclamation or explicit endorsement. Recipient states rarely attribute their governance choices to Chinese influence, and the relevant similarity is often structural rather than verbal: a law may share the Chinese configuration's hierarchical data classification, state access obligations and conditionality of cross-border transfers while employing entirely different legal language and citing entirely different reference points. The relevant comparanda, drawn from Chapter 1's analysis of China's domestic architecture, are therefore structural: does the law establish state sovereignty over cyberspace as a jurisdictional foundation? Does it impose security-cooperation obligations on private operators? Does it condition cross-border data flows on state-determined security requirements rather than adequacy assessments? Does it define critical information infrastructure broadly enough to encompass commercial platforms? These structural features – not vocabulary, not formal citation – are the test at the bilateral level, because selective adaptation regularly produces governance arrangements that share Chinese structural logic while presenting an entirely different surface. Mechanism tracing at this level should not simply work backward from similarities. It should first enumerate plausible Chinese, European, American, regional, and endogenous pathways and then use temporal and process evidence to adjudicate among them. It may then trace observed structural similarities to the specific bilateral channels ——– infrastructure contracts, cooperation agreements, training programmes, personnel networks ——– through which those features might plausibly have traveled.

At the regional level, the analytical task shifts. The mechanisms through which China operates in regional forums – institutional anchoring, declaratory legitimation, agenda-setting – are more directly observable than the diffuse channels of bilateral transfer, because China's role as proposer, host or dominant institutional actor is typically a matter of record. The evidentiary focus therefore moves from inferring influence through structural similarity to documenting what China specifically introduces, proposes and embeds in regional instruments, and what institutional form those contributions take. The question is not whether a regional framework resembles Chinese governance preferences – it is whether China actively shaped the framework's's architecture, through what mechanism, and whether the structural features it introduced subsequently appear in member states' domestic governance choices. The SCO Code of Conduct (UNGA, 2015), the BRICS Beijing and Kazan Declarations (BRICS, 2022, 2024), the ASEAN-China Joint Statement (2023) and the RCEP digital economy chapter (Association of Southeast Asian Nations [ASEAN], 2020) each leave some traceable record of Chinese input and institutional positioning. Analysis at this level therefore combines document-level reading – what structural features appear, how they are embedded – with institutional tracing of China's role in producing those documents. The distinction between explicit and implicit sovereignty language across successive iterations of the same framework is a particularly productive evidentiary test, because the progression from implicit structural encoding to explicit normative endorsement across institutional cycles is a signature of deliberate normative strategy rather than incidental convergence.

At the international level, the focus narrows further to specific, documentable acts of Chinese norm promotion: proposals submitted to standards bodies, positions taken in UN negotiations, drafting interventions, and coalition-building exercises. Attribution is more tractable where proposal records, votes, statements, and adopted texts are public. The negotiations leading to the 2024 UN Convention against Cybercrime provide an important case of coalition expansion, but not a straightforward case of Chinese normative transmission. The process originated in a Russian-sponsored resolution adopted in 2019 with Chinese support and over substantial opposition. The Convention was adopted by consensus by the General Assembly in December 2024 after extended negotiations and substantial textual compromise. Attribution is more tractable where proposal records, votes, statements, and adopted texts are public. The negotiations leading to the 2024 UN Convention against Cybercrime provide an important case of coalition expansion, but not a straightforward case of Chinese normative transmission. The process originated in a Russian-sponsored resolution adopted in 2019 with Chinese support and over substantial opposition. The Convention was adopted by consensus by the General Assembly in December 2024 after extended negotiations and substantial textual compromise (Polyakova and Meserole, 2019; UN, 2020).

The method is explicitly comparative across levels, but the comparison is asymmetric in the way the analysis just described. At the bilateral level, it asks whether structural similarity exists and whether mechanism tracing supports a Chinese-influence account over alternatives. At the regional level, it asks what China specifically introduced into institutional frameworks and whether those introductions spread to member states. At the international level, it asks whether Chinese positions achieved documented institutional traction, through what coalition mechanisms and whether the push–pull interaction accounts for the breadth of support those positions received. These are different questions requiring different evidence, and conflating them – treating structural similarity at the bilateral level as equivalent to documented institutional embedding at the regional level – would misrepresent both the strength and the character of the evidence.

This method is subject to limitations. Mechanism tracing is constrained by the opacity of governance processes: cooperation agreements are often unpublished, training curricula inaccessible and officials rarely document the full range of reference points consulted when drafting legislation. At the bilateral level, structural similarity consistent with Chinese influence is also consistent with independent parallel development, and the distinction requires interpretive judgment. These limitations define the method's scope rather than undermining it. The empirical chapters do not claim that Chinese normative influence explains every governance shift that resembles its configuration. The claim is more precise: that across bilateral, regional, and international levels, a recognisable Chinese-origin governance configuration moves through identifiable mechanisms, produces observable effects in recipient governance arrangements and constitutes a form of normative power that is consequential for the shape of the emerging digital order – even when its effects are partial, mediated by recipient agency and hybridised by the normative environment through which they travel.

6. Conclusion: From Theory to Empirical Inquiry

The framework developed in this chapter establishes three things that the empirical chapters must work with, test and in some cases qualify.

The first is a concept. Normative power, as defined here, is neither coercion nor attraction but the stabilisation of a governance repertoire – the condition in which Chinese-origin instruments, logics and vocabularies become available, legitimate and practically usable in other actors' governance choices, regardless of whether those actors endorse or even recognise their provenance. The concept is relational and constituted through interaction rather than unilateral projection. China supplies governance instruments – through infrastructure, framing, epistemic socialisation, institutional embedding and standard-setting – but what those instruments produce in any given context depends as much on what recipient states, regional organisations and international institutions bring to that supply as on what China intends to project. Recipient governments have their own governance priorities, institutional constraints, and strategic calculations, and their decisions about which elements of the Chinese repertoire to adopt, adapt, or reject are analytically as important as China's decisions about what to promote. This means that normative power, in the sense used here, is always co-produced: its outcomes are the joint product of Chinese supply and recipient demand, and neither side alone determines the result.

The concept is also distinct from soft power in Nye's sense (1990), and the distinction matters for how the empirical chapters read their evidence. Soft power is a pull phenomenon: it depends on the attractiveness of a state's political model, culture and values, and its operation requires that recipients find the promoting state worth emulating. Normative power does not require attractiveness or emulation. Recipient governments may adopt Chinese-aligned governance instruments because they reduce infrastructure costs, because regional frameworks have embedded them as defaults, because training programmes have made them the reference vocabulary of a domestic regulatory community, or because financing relationships have generated the kind of goodwill that Repnikova (2022) identifies as the practical foundation of Chinese influence in the Global South – none of which requires that recipients find the Chinese political model attractive or consciously seek to replicate it. This distinction is not merely theoretical: it shapes what counts as evidence. A government that adopts data localisation requirements while expressing no admiration for China and citing RCEP rather than Chinese law as its reference point may nonetheless be exhibiting the effect of Chinese normative power, if the structural logic of its regulatory choice reflects Chinese-origin design features embedded in the regional framework it is implementing.

The second contribution is a mechanism framework organised around the push–pull distinction and operating across three levels. At the bilateral level, China-anchored push mechanisms – infrastructure entanglement (C1), bilateral agreements and standard-alignment clauses, and epistemic socialisation – supply governance instruments, embed them in institutional relationships, and shape the reference vocabularies available to recipient officials. Host-anchored mechanisms – hedging and diversification (H1), selective adaptation and recombination

(H2) and strategic negotiation (H3) – shape what is actually adopted, in what form and under what conditions. At the regional level, institutional anchoring, declaratory legitimation, regulatory contagion and counter-mobilisation amplify, filter and transform what travels between bilateral and international settings. At the international level, three mechanisms – multilateral forum engagement and institutional positioning (I1), technical standard-setting (I2) and South–South coalition construction (I3) – operate through positional power rather than direct transfer. Critically, the international mechanisms produce durable normative effects only where they interact with demand-side conditions – the representation deficit, practical governance challenges and backlash against Western interventionism – that generate genuine pull from the states whose support Chinese coalition-building requires. The push–pull dynamic is not a separate mechanism but the structural condition that determines whether the mechanisms produce lasting institutional outcomes or merely ephemeral diplomatic positioning.

The recursive relationships between levels mean that these mechanisms do not operate in isolation. Bilateral implementation experience informs what China promotes in regional and international forums; regional endorsements create the legitimating context that reduces the political cost of bilateral adoption; international standard-setting produces structural baselines that shape bilateral governance choices without requiring any direct Chinese engagement. The cumulative force of the framework is therefore greater than the sum of its individual pathways, and tracing that cumulation – across levels, mechanisms, and cases – is what the empirical chapters aim to do.

The third contribution is a method whose evidentiary demands vary systematically across levels. At the bilateral level, where diffusion operates through indirect and often invisible channels, the primary analytical task is structural comparison between Chinese governance architecture and recipient governance choices: establishing whether the instruments a state adopts share the structural logic of the Chinese configuration – jurisdictional framing of cyberspace, state access obligations, conditionality of cross-border flows, comprehensive security rationales for regulatory authority – regardless of the surface vocabulary in which they are expressed, and working backward from observed structural similarities to the specific bilateral channels through which those features might plausibly have travelled. At the regional level, where China's role as proposer, host or dominant institutional actor is typically a matter of record, the task shifts from inferring influence through structural similarity to documenting what China specifically introduced into institutional frameworks, through what mechanism and whether those introductions spread to member states. At the international level, where Chinese positions in standards bodies and multilateral forums are documented in proposal records, vote tallies and adopted texts, the task narrows further to tracing the institutional traction of specific Chinese proposals, the coalition-building mechanisms through which that traction was achieved and whether the push–pull interaction accounts for the breadth of support. These are different questions requiring different evidence, and the method is designed to apply them at the appropriate level rather than treating structural similarity and documented institutional embedding as interchangeable forms of evidence.

What the framework cannot do is supply the empirical content. It specifies what to look for and how to look for it – and it establishes an asymmetric evidentiary standard that is appropriately demanding at each level without requiring a uniformity of evidence that the material cannot provide. Whether the pattern it anticipates holds, how strongly, in which domains and subject to what exceptions is the work of the chapters that follow. Those chapters may find that some mechanisms produce stronger effects than others, that recipient agency modifies Chinese influence more substantially in some contexts than the framework predicts, or that the crowded normative environment makes attribution to specifically Chinese sources less tractable than the two-stage method assumes. The framework is designed to accommodate those findings rather than to foreclose them: it defines the conditions of attribution rigorously enough to distinguish genuine normative power from coincidental convergence, while remaining open to the possibility that the pattern, where it exists, is always partial, always mediated and always contested.

References

Acharya, A. (2004) How Ideas Spread: Whose Norms Matter? Norm Localization and Institutional Change in Asian Regionalism. *International Organization*, 58(2), pp. 239–275.

Agbebi, M. (2023) *China's Digital Silk Road and Africa's Technological Future*. New York, NY: Council on Foreign Relations.

Association of Southeast Asian Nations (ASEAN) (2020) *Regional Comprehensive Economic Partnership (RCEP) Agreement*. Jakarta: ASEAN Secretariat. Available at: https://asean.org/our-communities/economic-community/integration-with-global-economy/regional-comprehensive-economic-partnership-rcep/

Benabdallah, L. (2020) *Shaping the Future of Power: Knowledge Production and Network-Building in China-Africa Relations*. Ann Arbor, MI: University of Michigan Press.

Barnett, M. and Duvall, R. (2005) 'Power in International Politics'. *International Organization*, 59(1), pp. 39–75.

Belli, L. (ed.). (2021) *CyberBRICS: Mapping Cybersecurity, Data Protection and Digital Identity in the BRICS Countries*. Cham: Springer Nature.

Bennett, A. and Checkel, J. T. (eds.). (2015) *Process Tracing: From Metaphor to Analytic Tool*. Cambridge: Cambridge University Press.

Bradford, A. (2020) *The Brussels Effect: How the European Union Rules the World*. Oxford: Oxford University Press.

Brautigam, D. (2009) *The Dragon's Gift: The Real Story of China in Africa*. Oxford: Oxford University Press.

BRICS. (2022) *XIV BRICS summit Beijing Declaration*. Toronto: BRICS Information Centre, University of Toronto. Available at: http://www.brics.utoronto.ca/docs/220623-declaration.html

BRICS. (2024) *XVI BRICS summit Kazan Declaration*. Toronto: BRICS Information Centre, University of Toronto. Available at: http://www.brics.utoronto.ca/docs/241023-declaration.html

Börzel, T. A. and Risse, T. (2012) 'From Europeanisation to Diffusion: Introduction'. *West European Politics*, 35(1), pp. 1–19. https://doi.org/10.1080/01402382.2012.631310

Chander, A. and Le, U. P. (2015) 'Data Nationalism'. *Emory Law Journal*, 64(6), pp. 677–739.
Checkel, J. T. (2005) 'International Institutions and Socialization in Europe: Introduction and Framework'. *International Organization*, 59(4), pp. 801–826.
Chen, X. and Gao, X. (2024) Norm Diffusion in Cyber Governance: China as an Emerging Norm Entrepreneur? *International Affairs*, 100(6), pp. 2419–2440.
Council of Europe (2001) *Convention on Cybercrime* (European Treaty Series No. 185). Available at: https://rm.coe.int/1680081561
Creemers R. J. E. H. (2020) 'China's Conception of Cyber Sovereignty: Rhetoric and Realization'. in Broeders, D. and van den Berg, B. (eds.) *Governing Cyberspace: Behavior, Power, and Diplomacy*. Digital Technologies and Global Politics. Lanham: Bloomsbury Publishing.
DeNardis, L. (2014) *The Global War for Internet Governance*. New Haven, CT: Yale University Press.
Custer, S.et al. (2021) *Tracking Chinese Development Finance: An Application of AidData's TUFF 2.0 Methodology*. Williamsburg, VA: AidData at William and Mary.
DiMaggio, P. J. and Powell, W. W. (1983) 'The Iron Cage Revisited: Institutional Isomorphism and Collective Rationality in Organizational Fields'. *American Sociological Review*, 48(2), pp. 147–160.
Drezner, D. W. (2005) 'Globalization, Harmonization, and Competition: The Different Pathways to Policy Convergence'. *Journal of European Public Policy*, 12(5), pp. 841–859.
El Kadi, T. H. (2022) 'How Huawei's Localization in North Africa Delivered Mixed Returns'. *Chatham House*, April 14, 2022. Available at: https://www.chathamhouse.org
Erie, M. S. and Streinz, T. (2021) 'The Beijing Effect: China's "Digital Silk Road" as Transnational Lawmaking'. *New York University Journal of International Law and Politics*, 54(2), pp. 1–71.
Expertise France (2025) *Digital for Development Hub*. Expertise France – Groupe AFD. Available at: https://www.expertisefrance.fr/en/projects/digital-development-hub
Farrell, H. and Newman, A. L. (2019) Weaponized Interdependence: How Global Economic Networks Shape State Coercion'. *International Security*, 44(1), pp. 42–79.
Feldstein, S. (2021) *The Rise of Digital Repression: How Technology Is Reshaping Power, Politics, and Resistance*. Oxford: Oxford University Press.
Fidler, D. P. (ed.). (2015) *The Snowden reader*. Bloomington, IN: Indiana University Press.
Finnemore, M. and Sikkink, K. (1998) International norm dynamics and political change. *International Organization*, 52(4), pp. 887–917.
Gagliardone, I. (2019) *China, Africa, and the Future of the Internet*. London: Zed Books.
George, A. L. and Bennett, A. (2005) *Case Studies and Theory Development in the Social Sciences*. Cambridge, MA: MIT Press.
Goertz, G. and Mahoney, J. (2012) *A Tale of Two Cultures: Qualitative and Quantitative Research in the Social Sciences*. Princeton, NJ: Princeton University Press.
Greitens, S. C. (2020) *Dealing with Demand for China's Global Surveillance Exports, Global China Report*. Washington, DC: Brookings Institution.
Gunitsky, S. (2015) Corrupting the Cyber-Commons: Social Media as a Tool of Autocratic Stability. *Perspectives on Politics*, 13(1), pp. 42–54.
Hartig, F. (2016) *Chinese Public Diplomacy: The Rise of the Confucius Institute*. London: Routledge.
Hill, J. F. (2014) 'The Growth of Data Localization Post-Snowden: Analysis and Recommendations for U.S. Policymakers and Industry Leaders'. *Lawfare Research Paper Series*, 2(3), pp. 1–41.
Hu, A. (2011) *China in 2020: A New Type of Superpower*. Washington, DC: Brookings Institution Press.

Jackson, J. (1975) 'Normative Power and Conflict Potential'. *Sociological Methods and Research*, 4(2), pp. 237–263.

Jasanoff, S. and Kim, S.-H. (2009) Containing the Atom: Sociotechnical Imaginaries and Nuclear Power in the United States and South Korea'. *Minerva*, 47(2), pp. 119–146.

Kang, D. C. (2007) *China Rising: Peace, Power, and Order in East Asia*. New York, NY: Columbia University Press.

Kavalski, E. (2013) The Struggle for Recognition of Normative Powers: Normative Power Europe and Normative Power China in Context'. *Cooperation and Conflict*, 48(2), pp. 247–267.

Li, W. and Chen, J. (2024) 'From Brussels Effect to Gravity Assists: Understanding the Evolution of the GDPR-Inspired Personal Information Protection Law in China'. *Computer Law and Security Review*, 54, p. 105994.

Manners, I. (2002) 'Normative Power Europe: A Contradiction in Terms?' *Journal of Common Market Studies*, 40(2), pp. 235–258.

Merry, S. E. (2006) *Human Rights and Gender Violence: Translating International Law into Local Justice*. Chicago, IL: University of Chicago Press.

Mueller, M. (2010) *Networks and States: The Global Politics of Internet Governance*. Cambridge, MA: MIT Press.

Nye, J. S. (1990) 'Soft Power'. *Foreign Policy*, 80, pp. 153–171.

Ong, A. and Collier, S. J. (2005) *Global Assemblages: Technology, Politics, and Ethics as Anthropological Problems*. Blackwell.

Peck, J. and Theodore, N. (2010) 'Mobilizing Policy: Models, Methods, and Mutations'. *Geoforum*, 41(2), pp. 169–174.

Pohle, J. and Thiel, T. (2020) 'Digital Sovereignty'. *Internet Policy Review*, 9(4). https://doi.org/10.14763/2020.4.1532

Polyakova, A. and Meserole, C. (2019) *Exporting Digital Authoritarianism: The Russian and Chinese Models*. Washington, DC: Brookings Institution.

Raymond, M. and DeNardis, L. (2015) 'Multistakeholderism: Anatomy of an Inchoate Global Institution'. *International Theory*, 7(3), pp. 572–616.

Repnikova, M. (2022) *Chinese Soft Power*. Cambridge: Cambridge University Press.

Schimmelfennig, F. and Sedelmeier, U. (2004) 'Governance by Conditionality: EU Rule Transfer to the Candidate Countries of Central and Eastern Europe'. *Journal of European Public Policy*, 11(4), pp. 661–679. https://doi.org/10.1080/1350176042000248089

Schirm, S. A. (2010) Leaders in Need of Followers: Emerging Powers in Global Governance'. *European Journal of International Relations*, 16(2), pp. 197–221.

Simmons, B., Dobbin, F. and Garrett, G. (2006) 'Introduction: The International Diffusion of Liberalism'. *International Organization*, 60(4), pp. 781–810.

Soulé, F. (2022) *Negotiating Africa's Digital Partnerships*. Waterloo, ON: Centre for International Governance Innovation.

Steinhilper, E. (2015) 'From "The Rest" to "The West"? Rights of Indigenous Peoples and the Western Bias in Norm Diffusion Research'. *International Studies Review*, 17(4), pp. 536–555.

Stone, D. (2012) 'Transfer and Translation of Policy'. *Policy Studies*, 33(6), pp. 483–499.

Towns, A. E. (2012) 'Norms and Social Hierarchies: Understanding International Policy Diffusion "From Below"'. *International Organization*, 66(2), pp. 179–209.

Tugendhat, H. and Voo, J. (2021) *China's Digital Silk Road in Africa and the Future of Internet Governance*. Working Paper 50. Oxford: Oxford Internet Institute.

United Nations General Assembly (UNGA) (2015) *Letter Dated 9 January 2015 from the Permanent Representatives of China, Kazakhstan, Kyrgyzstan, the Russian Federation, Tajikistan and Uzbekistan to the United Nations Addressed to the Secretary-General (A/69/723)*. United Nations Digital Library. Available at: https://digitallibrary.un.org/record/786846

United States Agency for International Development (USAID). (2020) *Digital Strategy 2020–2024*. Available at: https://www.ictworks.org/wp-content/uploads/2020/04/USAID_Digital_Strategy.pdf

Weyland, K. (2005) 'Theories of Policy Diffusion: Lessons from Latin American Pension Reform'. *World Politics*, 57(2), pp. 262–295.

Zeng, J., Stevens, T. and Chen, Y. (2017) 'China's Solution to Global Cyber Governance: Unpacking the Domestic Discourse of "Internet Sovereignty"'. *Politics and Policy*, 45, pp. 432–464. https://doi.org/10.1111/polp.12202

Zürn, M. (2018) *A Theory of Global Governance*. Oxford: Oxford University Press.

3 Mechanisms in Practice

Mapping Chinese Normative Power across Bilateral Cases

The framework developed in Chapter 2 disaggregated normative power into supply-side mechanisms anchored in Chinese agency, infrastructure entanglement (C1), bilateral agreements and standard-alignment clauses (C2), epistemic socialisation (C3) and demand-side mechanisms anchored in recipient agency: hedging and diversification (H1), selective adaptation and recombination (H2), and strategic negotiation and institutional bargaining (H3). The framework is analytically tractable in principle, but its empirical traction depends on whether each mechanism leaves observable traces and whether those traces satisfy the attribution conditions developed in Chapter 2: coherence, channel specificity, and cumulativity. This chapter undertakes that empirical work. It moves through eight bilateral cases for which sufficient evidence has been assembled: Vietnam, Chile, Malaysia, Zambia, Egypt, Kazakhstan, the Philippines and Laos, drawing on three evidentiary streams integrated through comparative process tracing. .

The first stream is quantitative, and it speaks primarily to the coherence condition rather than to attribution on its own. A computational text-similarity analysis compares the full English-language texts of cyber and data-protection laws across thirty documents from twenty-three jurisdictions, calibrated against China's three foundational instruments as outlined in Chapter 1: the Cybersecurity Law of 2017 (CSL), the Data Security Law of 2021 (DSL) and the Personal Information Protection Law of 2021 (PIPL). The procedure yields lexical-similarity scores that, while not themselves evidence of influence, mark out the empirical terrain on which mechanism analysis must operate. The second stream is documentary. For the selected cases, chosen as the union of high-scoring cases and theoretically informative low-similarity contrasts, project-level records from AidData Global Chinese Development Finance Dataset (Custer et al., 2021), treaty and memorandum-of-understanding texts disclosed through Chinese ministerial channels and host-country gazettes, training-program rosters from Huawei's ICT Academy (El Kadi, 2022) and the China Scholarship Council, and procurement and parliamentary records from each case country together permit reasonably granular reconstruction of when, where and on what terms Chinese governance instruments entered the relevant policy space. The third stream is qualitative. The chapter draws on a wider corpus of semi-structured interviews conducted with regional experts on data protection, cybersecurity law and digital infrastructure across the case regions, including specialists in Southeast Asia, Central Asia, sub-Saharan Africa, North Africa

DOI: 10.4324/9781042023738-4

and the United States, as well as a comparative practitioner perspective from a major US-based law firm. Quotations cited in this chapter are drawn from a subset of those interviews where the interviewee had detailed first-hand knowledge of the case country's regulatory drafting, implementation, or commercial environment. The full list of interviews, including code, country, role, format and date, is given in Appendix A; quotations are attributed by interview code rather than by name to protect interviewees who agreed to speak on a not-for-attribution basis. The qualitative material supplies texture and motivation that the documentary record cannot, particularly on how recipient actors interpret Chinese engagement and the regulatory choices that follow; it does not substitute for documentary evidence where attribution remains uncertain. A note on the corpus and its evidentiary status closes Section 1.

These streams converge unevenly across cases, and the chapter does not pretend otherwise. In some cases, Vietnam most clearly, the three streams reinforce one another: high lexical similarity, dense bilateral and infrastructural engagement, and an interview that frames the regulatory architecture as ideologically continuous with Chinese state-centric assumptions. In others, Zambia is the paradigmatic instance, the documentary record is thick on infrastructure and thin on governance frameworks, lexical similarity is low and the interview foregrounds practical receptivity rather than wholesale alignment. In still others, Kazakhstan and the Philippines, temporal sequencing rules out direct Chinese influence on the laws as initially enacted, and the analytic interest shifts to the mechanism patterns themselves. The argument the chapter develops is therefore not a uniform thesis about Chinese normative power but a typology: across the eight cases, distinct configurations of push and pull produce qualitatively different governance outcomes, and the framework is most useful when it discriminates among configurations rather than collapses them.

1. The Lexical Imprint: A Comparative Similarity Analysis

Norm diffusion in international law has historically been studied through case-by-case textual comparison, an approach that yields rich qualitative readings but does not scale and cannot easily distinguish similarity that reflects shared modelling from similarity that reflects shared topic. Computational text analysis offers a complement, not a replacement, that scales to larger corpora and permits reasonably objective cross-case comparison of lexical proximity. Before reporting the findings, this section explains in plain terms what the procedure measures and what its outputs mean.

1.1 What TF-IDF cosine similarity is, and what 0.175 means

The procedure used is Term Frequency-Inverse Document Frequency (TF-IDF) vectorisation followed by cosine similarity measurement, implemented with scikit-learn using 5,000 features, one- to three-word n-grams and standard English stopword filtering. The TF-IDF transformation weights each term by its frequency within a document and its rarity across the corpus, so that common legal boilerplate ('shall', 'article', 'law') receives low weight while distinctive vocabulary ('critical information infrastructure', 'network operator', 'important data') receives high weight. Cosine similarity then measures the angle between document vectors, yielding values from 0 (no shared distinctive vocabulary) to 1 (identical vocabulary). The procedure is agnostic about word order, syntactic structure, and semantic content. Two laws that use the same terms in different ways will score high; two laws that use different terms to express the same governance logic will score low.

A naive reading of cosine similarity scores would treat any value above 0 as evidence of influence. That reading is not available. Cyber and data-protection laws share common subject matter, and some convergence in vocabulary is expected even when no influence relationship exists. To establish what unsurprising similarity looks like in this corpus, mean pairwise similarity was calculated across the pooled corpus of cyber and data-protection laws, excluding the relevant Chinese reference text, yielding a baseline value of 0.175 (range 0.047 to 0.461). Because this pooled baseline mixes legal domains, it is used as an exploratory reference point rather than as a dispositive threshold. This number is the average lexical proximity that any two cyber or data-protection laws in the corpus would be expected to have given that they share the topic; it is not a threshold above which influence is demonstrated. It is the value against which individual scores are read.

The baseline operates as follows. A score *meaningfully above* 0.175 marks a case whose vocabulary is unusually proximate to the Chinese reference and therefore demands explanation, though the chapter avoids treating it as a statistical outlier unless distributional evidence is reported. A score at or near 0.175 is consistent with topical convergence and does not by itself support an inference of borrowing. A score *below* 0.175 means the law in question shares less distinctive vocabulary with the Chinese reference than the average law in the corpus does. None of these readings substitutes for mechanism analysis. The lexical signal flags cases for investigation; it does not establish what produced the proximity it identifies.

The chapter uses three baselines, one for each Chinese reference text. The Cybersecurity-Law baseline is 0.175 against the pooled corpus of cyber and data-protection laws; the PIPL baseline is computed against the same corpus and reported with each case; the DSL baseline is approximately 0.037 across the corpus. Because the DSL comparison uses a narrower and more technically specific vocabulary, elevated scores against that baseline are interpreted cautiously rather than treated as direct evidence of diffusion. Throughout the case studies, scores against all three Chinese reference instruments (CSL, PIPL, DSL) are reported in that order so that readers can evaluate the lexical pattern across China's full legal stack rather than treating any single law as a proxy.

1.2 The Corpus and the Three Parallel Analyses

The corpus comprises thirty analysable documents drawn from twenty-three jurisdictions: the EU's GDPR; seven Southeast Asian countries (Indonesia, Laos, Malaysia, the Philippines, Singapore, Thailand and Vietnam, with Vietnam represented by both its 2018 Cybersecurity Law and its 2023 Personal Data Protection Decree); six African states (Angola, Egypt, Kenya, Nigeria, Zambia and Zimbabwe, with Zambia and Zimbabwe each represented by separate cyber and data-protection statutes); two South Asian states (India and Pakistan); the United Arab Emirates and Saudi Arabia; three Latin American states (Chile, Ecuador and Peru); and Kazakhstan as a Central Asian comparator. Texts were collected primarily from the DLA Piper Data Protection Laws database and official government repositories, with PDF extraction and OCR applied where necessary. All similarity scores are computed against three Chinese reference texts: the 2017 Cybersecurity Law (CSL), the 2021 Data Security Law (DSL) and the 2021 Personal Information Protection Law (PIPL).

Three parallel analyses are conducted, one per Chinese reference instrument. The choice to run the analysis three times separately, rather than computing a single combined Chinese-corpus score, is methodologically deliberate. The three Chinese laws differ substantially in scope, vocabulary and international promotion, and combining them would obscure that the same recipient state may track one Chinese instrument closely while diverging from another. Reporting all three lets the reader see the polarisation, where it exists, and disciplines any inference of 'Chinese influence' against the question: influence on which Chinese instrument, and through which channel?

1.3 Findings across the Three Chinese Reference Instruments

Three findings emerge from the comparative analysis. The first concerns the Cybersecurity Law (CSL), against which the corpus baseline is 0.175: two countries score substantially above baseline and the rest cluster well below it. Vietnam scores 0.309 and Chile scores 0.224, the two highest CSL-proximity scores in the corpus. Malaysia scores 0.095, Zambia 0.078 and the Philippines 0.065, all below baseline. The polarisation is striking. The diffusion of China's state-centric cybersecurity vocabulary is not gradual or uniform but concentrated in particular cases, and the standard global cybersecurity discourse departs significantly from the Chinese model on the lexical surface.

The second finding concerns the Personal Information Protection Law (PIPL): the Philippines' 2012 Data Privacy Act produces a score of 0.388 against PIPL, more than twice the baseline, while no other case approaches that level. Notably, the Philippines scores almost exactly at baseline against the CSL (0.065), revealing a striking asymmetry between cybersecurity-domain and personal-information-domain alignment that the Philippines case study below probes in detail. The asymmetry already cautions against treating the lexical signal as a proxy for 'Chinese influence' in any general sense: a law may be lexically proximate to one Chinese instrument and remote from another, and the temporal sequence rules out direct Chinese influence on the Philippine instrument as enacted.

The third finding concerns the Data Security Law (DSL), against which the corpus baseline is approximately 0.037: Egypt produces the highest DSL score, at 0.095, substantially above the DSL corpus mean but still modest in absolute terms and well below the strongest CSL and PIPL similarities. The DSL is therefore the weakest channel of textual diffusion among China's three foundational instruments and is so reported throughout the case studies.

Table 3.1 summarises similarity scores for the cases examined in detail in this chapter.

1.4 Caveats That Discipline the Interpretation

Three caveats discipline the interpretation of these scores. First, TF-IDF measures *lexical* similarity, *not conceptual* similarity. A law could embed Chinese-style governance architecture using GDPR vocabulary and produce a low similarity score; conversely, a law could use Chinese vocabulary while implementing GDPR-style rights. Low similarity scores cannot decisively rule out conceptual influence, and high scores cannot by themselves establish it.

Second, the temporal direction of any inferred influence must be checked against enactment dates. Both the Philippines' 2012 Data Privacy Act and Kazakhstan's 2013 personal-data law predate China's most directly comparable instruments, making any direct causal pathway from the Chinese laws to those texts impossible by elementary chronology. In such cases, the analytic interest shifts to subsequent regulatory development, which the case studies trace.

Third, the corpus excludes implementing regulations, administrative interpretations, and enforcement guidance, which often carry the operational substance of governance frameworks. Two laws that look textually similar may diverge dramatically in practice; two that look textually distinct may converge through implementation. The similarity index is therefore a starting point for case analysis, not a conclusion. It identifies the cases where lexical alignment is strong enough to demand explanation (Vietnam, Chile against CSL; Philippines and to a lesser extent Egypt against PIPL) and the cases where lexical alignment is weak enough that any account of Chinese influence must travel through structural channels

Table 3.1 Lexical similarity scores against China's three foundational laws (selected cases)

Case	*CSL (baseline 0.175)*	*PIPL (baseline ~0.175)*	*DSL (baseline ~0.037)*
Vietnam (2018 CSL)	0.309	not applicable	0.041
Vietnam (2023 PDPD)	0.072	0.198	0.038
Chile (2024 CSL Ley 21.663)	0.224	0.061	0.044
Malaysia (2024 CSL + PDPA reforms)	0.095	0.123	0.031
Zambia (2025 CSL)	0.078	0.068	0.029
Egypt (2020 PDPL)	0.060	0.151	0.095
Kazakhstan (2013 PDP Law)	0.041	0.031	0.025
Philippines (2012 DPA)	0.065	0.388	0.033
Laos (2015 Cybercrime Law)	0.052	not applicable	0.029

rather than the legal text itself (Zambia, Malaysia, Kazakhstan against CSL; everyone against DSL).

A note on the interview corpus is necessary before the case studies begin. Interviews were semi-structured and conducted via Zoom or in person between March 2024 and July 2025. Interviewees were selected on the basis of demonstrated subject-matter expertise (academic publication, regulatory practice or senior civil-service experience in data protection or cybersecurity) and willingness to speak on the record about regulatory drafting, implementation or commercial environment in the case country. Interviews were recorded with consent and partially transcribed; quotations used in this chapter are taken from those transcriptions, lightly edited for readability and verified against the recording. Interviewees are referred to throughout by code (Interview-XX-N, where XX is the country code) rather than by name. The relationship between the corpus and the chapter is one of triangulation rather than statistical inference: interview testimony is used to confirm, complicate or contextualise patterns visible in the quantitative and documentary streams, not to substitute for them. Where a claim rests substantially on interview testimony, this is noted in the case study, and the claim is supported by reference to the secondary literature where comparable empirical evidence is available. The full corpus is documented in Appendix A.

2. Vietnam: Multi-Channel Convergence at the Highest Intensity

Vietnam is the case in which all three Chinese push mechanisms operate simultaneously and at high intensity, in which the lexical signal against the Chinese CSL is the strongest in the corpus, and in which recipient resistance is real but structurally constrained. Vietnam's 2018 Cybersecurity Law (Law No. 24/2018/QH14, passed June 2018, in force January 2019) scores 0.309 against the Chinese CSL: 1.77 times the cross-case baseline of 0.175, and substantially higher than every other Southeast Asian peer (Thailand 0.031, Singapore 0.013, Indonesia 0.020). The intra-regional outlier status is itself analytically important: if the Vietnamese score reflected generic ASEAN convergence on cybersecurity vocabulary, regional peers would cluster near similar values. They do not, which makes a country-specific explanation necessary.

The lexical signal does not fall away when the analysis shifts to other Chinese instruments. Vietnam's 2023 Personal Data Protection Decree (PDPD, Decree 13/2023/ND-CP) scores 0.198 against China's PIPL, well above the corpus mean for PIPL comparisons and indicating that the cyber sovereignty architecture of the 2018 law has been extended into the personal-information domain. Both the 2018 CSL and the 2023 PDPD score below or near the DSL baseline, consistent with the chapter's general finding that the DSL is the weakest channel of textual diffusion. Across China's three foundational instruments, then, Vietnam tracks the CSL most closely, the PIPL substantially and the DSL only marginally.

2.1 Predispositions: Why Vietnamese Governance Was Receptive

Before the mechanisms are traced, the Vietnamese political-economic conditions that predispose the state toward Chinese-style governance instruments deserve specification. The literature on contemporary Vietnamese politics consistently identifies three structural features that recur in this case (London, 2014; Vu, 2010; Beresford, 2008). First, single-party rule under the Communist Party of Vietnam treats information control and regime stability as primary state functions, with the Ministry of Public Security exercising enforcement authority over the digital sphere comparable in role, though not in scale, to China's Cyberspace Administration (Kerkvliet, 2019). Second, Vietnam's state-led developmentalism privileges strong administrative authority over digital infrastructure as a tool of economic transformation rather than as a constraint on it, an orientation that Chinese governance instruments fit naturally. Third, the post-Doi Moi political economy combines selective market opening with continuing state control over strategically important sectors, producing a regulatory disposition that resists wholesale liberal-market-and-rights frameworks while welcoming hybrid arrangements that preserve state authority. None of these conditions is sufficient to explain why Vietnam adopted Chinese-modelled provisions specifically, but they constitute the receptive ground on which the supply-side mechanisms operated.

2.2 Article-by-Article Structural Comparison

The 0.309 lexical similarity reflects more than topical convergence. Comparative-legal analysis (Bui and Lee, 2022) identifies several Vietnamese articles whose substantive provisions track specific Chinese articles. Four pairings warrant attention.

- *Vietnam Article 26 (data localisation) and China CSL Article 37 (cross-border data transfer for CIIO data).* Vietnam's Article 26 imposes data-storage and local-presence obligations on domestic and foreign service providers; China's Article 37 imposes localisation on Critical Information Infrastructure Operators for personal information and 'important data'. Both create national-territory storage obligations triggered by classification of the data and the operator. The Vietnamese provision was operationalised through Decree 53/2022/ND-CP, which substitutes a self-assessment and reporting mechanism for the pre-approval regime that China's Cyberspace Administration administers, an attenuation that the next sub-section addresses.
- *Vietnam Article 8 (prohibited acts) and China CSL Article 12.* Vietnam's Article 8 enumerates prohibited acts that include opposition to the Socialist Republic of Vietnam, distortion of historical truth, denial of revolutionary achievements and undermining national unity, language that has no direct analogue in liberal-democratic cybersecurity statutes. China's CSL Article 12 establishes parallel content prohibitions, with content-related acts elaborated further in CSL Article 47. The substantive parallel is the open-ended national-security and social-order trigger, with both regimes leaving the operative scope of 'prohibited content' to administrative determination.

- *Vietnam Articles 36–38 (responsibilities of state authorities) and China CSL Article 8.* Vietnam's Articles 36–38 allocate cybersecurity authority across the Ministry of Public Security, the Ministry of National Defence and the Government Cipher Committee. China's CSL Article 8 establishes a parallel division across the Cyberspace Administration of China, the Ministry of Industry and Information Technology, the Ministry of Public Security and sector regulators. The Vietnamese architecture concentrates more authority in the Ministry of Public Security than the Chinese architecture concentrates in any single agency, but the underlying logic of multi-agency state primacy with security-ministry leadership is shared.
- *Vietnamese provisions on critical infrastructure and network-operator obligations.* Vietnam's Articles 9–13 designate 'information systems important for national security' and Articles 24–25 specify their cybersecurity protection, paralleling China's Chapter III (Articles 31–39) on Critical Information Infrastructure. Vietnam's Articles 41–43 and Article 26 specify enterprise responsibilities including real-name registration and technical assistance to public-security organs, paralleling China's Articles 21 (multi-level protection scheme), 24 (real-name registration), 28 (technical assistance) and 47 (content management). The real-name registration parallel is particularly tight: both regimes require user-identity verification at account creation, an obligation that combines a content-control function with an identity-architecture function.

These article-pairings are not exhaustive, and the chapter does not claim that Vietnam's law is a clause-by-clause copy of the Chinese statute. What it shows is that the Vietnamese architecture is built around the same governance instruments that the Chinese architecture is built around, in ways that the lexical signal confirms and that comparative-legal analysis specifies. This is a stronger empirical claim than the lexical signal alone would license.

2.3 Mechanisms: Infrastructure, Bilateral Coordination and Epistemic Socialisation

The three Chinese push mechanisms operate at high intensity in the Vietnamese case. Infrastructure entanglement (C1) operates through sustained Chinese telecommunications financing extending back nearly two decades before the 2018 law's enactment. The AidData GCDF dataset records Chinese development-finance commitments to Vietnam's communications sector across the period 2002 to 2022, with China Development Bank concessional financing for EVNTelecom's 3G network expansion and additional smaller projects. Vietnamese telecommunications operators became operationally familiar with Huawei equipment standards across the 4G build-out period that preceded the 2017–18 cybersecurity drafting cycle. By the time draft text was being prepared, regulatory frameworks compatible with the installed base represented the path of least resistance both technically and economically. The 2025 award of new 5G equipment contracts exceeding USD 40 million to Huawei and ZTE despite sustained Western diplomatic pressure

(Guarascio, 2025), and Huawei's 2026 strategic cooperation agreements with Vietnamese financial institutions (Vu, 2026), are consistent with the proposition that the lock-in established in the 4G era has extended forward rather than receded with security warnings; whether this pattern proves durable across the next procurement cycle is a hypothesis for further longitudinal study, not a settled finding the present chapter establishes.

Bilateral cooperation frameworks (C2) have provided the second transmission pathway. China established bilateral digital economic cooperation mechanisms with Vietnam alongside other ASEAN partners (Liang et al., 2025). In September 2023, the two countries signed a memorandum of understanding on cooperation in combating cross-border gambling and cybersecurity, improving coordination under multilateral frameworks and enhancing law-enforcement capacity-building (Xinhua, 2023). The November 2022 China-ASEAN Summit produced a Digital Talent Cultivation Plan committing to train 1,000 ASEAN digital professionals over three years, with Vietnam an active participant (Li, 2022). Full agreement texts specifying the exact governance commitments are rarely publicly available, which limits the precision with which specific bilateral provisions can be linked to specific articles of Vietnamese law. But the documented existence of these channels, their operation during Vietnam's drafting period and their substantive focus on relevant policy domains together establish a plausible transmission pathway.

Epistemic socialisation (C3) operates at unusually high intensity in Vietnam. Huawei's ICT Academy maintains partnerships with at least three major Vietnamese universities (Hanoi University of Science and Technology, Polytechnic University of Ho Chi Minh City, and Industrial University of Ho Chi Minh City), providing ICT talent development, 5G and AI training and faculty development programmes (HUST, 2025). The Chinese Embassy in Hanoi reports approximately 23,000 Vietnamese students in China during the 2022–23 academic year, with the British Council's monitoring of South-East Asian student mobility flows corroborating the order of magnitude (British Council, 2024). Not all of these students study cybersecurity, but the cumulative volume of professional and academic socialisation makes Vietnam unusual among the cases for the depth of its Chinese-trained technical workforce.

2.4 Qualitative Evidence and Its Limits

The qualitative interview with a Vietnamese personal-data-protection specialist (Interview-VN-1, 2025) complicates the picture in two directions. The interviewee was emphatic that direct Chinese influence on Vietnam's legal drafting cannot be evidenced from the public record: Vietnamese lawmakers do not cite China as an example, and there is no documented exchange between Vietnamese drafters and Chinese counterparts. This is an important caution against over-reading the lexical signal. The absence of explicit attribution in the legislative record is itself evidence that the influence relationship, if it exists, operates below the surface of formal legal-process documentation.

Yet the same interview offered a structural reading of the law that is difficult to reconcile with independent convergence. The interviewee framed the underlying logic of Vietnamese cyber and data legislation as ideologically continuous with the Chinese model: a state-dominant regime in which the government acts as ultimate protector of data, in which national security takes priority over data flows and in which enforcement is centralised in a security ministry that performs functions distributed in China across the Cyberspace Administration of China, the Ministry of Public Security, and other sectoral authorities. On data localisation, the interviewee described Vietnamese practice as partial adoption: the PDPD mandates self-assessment and reporting for cross-border transfers, less stringent than China's pre-approval regime, but critical data must remain in Vietnam under a national-security justification. The earliest Vietnamese drafting reportedly mirrored China's pre-approval model and was relaxed only after sustained industry backlash.

Because a single interview cannot bear the weight of an attribution claim, the chapter triangulates against the comparative-legal record. The article-pairings developed in §2.2 (Bui and Lee, 2022) are independent documentary evidence that the Vietnamese instrument tracks the Chinese one structurally; the political-economic literature in §2.1 establishes that Vietnam's regime-security predispositions made such tracking attractive; and the regional and bilateral channels in §2.3 establish the transmission pathways through which it could have occurred. The interview supplies the practitioner-level interpretation that ties the documentary record together. None of these streams is dispositive on its own; together, they make Chinese normative influence the most parsimonious account of the observed pattern.

2.5 Recipient Agency

Vietnamese host-side responses (H1, H2, H3) display real but constrained agency. Hedging is most visible in the deliberate compartmentalisation between civilian and military telecommunications procurement: Vietnam's Military Industry Telecommunications Group has explicitly avoided partnering with Huawei for 5G infrastructure, even as civilian operators have continued Huawei relationships (EIAS, 2024; Liang et al., 2025). The 2025 5G contracts going to Huawei and ZTE rather than to European alternatives (Tran, 2025) suggest that hedging is more aspirational than fully operational on the civilian side, with cost and infrastructure compatibility outweighing diversification.

Selective adaptation (H2) appears notably weak. The 0.309 lexical similarity score, combined with the structural article-pairings developed above, indicates that Vietnam reproduced Chinese architecture with high fidelity rather than recombined it creatively. The PDPD's relaxation of pre-approval for cross-border transfers is the principal observed adaptation; outside that domain, the architecture is faithful. Strategic negotiation capacity (H3) exists, as Vietnam has demonstrated in renegotiating BRI debt obligations (Brautigam, 2009), but evidence of its application to cybersecurity governance terms specifically is limited. The interview's observation that Vietnamese civil society and the private sector view Chinese technology with pronounced scepticism, driven by nationalism and security concerns rather than by direct contestation of regulatory borrowing, points to a domestic constituency that does not endorse the Chinese model even as the state has built regulatory architecture compatible with it.

The cumulative pattern across the three streams (lexical, documentary, qualitative) makes independent convergence implausible. The temporal sequence (Vietnamese law drafted 2017–18, one year after China's 2017 instrument), the simultaneous operation of three documented bilateral channels during the drafting period, the article-by-article structural alignment, the divergence from both ASEAN peers and Western templates and the qualitative testimony that the underlying logic is continuous with Chinese state-centric assumptions, together support the inference that Chinese normative influence is the most parsimonious account of the observed pattern. Vietnam emerges as the strongest case in the corpus: Chinese push mechanisms (C1, C2, C3) all operated at high intensity, host-side selective adaptation (H2) was limited, and the resulting normative outcome shows the closest lexical and structural alignment with the Chinese cybersecurity model. The evidence makes an explanation based solely on independent convergence difficult to sustain, even if the public drafting record does not prove direct copying.

3. Chile: Distance, Asymmetry and the Limits of the Public Record

If Vietnam shows multi-channel push meeting partial pull, Chile presents a different configuration: high infrastructure investment combined with extreme economic asymmetry, weaker bilateral governance frameworks, moderate epistemic engagement and stronger institutional capacity for hedging. Chile's Cybersecurity Law (Ley 21.663), promulgated 26 March 2024 and published 8 April 2024, scores 0.224 against China's 2017 CSL: the second-highest score in the corpus and substantially above the 0.175 baseline. The pattern is analytically puzzling on its face. Chile is geographically distant from China, lacks a comprehensive bilateral cybersecurity framework comparable to the China-ASEAN architecture and exists within a Latin American legal tradition more naturally aligned with European and inter-American instruments (OAS, 2018). The high similarity score therefore demands an explanation that does not rely on the multi-channel bilateral engagement pattern visible in Vietnam.

Against the other two Chinese reference instruments, the Chilean signal is much weaker: 0.061 against PIPL and 0.044 against DSL. The Chilean lexical signal, in other words, is concentrated on the cybersecurity-domain instrument and does not extend into personal-information or data-security domains. This polarisation is itself a finding. It suggests that whatever produced the proximity to the Chinese CSL did not simultaneously produce proximity to the personal-information regulatory architecture that the GDPR and the broader European framework anchor in Chilean and Latin American practice. The case study below treats the polarisation as evidence that the Chilean signal reflects a narrow set of cybersecurity-specific considerations rather than a wholesale alignment with the Chinese governance stack.

3.1 Predispositions: Copper, Asymmetric Trade and a Contested Digital Sovereignty Discourse

Chile's economic relationship with China is the structural condition against which the case must be read. China is Chile's largest export destination, with bilateral trade dominated by copper exports. UN COMTRADE and the Observatorio Económico Complejo (OEC) report Chilean exports to China at USD 37.82 billion in 2024. China is the largest single destination for Chilean copper. The unqualified claim that '70 per cent of Chilean copper goes to China' overstates the position; the more defensible formulation is that China is Chile's largest single copper customer and the most important destination for Chilean copper exports going to Asia, with trade-data sources consistently identifying China as the dominant Asian destination but not as the destination for an absolute majority of Chilean copper exports by value (Cochilco, 2024; IndexBox, 2024). The asymmetry is real even in the more conservative framing: Chile's macroeconomic exposure to Chinese demand is substantial enough that policy-makers consider the China relationship in routine economic decision-making, and the China–Chile Free Trade Agreement of 2005, expanded through subsequent protocols, anchors the relationship in legal instruments (Wise, 2020).

The literature on Chile–China relations characterises Chile as a multi-vector state that engages China commercially while maintaining policy autonomy on governance questions (Wise, 2020; Ellis, 2020; Stuenkel, 2020). The 2020 decision to award the Chile-Asia Trans-Pacific submarine-cable contract to Japan's NEC Corporation rather than to Huawei, attributed by analysts to United States diplomatic pressure rather than to commercial accommodation toward China (Zheng, 2020), illustrates the multi-vector posture. Chile is not, on the available evidence, a state predisposed to wholesale alignment with Chinese governance preferences; it is a state whose commercial relationships with China create structural conditions under which anti-China regulatory choices carry economic risk that Chilean policymakers are demonstrably unwilling to accept.

The chapter's earlier framing claimed that this structural asymmetry produced 'anticipatory accommodation' of Chinese commercial preferences in the Chilean cybersecurity legislation. That formulation deserves softening. A search of the Biblioteca del Congreso Nacional record for Ley 21.663, ministerial communications from Subtel and the Ministry of Foreign Affairs, and statements from Chilean industry actors on the cybersecurity law produces no statement explicitly attributing Chilean cyber policy choices to Chinese commercial relations or to copper-export considerations (BCN, 2024). What the public record establishes is that Chilean cybersecurity policymaking unfolded in the context of substantial copper trade and infrastructure financing relationships with China, and that the legal text bears structural similarities to the Chinese model that may reflect this context. The available evidence does not support a stronger attribution claim. Chilean cybersecurity policy may have been shaped by these structural conditions through routes that the public legislative record does not directly document. That is a reasonable hypothesis to develop. It is not a finding the public record establishes.

3.2 Mechanisms: Infrastructure Substantial, Bilateral Coordination Thin, Epistemic Moderate

Infrastructure entanglement (C1) in Chile is, in absolute terms, larger than in Vietnam. AidData records Chinese development-finance commitments to Chile's communications sector across the period 2007–23, with notable spikes in 2010 (a CDB-syndicated facility to Nextel Chile of approximately USD 96 million within a USD 150 million total syndicated loan, AidData Project 69152), 2016 (financing to WOM telecommunications) and 2019 (additional WOM financing). Beyond financing, Chinese companies have deployed physical infrastructure that creates technical path dependencies. The Fibre Optic Austral submarine-cable system, deployed across 2018–19, was a partnership between Huawei Marine and the Chilean telecommunications provider CTR with investment from Subtel; at the time of completion, it became the world's southernmost submarine cable, connecting southern Chilean regions to international networks via Chinese-supplied equipment (Offshore Energy, 2018). Huawei established partnerships with Movistar, a major Chilean carrier, to deploy 5G and 4G technology in remote locations including Puerto Williams, and in 2022 partnered with the Universidad de Chile and Movistar on a 5G laboratory at the Carén campus (Huawei, 2023; Universidad de Chile, 2022). The July 2025 memorandum of understanding between Huawei Chile and Codelco, Chile's state-owned copper corporation, to explore 5G-powered AI, automation and cloud services for mining operations, signed after the cybersecurity law's enactment, suggests that infrastructure engagement is now extending into Chile's most strategically critical economic sector (International Mining, 2025).

The path-dependency mechanism in Chile operates at three levels that warrant specification. At the physical-infrastructure layer, Huawei equipment is embedded in mobile and fixed-line networks across multiple operators, with maintenance, software updates and interoperability requirements that lock in vendor-specific design assumptions. Replacing this base would require capital expenditure that no Chilean operator has signalled willingness to undertake. At the regulatory-compatibility layer, vendor-specific maintenance arrangements, software updates, interoperability requirements, and operator training may make some regulatory choices easier to maintain than alternatives that would require costly reconfiguration. A Chilean cybersecurity statute compatible with the installed base imposes lower transition costs than one requiring infrastructure reconfiguration. At the operational-personnel layer, Chilean telecommunications engineers trained on Huawei equipment, certified through Huawei's professional programmes and embedded in Chinese-vendor support networks constitute a domestic technical workforce whose expertise is partly Chinese-specific. The path dependency these three layers jointly produce is not a coercion mechanism; it is a structural condition that lowers the cost of regulatory choices compatible with Chinese architecture and raises the cost of choices incompatible with it.

Bilateral cooperation frameworks (C2) operate at substantially lower intensity than in Vietnam. In May 2017, then-President Xi Jinping met then-President

Michelle Bachelet, agreeing to deepen the China-Chile comprehensive strategic partnership and push forward cooperation in infrastructure construction, regional connectivity and information and communication sectors (Chinese Consulate Los Angeles, 2017). The 2005 Chile-China Free Trade Agreement, while establishing broad economic partnership and including technology-cooperation provisions in Article 106, contains no cybersecurity governance or data governance clauses (Government of Chile and Government of the People's Republic of China, 2005). A 2017 Protocol amending the FTA added e-commerce facilitation provisions but, like the 2005 instrument, no cybersecurity or data governance clauses (Morosini et al., 2024). Searches of Chinese MFA archives, Chilean government sources and news reporting identify no published bilateral agreements or memoranda specifically addressing cybersecurity cooperation comparable to the China-ASEAN instruments. The absence of cyber-specific bilateral agreements distinguishes Chile from Vietnam materially. Whatever explains Chile's textual alignment with the Chinese cybersecurity model, it is not the comprehensive bilateral coordination architecture that operates in the ASEAN cases.

Epistemic socialisation (C3) operates at moderate levels. Four Confucius Institute platforms in Chile (Santo Tomás University 2007, Catholic University of Chile 2008, a National Institute classroom 2011 and the Latin American Regional Centre for Confucius Institutes established in 2014) make Chile a regional hub for Chinese language and cultural programming across Latin America. ZTE financed the installation of a technology laboratory at the University of Chile in 2011 valued at USD 11 million (ZTE, 2013), and Huawei established its 5G laboratory partnership at the Carén campus in 2022 (Universidad de Chile, 2022). China Scholarship Council data shows only 18 Chilean students received Chinese government scholarships in 2023, and additional Chilean graduates received Ministry of Commerce scholarships in 2021. Compared to the 23,000 Vietnamese students in China during the same period, the scale of Chilean educational exchange with China is small by orders of magnitude. The epistemic channel operates, but not at a level that would by itself explain regulatory architecture.

3.3 Recipient Agency

Chilean hedging (H1) is the strongest among the high-similarity cases. The 2020 Chile-Asia trans-Pacific cable contract awarded to NEC over Huawei demonstrates that Chilean procurement remains contested and subject to geopolitical considerations rather than reflecting automatic Chinese vendor preference (Zheng, 2020). The 2021 decision to allow Huawei to bid on 5G network contracts under a 'technology-standards-based approach', rather than implementing a blanket geopolitical exclusion, indicates deliberate policy autonomy: Chile rejected an automatic US-aligned exclusion and an automatic Chinese inclusion, choosing a procedural rule that maintains optionality (RCR Wireless, 2021; Stuenkel, 2020). This is institutionally meaningful hedging that distinguishes Chile from cases like Vietnam where infrastructure compatibility and political-economic constraints have produced more uniform vendor outcomes.

Selective adaptation (H2) appears more substantial than in Vietnam. The 0.224 lexical similarity score, while elevated above the 0.175 baseline, is notably lower than Vietnam's 0.309, suggesting greater modification of Chinese legal templates or hybrid incorporation of alternative governance vocabularies. Without granular structural analysis comparing Chile's law against Chinese and European reference architectures on hierarchical data classification, state-access obligations, cross-border-transfer conditionality and critical-infrastructure scope, the precise degree of adaptation cannot be definitively established. The chapter does not claim, for instance, that Chile's law builds the same multi-level protection scheme that anchors China's CSL. The gap between Vietnam's 0.309 and Chile's 0.224 is itself meaningful: it suggests that Chilean adaptation operated more substantially on the legal text than Vietnamese adaptation did. Strategic negotiation capacity (H3) is institutionally available; the Chilean Congress has developed oversight mechanisms for Chinese technology agreements and has paid parliamentary attention to national-security implications of Chinese telecommunications infrastructure (Cambero, 2021). Whether comparable bargaining occurred in contexts directly relevant to the drafting of Ley 21.663 is not established in the public record.

3.4 What the Chile Case Shows

Among possible explanations of Chile's lexical similarity to the Chinese model, four are non-mutually exclusive: infrastructure path dependency, in which the Chinese telecommunications financing made Chinese-compatible regulation operationally easier than alternatives requiring infrastructure replacement; structural economic context, in which copper-export dependence creates incentives that may, but need not, shape policy choices on the margin; legal borrowing through observation, in which Chile drafted from publicly available Chinese reference texts attracted by their comprehensiveness without bilateral coordination; and global convergence, in which Chile independently developed similar frameworks in response to similar security pressures.

Pure convergence cannot be ruled out: Chile's law was enacted seven years after China's, Chinese infrastructure financing preceded the drafting period, and Chile's legal approach differs in some respects from other Latin American and OECD-oriented frameworks, but the public record does not establish that Chilean drafters consulted Chinese legal texts. The most defensible reading of the available evidence is more cautious: infrastructure path dependency and the structural economic context may have made Chinese-compatible regulatory options more attractive, but the record supports a hypothesis of possible observational borrowing rather than a finding that Chile drafted from Chinese templates. Whether the structural economic context shaped that choice through anticipatory accommodation, or only through the more general background condition that policy hostility to China carries economic risk, the public record does not adjudicate. The mechanism pattern, strong C1, weak C2, moderate C3, strong H1, moderate H2, with H3 institutionally available but rarely exercised in the cyber domain, produces moderate rather than high similarity, but similarity nonetheless in a context where geographic distance would predict its absence. Chile is therefore best treated as a case of unresolved or multiply determined lexical proximity. A stronger attribution claim would require drafting records, official statements, or interview evidence that the public record does not currently provide.

4. Malaysia: Selective Hedging and the Architecture of Hybrid Frameworks

Malaysia is in some respects the most analytically valuable case, because it combines comprehensive Chinese push across all three mechanisms with a low lexical similarity score. The 2024 Cybersecurity Act registers 0.095 against the Chinese CSL, just below the 0.175 baseline. Against PIPL the score rises to 0.123, still below baseline but higher than the cybersecurity-domain score, reflecting the 2024 amendments to Malaysia's Personal Data Protection Act that introduced GDPR- and PIPL-aligned provisions. Against DSL the score is 0.031, near the corpus DSL baseline. The puzzle is direct: how can dense bilateral, infrastructural and epistemic engagement coexist with a regulatory text that does not lexically resemble the Chinese model? The case suggests that selective adaptation can transform the surface of borrowed frameworks substantially, and that diffusion patterns in plural legal-political contexts may operate through implementation rather than text.

4.1 Mechanisms

Bilateral frameworks (C2) operate at exceptionally high intensity. On 16 April 2025, Malaysia signed two memoranda of understanding with China's National Development and Reform Commission, witnessed by Prime Minister Anwar Ibrahim and President Xi Jinping. The digital economy MOU explicitly addresses 'policy coordination and regulatory alignment, industrial digital transformation, digital technology innovation and talent development' (Sekaran, 2025); the AI cooperation MOU establishes complementary technology partnership frameworks. The inclusion of explicit 'regulatory alignment' language at the level of intergovernmental agreement is unusual: most bilateral digital cooperation instruments in the corpus describe technical and commercial cooperation without naming regulatory alignment as an objective. The temporal coincidence of these MOUs with Malaysia's April 2025 award of a second wholesale 5G network to Huawei and ZTE, signed in the same month (Wood, 2025), suggests coordination between the commercial and the regulatory tracks rather than independent developments.

Infrastructure engagement (C1) is moderate but accelerating. AidData records Bank of China Malaysia's syndicated share of approximately USD 68 million within a USD 270 million green-financing facility for the GDS Nusajaya Tech Park Data Centre Project (AidData Project 106768, 2023; Butler, 2023). The April 2025 5G award to Huawei and ZTE for U Mobile's second wholesale network targets 90 per cent population coverage within twenty-four months, materialising despite Western pressure and indicating pragmatic vendor selection prioritising cost and technical capability over geopolitical considerations (Wood, 2025). Chinese platforms are integrated into Malaysian fintech systems, including Touch‘n Go e-wallet partnerships with Chinese partners, and Malaysia serves as a regional data-centre hub for several Chinese firms (Qu, 2023).

Epistemic socialisation (C3) operates at notably high levels. AidData records substantial education-sector engagement between 2009 and 2023. Major initiatives include the construction of the Xiamen University Malaysia Campus, with a CDB loan of approximately USD 170 million in 2013 (AidData Project 49402, 2013) supplemented by a CCB facility in 2015; Confucius Institutes at the University of Malaysia (2009) and SEGi University (2014); recurring scholarship programmes; and the East Coast Rail Link Industrial Skills Training initiative (2017) (Xinhua, 2022). The April 2025 MOUs commit to expanded talent-development cooperation, extending educational engagement into digital technologies (Sekaran, 2025).

4.2 The Hybrid Architecture, Specified

Despite this dense engagement, the lexical signal is weak. The interpretation supplied by a Malaysian privacy practitioner working in regulatory compliance (Interview-MY-1, 2025) is that Malaysia's approach is deliberately hybrid: aligning with EU GDPR-style regulation as the primary template while drawing practical lessons from Chinese frameworks. This hybrid pattern is consistent with the broader literature on selective adaptation in non-Western jurisdictions, in which legal systems borrow from multiple foreign reference points while reshaping them to fit domestic political and institutional conditions (Potter, 2003; Acharya, 2004) and with the comparative regulatory literature on the Beijing Effect, which predicts that Chinese-aligned governance frameworks will travel abroad in modular form rather than as wholesale legal transplants (Erie and Streinz, 2021; Bradford, 2023).

The 2024 amendments to Malaysia's Personal Data Protection Act introduced data-controller terminology, mandatory breach notification, data-protection-officer obligations, and a right to data portability. Subsequent commissioner guidance and consultation processes have elaborated breach-notification procedures, DPO requirements, cross-border-transfer rules, and data-protection impact-assessment expectations. On terminology, Malaysia replaced the term ‘data user’ (a feature of the 2010 PDPA inherited from earlier UK legislation) with ‘data controller’, the GDPR term, in the 2024 amendments, a small but symbolically European choice. On data localisation, the interviewee was emphatic that Malaysia did not impose direct localisation requirements but instead adopted transfer impact assessments to evaluate whether the recipient country provides equivalent protection, a procedural mechanism that operates as indirect alignment with the cautious cross-border posture characteristic of both Chinese and European frameworks without adopting either's specific architecture. On cyber sovereignty, the interviewee observed that Malaysia's 2024 Cybersecurity Act reflects a growing emphasis on cyber sovereignty defined territorially and extended to the protection of cyberspace, echoing China's expanded conception of sovereignty without adopting Chinese terminology wholesale.

What Malaysia adapts and what it preserves can be summarised more sharply. Malaysian provisions that lean European: the controller/processor terminology, the rights-protective architecture of the PDPA amendments, the breach-notification mechanism, the data-protection-officer requirement. Malaysian provisions that lean Chinese: the cyber sovereignty framing of the 2024 Cybersecurity Act, the broad designation of critical national information infrastructure, the security-centred regulatory rationale. Malaysian provisions that are genuinely hybrid: the transfer-impact-assessment mechanism, which is procedurally European but operationally permits the cautious cross-border posture characteristic of both Chinese and European regimes; the Data Protection Officer role, modelled on GDPR but situated in a regulatory environment that emphasises state oversight more than European practice does. This is hybridisation in a precise sense: not random eclecticism, but deliberate selection of which architecture supplies which provision, calibrated to Malaysia's plural political institutions and its regulatory market position between European trade partners and Chinese commercial partners.

4.3 Recipient Agency

Malaysian hedging (H1) is institutionally robust and visible across multiple decision points. While the 5G award to Huawei and ZTE indicates Chinese vendors retain market access, Malaysia simultaneously explores ASEAN Model Contractual Clauses as alternative tools for regional data flows, signalling a preference for regional rather than bilateral coordination architectures. The interviewee noted that privacy professionals and multinational companies face genuine dilemmas navigating between China's stricter data governance frameworks and looser regulations elsewhere, indicating that the regulatory environment is treated as plural rather than aligned with any single foreign reference. Selective adaptation (H2) is unusually strong, as the architectural specification above demonstrates: Malaysia substantively rebuilt its data governance architecture by drawing on multiple sources without privileging any. This is selective adaptation in its most articulated form: a deliberate policy of regulatory bricolage. Strategic negotiation (H3) is supported by Malaysia's plural political institutions, with parliamentary oversight and active civil society. The interviewee described a recognisable 'privacy paradox' in Malaysian society, with citizens voicing concern over data misuse yet often trading privacy for convenience, creating space for regulatory development without strong electoral pressure for a particular foreign template.

The Malaysia case therefore suggests that Chinese push can be high across all three supply mechanisms while host-side adaptation, hedging, and institutional plurality combine to produce a textually distinctive but conceptually convergent regulatory framework. The low CSL similarity score (0.095) understates the depth of substantive engagement: it indicates that Malaysian drafters did not work from Chinese text, but that they built a hybrid architecture in which implementation rather than legislation may prove the more consequential locus of Chinese influence – a proposition the present chapter cannot test on the available evidence and which is flagged here as a hypothesis for further research, to be assessed once the

2024 amendments and the April 2025 MOUs have generated a sufficient implementation record. Malaysia is, in this sense, what successful selective adaptation looks like at the level of the legal text, and a corrective to any account that would read low lexical similarity as evidence of low influence; what closer Sino-Malaysian regulatory practice will look like in operation is the question further work would need to address.

5. Kazakhstan: Pull without Available Push, Then Documented Borrowing

Kazakhstan presents a temporally bifurcated case that stresses the framework in productive ways. The country's primary personal-data legislation, Law No. 94-V of 21 May 2013 'On Personal Data and Their Protection', was enacted four years before China's Cybersecurity Law and eight years before its PIPL (Republic of Kazakhstan, 2013). Lexical similarity scores against the three Chinese reference instruments are 0.041 against the CSL, 0.031 against the PIPL and 0.025 against the DSL: all near the corpus baseline for each instrument, and the temporal sequence rules out direct Chinese textual influence on the original 2013 instrument. Kazakhstan was drafting from European Directive 95/46/EC, OECD Privacy Principles, the APEC Framework and Russian and Eurasian Economic Union models that pre-date Belt and Road digital expansion.

Yet the qualitative evidence and the post-2013 regulatory record together indicate that Chinese normative influence on Kazakhstan's subsequent data localisation policy has been substantial. The case is not one of textual borrowing in the foundational statute but of selective adoption through subsequent amendment, supported by the comparative-legal literature on Central Asian data law (Greenleaf and Kaldani, 2025) and corroborated by the Kazakhstani regulatory enforcement record.

5.1 Predispositions: Post-Soviet, Multi-Vector, between Russia and China

The literature on Kazakhstani foreign policy and political economy characterises Astana's posture as multi-vector, with strategic relationships maintained simultaneously with Russia, China, the European Union and the United States, calibrated to preserve policy autonomy in the face of much larger neighbours (Cooley, 2012; Laruelle, 2018). On digital policy specifically, Kazakhstan participates in the Eurasian Economic Union (EAEU) regulatory acquis, which carries Russian-derived principles, while also engaging Chinese digital infrastructure cooperation through the Belt and Road framework. The 2013 personal-data law itself reflects this multi-vector inheritance: it draws from European data-protection vocabulary, OECD principles, and Russian-and-Soviet legal traditions on state administrative authority, producing a regulatory architecture distinctly different from either a wholesale European or a wholesale Chinese template (Greenleaf and Kaldani, 2025).

These predispositions matter for the case in two ways. First, they specify why the 2013 statute scored at corpus baseline on all three Chinese reference instruments:

there was no Chinese model to borrow from at that date, and the available models came from elsewhere. Second, they explain why Kazakhstan was institutionally capable of selective borrowing on a specific policy element after Chinese frameworks became available: the multi-vector posture treats foreign legal models as resources to be combined rather than as packages to be adopted whole.

5.2 The Post-2013 Trajectory: Law No. 419-V and the Data-Localisation Amendment

Kazakhstan amended its 2013 law to add a data-localisation requirement in late 2015, before China enacted the Cybersecurity Law in November 2016 and before that law entered into force in June 2017. Law No. 419-V 'On Amendments to Certain Legislative Acts on Informatization', published 26 November 2015 and entering into force 1 January 2016, introduced an obligation that owners and operators of personal-data databases store those databases on the territory of Kazakhstan (Republic of Kazakhstan, 2015). The localisation rule has been variously codified in Article 12 (storage) and the closely related Article 25–1 of the consolidated Personal Data Protection Act, with subsequent amendments through the 2020s clarifying enforcement (Morgan Lewis, 2023).

The temporal sequencing is analytically important because it rules out direct borrowing from the enacted Chinese CSL. Any Chinese influence on the 2015 Kazakhstani amendment would have to run through earlier Chinese policy practice, draft legislation, cyber-sovereignty discourse, or bilateral policy exchange. The chronology therefore narrows rather than proves the possible pathway.

5.3 Qualitative Attribution and its Corroborating Documentary Record

The most direct attribution comes from the interview with a Kazakhstani academic specialist in cybersecurity policy who previously served as a senior civil servant (Interview-KZ-1, 2025). The interviewee was unambiguous: 'After studying Chinese policy in terms of cyber security, we took experience that all personal data of Kazakhstan should be saved in the location of Kazakhstan territory. In the local, I mean, server… This policy was applied from Chinese experience, from Chinese policy. We applied in Kazakhstan'. This is the most explicit attribution of Chinese policy borrowing recorded in any of the interviews conducted for this study.

A single interview cannot bear the full weight of an attribution claim. The chapter therefore corroborates the interview against three documentary sources. First, Greenleaf and Kaldani (2025), in the first systematic comparative study of all six Central Asian data-protection laws, situate Kazakhstan's regime between Russian and ex-Soviet legacy law, the Council of Europe Convention 108+ tradition and Chinese Belt and Road infrastructure influence, identifying data localisation as a dimension where Chinese policy has had traceable impact in the region, while characterising the principal Chinese channel as infrastructure dominance and surveillance technology rather than direct legal-text borrowing. Russia's 2014 data-localisation law, effective in 2015, remains an important alternative pathway that the chapter must treat seriously rather than dismiss. Second, the regulatory enforcement record corroborates the operational reach of the localisation rule. In August 2023, Kazakhstani regulators briefly blocked yandex.kz because the site's servers were located outside Kazakhstan, and Yandex agreed to relocate its Kazakhstan-branch servers to Kazakhstani territory; Yandex Go (the ride-hailing service) had already been compelled to comply earlier (Meduza, 2023). The enforcement record demonstrates that the Chinese-modelled localisation rule has been operationalised against non-Chinese commercial actors. Third, the cross-border governance literature on Russian and Chinese data-localisation regimes (Khasanova and Tai, 2024) helps distinguish the Chinese-modelled localisation rule the interviewee describes from the Russian-modelled rules that Kazakhstan's earlier legislation absorbed through EAEU integration: although both Russian and Chinese regimes share sovereignty-first rhetoric, they diverge institutionally, and the Kazakhstani 2015 amendment more closely tracks the Chinese architecture than the Russian one on the specific dimension of national-territory storage of personal data of Kazakhstani citizens.

The Yandex enforcement case is itself analytically significant. Russian platforms, particularly Yandex Go and Yandex's broader product suite, were required to comply with the Kazakhstani localisation requirement by storing Kazakhstani user personal data, including card numbers and other sensitive information, on Kazakhstani servers, on pain of fines or business bans. The case applies a Chinese-modelled data-sovereignty regime to a non-Chinese commercial actor (a Russian one), which complicates the geopolitical reading. The Chinese-derived rule was used in a regulatory context where its principal effect was to constrain Russian services, demonstrating that recipient states can deploy borrowed Chinese governance instruments towards their own strategic objectives unrelated to Sino-recipient bilateral relations.

5.4 Mechanisms

Infrastructure engagement (C1) in Kazakhstan is substantial, though the chapter's earlier dollar figures require correction against the AidData record. AidData records substantial Chinese telecommunications financing committed primarily between 2005 and 2011, including a CDB facility for CDMA-450 network expansion (AidData Project 40103, 2023), Huawei equipment financing in 2007 and 2011 and a CDB loan of approximately USD 300 million to KazakhTelecom in 2009 (AidData Project 70862, 2009). Pre-law infrastructure created technical dependencies and vendor relationships before the 2013 drafting of the personal-data law. The crucial constraint, however, is temporal not infrastructural: in 2013, no Chinese cyber or data-protection template existed in mature form to reference. The pre-law infrastructure created conditions potentially receptive to Chinese influence, but absent available Chinese legal frameworks these conditions remained latent. The interview testimony shows them activating later, in the data-localisation domain, once Chinese policy became available as a reference point.

The interviewee offered a notable observation on the limits of Chinese commercial presence in Kazakhstan's telecommunications sector specifically: 'We don' have Chinese companies in Kazakhstan… I personally, I haven't heard anything about Chinese companies in the mobile networking industry', identifying Russian companies (Beeline) and Kazakhstani national operators as the dominant market actors. This is in some tension with the AidData record of large Huawei-linked financing, and likely reflects the distinction between equipment provision (Huawei as an upstream supplier) and consumer-facing telecommunications operation (where the Chinese presence is genuinely limited). The implication for the framework is that infrastructure entanglement (C1) operates at the equipment and standards layer rather than the operator layer, which may explain why Kazakhstani public perception of Chinese technological influence is less salient than in cases where Chinese operators provide consumer services directly.

Bilateral cooperation (C2) and epistemic socialisation (C3) operate at lower documented intensity than in the high-similarity cases. Kazakhstan participates in what the interviewee described as a 'silk road in terms of digitalisation', an explicit identification with the BRI Digital Silk Road framework. The interviewee framed the working relationship in cooperative terms: 'We try to work with China very closely'. The stated rationale was epistemic, China's 'powerful experience in terms of digitalisation and cyber security', rather than ideological alignment. This pragmatic framing is consistent with Greitens (2020), who argues that Global South governments adopt elements of Chinese surveillance and digital-governance toolkits primarily for instrumental and capacity-building reasons rather than out of ideological alignment with Beijing. C3 operates at moderate scale, with educational exchange channels established but not at the volume documented for ASEAN cases.

5.5 Recipient Agency and What the Kazakhstan Case Establishes

Recipient agency (H1, H2, H3) is strong across all three dimensions. Kazakhstan exemplifies pragmatic openness rather than alignment to any external bloc: it learns from China where Chinese practice is useful (data localisation), from Estonia on digitisation governance and from the EU on principles it nevertheless does not yet codify. The 2013 law, drawing from European and OECD frameworks, embodies adaptation more than borrowing. The 2015 amendment, however, demonstrates institutional capacity to add Chinese-modelled provisions selectively when those provisions become useful for purposes the recipient state itself defines. The data-localisation rule applied to Russian services (the Yandex enforcement case) demonstrates capacity to deploy borrowed frameworks against actors who are themselves geopolitical near-peers.

Kazakhstan is therefore a case in which the lexical signal points away from Chinese influence on the foundational 2013 statute, while the interview evidence and subsequent enforcement record suggest possible Chinese influence on a specific later policy element. Because the 2015 localisation amendment predates China's enacted CSL and overlaps chronologically with Russian localisation law, the attribution should be framed as contested rather than settled. The case demonstrates two methodological points.

First, attribution at the level of foundational legislation is not the only scale at which Chinese normative influence operates. Subsequent amendments, secondary regulation, ministerial directives and enforcement choices may carry the operative borrowing without registering in the lexical signal of the founding statute. Capturing this requires extending the corpus to include implementing regulations and amendments, work that the present chapter has not undertaken at scale. Second, recipient-side framing of the borrowing relationship can be openly attributional, 'we took experience from Chinese policy', without producing the politicisation around Chinese influence that observers might expect, particularly where the borrowing is framed as a pragmatic choice among multiple available models. The mechanism configuration in Kazakhstan is moderate C1 (concentrated at the equipment and standards layer), low C2, moderate C3, with strong recipient agency across H1, H2 and H3, producing low lexical similarity on the foundational text but documented borrowing on a specific policy element of considerable operational significance.

6. Zambia: Infrastructure-Heavy, Norm-Light

Zambia is the case in which the framework's asymmetric configurations are most clearly visible. Zambia exhibits among the highest documented Chinese telecommunications-infrastructure investments in the case set across 2001 to 2017, yet the lexical similarity of its 2025 Cyber Security Act to China's 2017 CSL is only 0.078, well below the 0.175 baseline. Against PIPL the score is 0.068; against DSL 0.029. Bilateral frameworks specifically dedicated to digital governance are not evidenced in available sources. Epistemic socialisation operates at moderate scale. The Zambia case therefore tests directly whether infrastructure intensity alone is sufficient to drive lexical convergence, and the answer is firmly negative.

6.1 Mechanisms

Infrastructure (C1) is exceptional. AidData records substantial Chinese commitments across the period, including approximately USD 280 to 302 million for the Phase II Communication Towers project (the figure varying between Zambian Ministry of Finance and Economic Planning sources and Ministry of Finance and National Planning sources, AidData adopting the higher figure), USD 133.5 million and USD 76.7 million for Digital Terrestrial Television Broadcasting Phases II and III (2016), USD 68.5 million for the Smart Zambia National ICT Development project (2015), USD 55 million for Fibre Optic Phase II (2011) and earlier renovation and equipment financing in 2001–06 (Custer et al., 2021). The Smart Zambia project deserves particular attention: its scale and its broad 'national ICT development' designation suggest integrated digital-governance infrastructure beyond simple connectivity provision. A particularly distinctive episode involves Zambia's 2014 government assumption of approximately USD 103 million in private LAP Green Networks debt to ZTE (Network World, 2014), converting a commercial obligation into sovereign debt and creating fiscal dependencies of a kind not observed elsewhere in the corpus. This debt assumption preceded the 2015 Smart Zambia financing by one year, suggesting potential conditionality between financial accommodation and subsequent infrastructure financing. Beyond the connectivity-and-broadcasting projects above, Chinese government funding also financed the renovation of the Mulungushi International Conference Centre in Lusaka, completed in 2020 at a reported cost of between USD 30 million and USD 60 million (the figure varies across sources, with Tech Policy Press, 2026, citing approximately USD 30 million and Human Rights Watch, 2026, the higher figure). The Mulungushi Centre is governance-relevant infrastructure of a kind distinct from telecommunications hardware: it is a venue for international convening, with no operational connection to the Zambian regulatory drafting record on which the lexical analysis is built. Its inclusion in the inventory is justified ex post by the events discussed in §6.2 below, in which the centre's funding source became operationally consequential. It also revises downward the precision of any claim that Chinese infrastructure presence in Zambia is concentrated in connectivity and broadcasting alone.

Bilateral cooperation frameworks (C2) specific to digital governance are not documented in accessible sources. The compliance lawyer interviewed for this study (Interview-ZM-1, 2024), in regulatory contact with the Zambian Data Protection Commissioner, was clear that she could not point to specific bilateral data-governance MOUs between Zambia and China: 'In terms of agreements between the government and them, I'm not in a position to say'. This contrasts sharply with Vietnam, Malaysia and Egypt, where formal MOUs explicitly addressing digital governance and regulatory cooperation are publicly disclosed.

Epistemic socialisation (C3) operates at moderate scale. AidData records approximately USD 14 million in education-sector engagement between 2007 and 2023, including a USD 11.4 million Confucius Institute building in 2013 and the Sinohydro Training Institute (USD 1.5 million) in 2017 (PowerChina, 2023). The infrastructure-to-education ratio sharply prioritises the former and inverts Malaysia's pattern. This skew is itself a structural feature of the Zambia case: engagement is mediated almost entirely through hardware and turnkey infrastructure rather than through people-to-people governance training.

6.2 The Interview, the Literature and the Absence of Public Controversy

The interview provides crucial qualitative texture. The interviewee's framing of Chinese influence in Zambian data protection is consistently positive but qualified: 'In terms of China's influence, China has been very helpful actually in terms of the African landscape of data protection'. The interviewee identified Huawei and ZTE as platforms that have helped to increase data-protection awareness and provided technology now used in Zambia's data-protection efforts, naming the National Data Centre and the Smart Zambia initiative as Chinese-supported projects. The reading of regulatory borrowing was straightforward: 'Our new Zambian regulation has borrowed a little bit from your regulation in China as well as the GDPR, except my observation is that your regulations in China are a little bit more stringent in terms of the penalties'. This is partial attribution, China alongside the GDPR as inspirations, and explicitly distinguishes the Chinese model on the dimension of penal stringency rather than treating it as identical.

The interview pattern is consistent with the broader empirical record on Chinese surveillance and digital governance in Africa. Jili (2022, 2023) documents that African governments procure Chinese surveillance and ICT infrastructure for instrumental rather than ideological reasons, and that the demand-side conditions (urbanisation pressures, weak local IT industries, regime-security incentives) are at least as significant as the supply-side push. The Australian Strategic Policy Institute's mapping of Chinese tech-firm deployments in Africa identifies Smart City and Safe City projects across more than 75 contracts, with Zambia among the recipients (ASPI, 2019). Hoffman (2019) shows that Chinese firms have systematically bundled technical infrastructure with governance assumptions about state-managed data environments, producing the kind of operational embedding the Zambian interview describes without requiring explicit regulatory MOUs. Brautigam's work on Chinese investment in Africa (Brautigam, 2009, 2020) characterises the Zambian and broader African pattern as substantial commercial and infrastructural engagement that does not translate automatically into governance alignment, a characterisation that the Zambian case bears out. Read together, these sources suggest that the Zambian pattern, where infrastructure intensity is high and regulatory borrowing is partial, observational, and politically depoliticised, is not idiosyncratic. It is the modal Sub-Saharan African pattern in the literature on Chinese digital-governance influence.

The interviewee's reading of legislative independence was robust: 'Zambian legislators have still been independent despite growing influence'. The trigger event invoked was the high-profile fines imposed on Google and other firms ('witnessing cases such as Google being fined 60 million pounds was it a few years ago over data-protection breaches'), which alerted regulators across Southern Africa to the imminence of data-protection challenges. On data sovereignty and public perception, the interviewee acknowledged that researchers raise concerns about 'the independence of how the data is being used in terms of the fact that we have an external country being able to have this amount of influence', and about 'data sovereignty, who controls the data, where is it stored' But the interviewee was clear that the 2024 regulation's requirement to store personal data locally answers those concerns at a structural level: 'I haven't seen any uproar in terms of Chinese influence at this point, no', citing collaborations such as the TopStar joint venture between Chinese and Zambian media, well received without significant controversy.

The 2024 interview reading on the absence of public controversy has been overtaken by events that the chapter must register, even at the cost of disturbing the case's analytic surface. On 28-29 April 2026, after the interview but before final revision of this chapter, the Zambian government postponed RightsCon 2026, the world's largest digital-rights summit, scheduled for 5-8 May 2026 at the Mulungushi International Conference Centre in Lusaka. The official justification cited 'pending administrative and security clearances' and the need for the summit's thematic content to be brought into 'full alignment with Zambia's national values, policy priorities, and broader public interest considerations' (Mutati, cited in Lusaka Times, 2026). Access Now, the convening organisation, declined the implied conditions and announced on 29 April 2026 that the summit would not proceed in Lusaka or online (Access Now, 2026). Civil-society reporting in Lusaka, Human Rights Watch's investigative summary, and several press accounts alleged that Chinese government pressure over Taiwanese participation and criticism of Chinese digital-governance practice contributed to the postponement, particularly because the event was scheduled to take place on Chinese-funded premises (Human Rights Watch, 2026; Tech Policy Press, 2026; China Digital Times, 2026; Semafor, 2026). The OHCHR Special Rapporteur on freedom of peaceful assembly characterised the postponement as a de facto cancellation and as a violation of the rights of assembly, association, and expression (OHCHR, 2026).

The episode is consequential for the chapter in three respects. First, it shows that Chinese influence in Zambia operates through a channel the lexical-similarity index by construction cannot register. The 2025 Cyber Security Act score of 0.078 against the CSL captured Zambian regulatory drafting; it could not have captured Zambian administrative discretion over which voices may convene on Chinese-funded premises. The discretion exercised on 28 April 2026 illustrates a potential modality of influence that lexical analysis cannot capture and that the chapter's cross-case analysis treats as a hypothesis for further research: implementation and administrative practice may matter more than statutory text. The episode is suggestive rather than dispositive because the public record does not establish the relative weight of Chinese pressure, domestic security politics, and pre-electoral restrictions. Second, the episode realises a configuration the framework predicts: very high C1 (infrastructure, including a now-explicitly-relevant convening venue), low C2 (no formal cyber-governance MOU is required for the leverage to operate) and constrained H3 (Zambian capacity to refuse the implied request appears to have been institutionally bounded by the prior fiscal and infrastructural relationship). The framework does not require revision; the case it explains has merely become more articulated. Third, the episode falls within the period of intensified pre-electoral political controversy that Zambian commentators (Sishuwa, 2026; Net Rights Coalition, 2026) had already flagged as constraining civil-society convening in advance of the August 2026 elections, which means that Chinese pressure and domestic political control explanations operate jointly rather than as alternatives. Disentangling their relative weight is beyond what the present chapter can establish on the available record; what it can establish is that the depoliticised reading captured in the 2024 interview no longer holds.

6.3 What Zambia Establishes

Zambia presents a configuration in which extreme infrastructure intensity coexists with weak governance frameworks and moderate epistemic engagement, producing low lexical similarity on all three Chinese reference instruments and substantial but qualified regulatory borrowing through observational rather than coordinated channels. The case demonstrates two general points. First, infrastructure provision is a necessary but not sufficient condition for substantial lexical convergence: without complementary bilateral frameworks or epistemic channels addressing governance specifically, infrastructure does not translate into legal-text borrowing. Second, the absence of public political controversy over Chinese influence does not require the absence of substantive influence; it may instead reflect the depoliticisation that comes when borrowing is framed as observational rather than ideological, and when the Chinese model is presented alongside other reference points rather than as the sole template. The April 2026 RightsCon cancellation discussed in §6.2 invites a stronger version of the same point. The depoliticised framing visible in the 2024 interview held only until an external occasion (the convening of Taiwanese voices on Chinese-funded premises) made suppression operationally relevant; once such an occasion arose, infrastructure-mediated influence surfaced through administrative discretion rather than statutory text. Zambia's case, on the available record, is therefore best characterised as lexically norm-light but potentially practice-heavy: the operative channel of influence may lie less in statutory borrowing than in the leverage infrastructure provision creates over administrative and convening decisions.

7. Limit Cases: The Philippines, Egypt and Laos

The remaining three cases occupy analytically distinct positions in the case set. The Philippines is a temporal null case in which high lexical similarity against PIPL coexists with chronological impossibility of direct Chinese influence on the law as enacted. Egypt is the case of comprehensive multi-channel Chinese engagement with anomalously low cybersecurity-domain lexical similarity but suggestive proximity in the under-diffused DSL domain. Laos is a temporal null case similar to the Philippines but lacking suggestive subsequent amendments. Treating the three together permits a sharper specification of the temporal and channel-specific constraints that the framework must respect.

7.1 The Philippines

The Philippines presents the highest single similarity score in the entire corpus, 0.388 between the 2012 Data Privacy Act and China's 2021 PIPL, more than twice the corpus baseline. Against the CSL, the score falls to 0.065, well below the corpus baseline; against the DSL, it is 0.033. The polarisation across instruments is itself diagnostic: the Philippine law tracks China's PIPL closely on the lexical surface but does not track the CSL or DSL.

Direct Chinese influence on the Philippine law as enacted is decisively ruled out by chronology. The Philippine Data Privacy Act was enacted in August 2012; China's PIPL was enacted in November 2021. The causal sequence necessary for Chinese influence on the Philippine instrument runs in the wrong direction by nearly a decade. The most plausible explanation is that both countries drew from common international privacy frameworks circulating in the late 2000s and early 2010s. The Philippine Data Privacy Act of 2012 was developed with explicit reference to the OECD Privacy Guidelines (originally 1980, updated 2013), the APEC Privacy Framework (Asia-Pacific Economic Cooperation, 2004), and the EU Data Protection Directive 95/46/EC. China's subsequent PIPL development drew from many of the same global reference points alongside emerging European GDPR-influenced practices. The 0.388 lexical similarity reflects parallel incorporation of globally circulating privacy norms, not bilateral transmission.

Chinese infrastructure and partnership engagement with the Philippines did intensify substantially during the Duterte administration (2016–22). AidData records substantial Chinese financing for Philippine telecommunications and digital projects, including Bank of China loans across multiple branches for 4G and 5G telecommunications projects with Dito Telecommunity, totalling approximately USD 500 million across 2019–23 (AidData Project 96036 and others), and a China Eximbank facility of USD 275.9 million for Phase 1 of the Safe City surveillance infrastructure project (AidData Project 63248). The Safe City project was subsequently cancelled under the Marcos administration; the AidData record now tags it '[Cancelled]', and any reading of the Philippine case must register that the surveillance project did not produce the operational embedding that comparable projects produced elsewhere. Most of the financing in any case postdates the 2012 Data Privacy Act and therefore cannot explain the law's initial structure.

There is suggestive evidence on the post-2012 trajectory that the chapter flags as a hypothesis for further research rather than as a finding the present record establishes. Legislative proposals to amend the 2012 Data Privacy Act were filed in 2021–22, incorporating provisions that align with Chinese PIPL concepts including biometric and genetic data definitions, extraterritorial application clarifications, and digital age-of-consent specifications (House Bills 892, 898; Senate Bill 1367). The temporal coincidence with PIPL enactment in November 2021 is striking. These amendments could reflect Chinese influence operating through post-law channels, including academic discussion, professional networks, comparative-law analysis or direct reference to the recently enacted PIPL as a reference text; equally, they could reflect parallel adoption of globally circulating personal-information vocabulary into which Chinese, European and other contributions have all flowed. The amendments remain pending before the Philippine Congress and have not been enacted into law as of writing. The present chapter cannot adjudicate between these alternatives and registers the convergence as a hypothesis to be tested by further research once enactment, drafting deliberations and any Chinese consultation footprint become more fully visible in the legislative record.

The Philippines therefore functions as a temporal null case in which the lexical signal could not have been produced by Chinese influence on the original instrument, with the suggestive amendments as a forward-looking consideration rather than a settled finding. The case disciplines the inference made about Vietnam and Chile by showing what high similarity can mean in the absence of possible direct influence. The methodological qualification that follows: when high similarity scores reflect parallel adoption of global frameworks rather than bilateral transmission, the appropriate inference is convergence on a common reference set, not Chinese normative influence specifically. Similarity scores must always be interpreted in conjunction with enactment chronology.

7.2 Egypt

Egypt sits at the opposite extreme. The country exhibits the most comprehensive multi-channel Chinese engagement of any case in the corpus, with exceptionally strong presence across infrastructure, bilateral frameworks, and epistemic socialisation. Yet its Personal Data Protection Law scores only 0.060 against the Chinese CSL and 0.151 against the PIPL. The DSL similarity, however, is the highest in the entire corpus: 0.095, more than 2.5 times the corpus DSL baseline.

The DSL pattern is analytically suggestive. The Egyptian instrument lexically tracks the Chinese law that has produced the weakest cross-corpus signal, in the case where Chinese multi-channel engagement is most comprehensive. Egypt's Personal Data Protection Law was issued in 2020; China's Data Security Law was adopted in 2021. The elevated DSL similarity therefore cannot reflect diffusion from the DSL into the Egyptian instrument, by the same chronological reasoning the chapter applies to the Philippines and Kazakhstan. Therefore the DSL proximity is explained as parallel drafting on shared vocabulary, with any diffusion hypothesis confined to Egypt's post-2020 regulatory development. Chinese infrastructure investment in Egypt is substantial across multiple AidData entries from 2002 to 2018, including Bank of China and Huawei financing for 4G infrastructure (2018), Industrial and Commercial Bank of China financing for Huawei's New Administrative Capital project (AidData Project 66598, 2017) and subsequent expansion through the September 2024 China–Africa Cooperation Summit MOUs covering the entire technology stack (ITIDA, 2024).

Bilateral frameworks display comprehensiveness without parallel in other cases. On 6 September 2024, Prime Minister Madbouly witnessed five MOUs at the China–Africa Cooperation Summit. The Huawei MOU expanded technical support from 800 to 1,400 professionals and committed to training 1,500 Egyptian staff in cloud and AI capabilities. The Tsinghua Unigroup MOU established chip-design R&D, jointly developed an Arabic Large Language Model, deployed Unigroup cloud infrastructure, and created a USD 300 million technology fund for Chinese investment, with Tsinghua Unigroup contributing 60–70 per cent of the fund (ITIDA, 2024). Additional MOUs with Fiberhome, ZTE and Hengtong established local manufacturing, R&D centres and training academies. These agreements create vertically integrated dependencies from hardware to software to AI, with explicit policy-coordination provisions positioning Chinese entities as embedded development partners rather than external vendors.

Epistemic channels combine historical educational infrastructure (the Egyptian-Chinese School for Applied Technology, the Egyptian Chinese University, two Confucius Institutes, scholarship programmes and two Luban Workshops) with massive 2024 expansion (Huang, 2023). The 1,500 Huawei cloud and AI trainees committed in the September 2024 MOU alone exceed prior scholarship programmes by a factor of four. Joint development of an Arabic LLM positions Chinese partners centrally in AI governance conceptualisation for Arabic-speaking contexts.

Combined with Egypt's comprehensive multi-channel engagement, the high DSL similarity supports a hypothesis that the chapter explicitly flags for further research rather than treats as a settled finding: that the September 2024 MOUs (particularly Tsinghua Unigroup's Arabic LLM development and the chip-design R&D framework) may operationalise governance dimensions that subsequent Egyptian regulation could codify (Anwar, 2024). On this hypothesis, which the present chapter does not claim to settle, Egypt is the most analytically interesting candidate among the cases for testing whether comprehensive multi-channel engagement eventually produces lexical convergence on a longer time horizon than the Vietnam case has so far displayed. Whether such convergence in fact materialises, and through which specific transmission pathway it would do so, are questions the available evidence cannot answer; they are research questions for subsequent work, and the chapter advances them as such rather than as findings on which the cumulative argument depends.

7.3 Laos

Laos's Law on Prevention and Combating Cyber Crime was enacted in 2015, two years before China's 2017 CSL. The TF-IDF score of 0.052 against the CSL is comfortably below baseline; PIPL and DSL scores are similarly low. AidData records substantial communications-sector investment in Laos, but the projects concentrate in 2015 (contemporaneous with the law) or later: financing for Electronic ID Cards in 2015, telecommunications construction in 2022 (AidData, 2025), and television reconstruction in 2017. No substantial pre-2015 Chinese infrastructure created path dependencies before the drafting period. The 2015 timing of major projects suggests that Chinese infrastructure engagement accelerated following the law's enactment rather than driving it. The case functions as a temporal control: it demonstrates that infrastructure engagement and moderate similarity scores cannot establish influence in the absence of both a causal sequence and available Chinese templates. The reversed timing makes independent development or convergence on global cyber-crime templates the most plausible explanations.

Laos is included in the case set primarily as a temporal null. Its principal value to the chapter is that it shows what infrastructure-led engagement looks like when the temporal sequence forecloses direct legal-text borrowing, and it disciplines the inference in the Vietnam and Chile cases by demonstrating that infrastructure engagement does not by itself produce textual convergence when the chronology rules out borrowing.

8. Cross-Case Configurations

The eight cases produce six distinct mechanism configurations that together discriminate among the empirical patterns Chapter 2's framework was designed to capture. Table 3.2 summarises the assessment, reporting the lexical signal against all three Chinese reference instruments rather than the cybersecurity domain alone.

The first configuration is dense multi-channel push meeting partial pull, exemplified by Vietnam: high values across all three Chinese mechanisms combine with moderate hedging, weak adaptation, and constrained negotiation to produce the corpus's highest cybersecurity-domain similarity, with strong signal extending into the personal-information domain. The second is infrastructure-and-context push meeting strong institutional pull, exemplified by Chile: substantial infrastructure investment combined with structural economic asymmetry produces high similarity in the cybersecurity domain through pathways the public legislative record does not directly document, while the polarisation of the lexical signal (high CSL, low PIPL, low DSL) suggests that Chinese influence is concentrated rather than wholesale. The third is comprehensive push meeting strong adaptation, exemplified by Malaysia: high values across all three Chinese mechanisms produce only moderate-to-low lexical similarity because recipient adaptation reorganises the inputs into a hybrid framework that draws as substantially on European templates. The fourth is infrastructure-dominant push with weak governance frameworks, exemplified by Zambia: very high infrastructure investment without complementary governance coordination produces low lexical similarity across all three reference instruments and qualified regulatory borrowing through observational rather than coordinated channels. The fifth is comprehensive push under temporal foreclosure, exemplified by the Philippines: even the most intensive Chinese engagement cannot produce lexical convergence on instruments that predate the relevant Chinese reference texts, although the chapter flags as a hypothesis for further research the proposition that subsequent diffusion may occur on longer horizons (Egypt's elevated DSL signal and the Philippines' pending PIPL-aligned amendments are advanced in this chapter as hypotheses for subsequent longitudinal study, not as settled findings on which the configuration's typological status depends). The sixth is sustained push with high recipient agency producing topic-specific borrowing, exemplified by Kazakhstan: substantial infrastructure and moderate epistemic engagement combine with strong recipient agency to produce attributable borrowing on a specific policy element (data localisation, added by 2015 amendment) without broader lexical convergence on the foundational text. The April 2026 RightsCon episode treated in §6 above qualifies the fourth configuration in a direction the framework anticipates rather than disturbs: where C1 is very high and C2 architecture is absent, the principal channel of Chinese normative influence is the leverage that infrastructure dependency creates over governance practice rather than the borrowing it produces in legal text. The lexical-similarity index by construction cannot register that channel. The Zambian case has now supplied, on the operational record, the implementation-rather-than-legislation evidence that the Malaysian closer in §4 had advanced as an open question, and on a specific dimension (administrative discretion over civic convening) that further work would need to test against comparable cases.

Across these configurations, several cross-cutting patterns emerge.

Infrastructure investment (C1) is necessary but not sufficient for lexical convergence. Vietnam, Chile, Egypt, Zambia and Kazakhstan all show high or very high

Table 3.2 Mechanism intensity and lexical signal across all three Chinese reference instruments

Case	*C1*	*C2*	*C3*	*H1*	*H2*	*H3*	*CSL*	*PIPL*	*DSL*
Vietnam	High	High	Very high	Moderate	Weak	Moderate	0.309	0.198	0.041
Chile	High	Low	Moderate	Strong	Moderate	Moderate	0.224	0.061	0.044
Malaysia	Moderate	Very high	High	Strong	Strong	Strong	0.095	0.123	0.031
Zambia	Very high	Low	Moderate	Moderate	Moderate	Weak	0.078	0.068	0.029
Egypt	High	Very high	High	Moderate	Moderate	Moderate	0.060	0.151	0.095
Kazakhstan	Moderate	Low	Moderate	Strong	Strong	Strong	0.041	0.031	0.025
Philippines	Moderate	Low (pre-2016)	Low	Strong	Moderate	Strong	0.065	0.388	0.033
Laos	Low (pre-2015)	Low	Low	Weak	Weak	Weak	0.052	n/a	0.029

infrastructure investment, but only Vietnam and Chile produce high CSL similarity scores. The other three cases demonstrate that infrastructure alone, without complementary bilateral coordination (C2) and where recipient agency is robust, translates into operational dependencies and regulatory receptivity but not into legal text borrowing.

Bilateral coordination frameworks (C2) are most consequential when they explicitly name regulatory alignment as an objective. The Malaysia April 2025 MOUs, which include explicit 'regulatory alignment' language, represent the strongest documented C2 channel and have not yet produced lexical convergence. The chapter advances as a hypothesis for further research, rather than as a settled finding, the proposition that even the most explicit bilateral coordination may operate primarily through implementation rather than legislation; testing this proposition requires sustained observation of post-MOU regulatory practice across the Malaysian and other comparable cases, work that the present chapter has not undertaken at scale. The Vietnam case, where bilateral cooperation is dense but rarely names regulatory alignment explicitly, has produced the strongest lexical convergence in the corpus. The relationship between explicit bilateral coordination and lexical outcome is therefore not linear, and the typology the chapter develops should be read as accommodating, rather than resolving, this non-linearity.

Epistemic socialisation (C3) operates at scales that vary by orders of magnitude across cases. Vietnam (approximately 23,000 students in China) and Egypt (1,500 Huawei trainees committed in 2024 alone, plus four prior epistemic platforms) sit at the high end; Chile (18 scholarship recipients in 2023) and Zambia (modest scholarship totals over a decade) sit considerably lower. The independent effect of C3 is difficult to isolate from the infrastructure and bilateral channels with which it co-occurs, but the comparative pattern suggests that very high C3 (Vietnam) is not separable from very high C1 and C2 in producing the strongest lexical signals.

On the recipient side, hedging (H1) varies sharply with institutional structure. Cases with parliamentary plurality and active civil society (Malaysia, Chile) display robust hedging; cases with concentrated executive authority and limited legislative oversight (Vietnam, Laos) display weaker hedging. Selective adaptation (H2) is the recipient mechanism with the most variable empirical signature: Vietnam shows weak adaptation (high lexical similarity reflects close textual borrowing), Malaysia shows strong adaptation (low lexical similarity despite dense engagement reflects substantial transformation) and the others sit between these poles. Strategic negotiation (H3) is rarely strongly evidenced in the cybersecurity-governance domain specifically, even where institutional capacity exists; the most documented instances of negotiation occur in infrastructure procurement (Chile's NEC cable choice, Vietnam's military-civilian compartmentalisation) rather than in regulatory drafting. This may reflect a real asymmetry: Chinese push in infrastructure faces direct vendor competition that makes negotiation visible, while Chinese push in governance operates through more diffuse channels where the negotiating object is harder to specify.

The lexical pattern across all three Chinese reference instruments is more informative than the cybersecurity-domain signal alone. Chile's polarisation (high CSL, low PIPL, low DSL) is meaningful: it suggests that Chilean cybersecurity policymaking responded to specifically cybersecurity-domain conditions, not to a wholesale alignment with the Chinese governance stack. Vietnam's signal extending across CSL and PIPL but not DSL is meaningful: it suggests that Vietnam tracks the Chinese architecture in domains where China has consistently promoted external uptake, but not in the domain (data security) where Chinese international promotion has been most limited. Egypt's elevated DSL signal in a context of comprehensive multi-channel engagement is meaningful: it raises the hypothesis – for which only further research can provide a settled finding – that Egypt may be entering a phase of DSL-specific norm diffusion that the cross-corpus pattern does not yet show. Reporting all three signals consistently across cases is therefore not a methodological convenience; it is the only way to read what the lexical record is actually saying.

8.1 What the Interview Corpus Adds, and What It Cannot

The four primary case-country interviews drawn on in this chapter offer a triangulating qualitative dimension that the quantitative and documentary streams cannot provide. Three points stand out across them. First, recipient experts vary in how willing they are to attribute regulatory developments to Chinese influence directly. The most explicit attribution comes from the Kazakhstani interview, which described data-localisation policy as taken directly 'from Chinese experience, from Chinese policy' (Interview-KZ-1, 2025). The most cautious comes from the Vietnamese interview, which insisted on the absence of documented Chinese influence on Vietnamese drafting while affirming structural ideological continuity (Interview-VN-1, 2025). The Zambian interview attributed inspiration to China alongside the GDPR while emphasising legislative independence (Interview-ZM-1, 2024); the Malaysian interview framed Chinese frameworks as one input among several in a deliberately hybrid architecture (Interview-MY-1, 2025).

Second, the interviews consistently identify implementation rather than legislation as the locus of substantive engagement. The Zambian interview noted that Zambian regulatory implementation began only in March 2025 and that informed opinions could be formed only once the regulation operates in practice. The Malaysian interview described privacy professionals navigating practical compliance challenges between Chinese and other regulatory regimes that no amount of legislative text would fully resolve. The Kazakhstani account of Russian services being forced to comply with the Kazakhstani localisation rule is essentially an implementation story. The Vietnamese interview emphasised that the operative architecture of the Vietnamese regime consists in the ministerial enforcement role of the Ministry of Public Security, not in the words of the law. Across the cases, the interviewees are unanimous that the question of Chinese influence cannot be settled by reading legal texts alone.

Third, the interviews suggest that public political mobilisation against Chinese influence is largely absent in the recipient countries, even where individual experts express concerns about data sovereignty. The Zambian interview reported 'no uproar' in Zambia despite extensive Chinese infrastructure presence. The Malaysian interview described a 'privacy paradox' in which citizens express concerns about data misuse but routinely trade privacy for convenience. The Kazakhstani interview reported not having seen 'any kind of negative stuff in terms of Chinese 'digitalisation' in Kazakhstani media. The Vietnamese interview described Vietnamese civil society sentiment as quietly sceptical of Chinese technology, driven by nationalism and security concerns, but oriented toward economic protectionism rather than direct contestation of regulatory borrowing. Across the cases, the political space for reactive opposition to Chinese normative influence is narrow and the depoliticisation of the borrowing relationship is itself a structural condition under which diffusion proceeds.

9. Conclusion

This chapter has applied the six-mechanism framework developed in Chapter 2 to eight bilateral cases, drawing on a corpus-wide computational similarity analysis against China's three foundational laws (CSL, PIPL, DSL), project-level documentary evidence, and qualitative interviews in four countries. The cumulative argument is twofold. First, Chinese normative power in cyberspace operates through identifiable, traceable mechanisms whose intensity varies by case, whose interaction is non-additive and whose outcomes depend as much on recipient configuration as on Chinese supply. Second, the framework is most useful when it is allowed to discriminate among configurations rather than aggregate them: a uniform thesis about Chinese normative reach mischaracterises both the cases of strong alignment (Vietnam, Chile) and the cases of muted, hybrid or absent alignment (Malaysia, Zambia, Kazakhstan, Egypt) in ways that obscure the actual analytic stakes.

The chapter also clarifies what the framework cannot resolve at the bilateral level. Infrastructure dependencies, bilateral agreements and epistemic socialisation each interact with recipient hedging, adaptation and negotiation in ways that produce country-specific outcomes, but they do not by themselves explain why Chinese governance vocabulary is more or less attractive in different regional or international contexts. The Vietnam-versus-Chile comparison shows that geographic distance and institutional structure can be overcome by economic and infrastructural channels combined with regime-security predispositions. The Malaysia-versus-Zambia comparison shows that comparable infrastructure intensity can produce divergent regulatory outcomes depending on the broader institutional environment. The Egypt-versus-Kazakhstan comparison shows that comprehensive multi-channel engagement can fail to produce lexical convergence when temporal sequencing forecloses diffusion in the foundational text; whether subsequent regulatory development will carry the operative borrowing on specific policy elements, as the Kazakhstan 2015 amendment did and as the Egypt and Philippines cases have been hypothesised in this chapter to potentially do, is a question the present record cannot settle and that this chapter has explicitly advanced as a hypothesis for further research. These second-order patterns point beyond the bilateral level toward regional dynamics, the role of ASEAN, the African Union, EU regulatory neighbourhood effects and toward international forums in which

Chinese normative claims are formally advanced and contested. Chapter 4 takes up these higher levels of analysis, treating regional organisations and international institutions not as sums of bilateral relations but as sites of normative production in their own right.

The empirical material assembled here also raises methodological points that bear on the rest of the book. Lexical-similarity analysis, treated cautiously and reported across all three Chinese reference instruments, identifies the cases that demand explanation but does not by itself adjudicate the source or content of that explanation. Project-level documentary evidence drawn from databases like AidData and from disclosed treaty texts provides the structural backbone for any account of mechanism operation. Qualitative interviews supply the interpretive layer that quantitative and documentary streams cannot generate, particularly on the question of how recipient actors themselves frame the borrowing relationship. None of these streams is dispositive on its own; together, they make possible the kind of disciplined inference about normative power that the framework was developed to support.

References

Access Now (2026) 'Statement on RightsCon 2026: Foreign Interference, the Postponement, and What Comes Next', 1 May. Available at: https://www.accessnow.org/ (accessed: 5 May 2026).

Acharya, A. (2004) 'How Ideas Spread: Whose Norms Matter? Norm Localization and Institutional Change in Asian Regionalism', *International Organization*, 58(2), pp. 239–275. https://doi.org/10.1017/S0020818304582024

AidData Project 106768 (2023) *Bank of China (Malaysia) Contributes to $272.12 Million Syndicated Green Loan for Phase 1 of GDS Nusajaya Tech Park Data Center Project.* Available at: https://china.aiddata.org/projects/106768 (accessed: 4 May 2026).

AidData Project 49402 (2013) *CDB Provides $170 Million Loan for Xiamen University Malaysia Campus Construction Project.* Available at: https://china.aiddata.org/projects/49402 (accessed: 4 May 2026).

AidData Project 66598 (2017) *ICBC Provides $100 Million Loan to Banque Misr.* Available at: https://china.aiddata.org/projects/66598/ (accessed: 4 May 2026).

AidData Project 70862 (2009) *China Development Bank Provides $300 Million Loan to KazakhTelecom to Form a Joint Venture.* Available at: https://china.aiddata.org/projects/70862 (accessed: 4 May 2026).

AidData Project 96036 (2019) *Bank of China Loans to Dito Telecommunity for 4G/5G Network.* Available at: https://china.aiddata.org/projects/96036/ (accessed: 4 May 2026).

AidData (2023) 'China Development Bank Provides $218 Million Loan to KazNurTel LLP for the CDMA-450 Network Expansion Project.' Global Chinese Development Finance Dataset, Version 3.0, Project ID 40103. Williamsburg, VA: AidData at William & Mary.

Anwar, A. (2024) 'Egypt, Tsinghua Unigroup Collaborate on $300m Tech Fund, Data Centre', *Amwal Al Ghad.* Available at: https://en.amwalalghad.com/egypt-tsinghua-unigroup-collaborate-on-300m-tech-fund-data-center/ (accessed: 4 May 2026).

AidData (2025) 'China Eximbank Provides $31.875 Million Preferential Buyer's Credit for Electronic Identification Card Project.' China's Loans and Grants to Low- and Middle-Income Countries Dataset, Version 1.0, Project ID 64136. Williamsburg, VA: AidData at William & Mary.

Asia-Pacific Economic Cooperation (2004) *APEC Privacy Framework* (2004/AMM/014rev1). 16th APEC Ministerial Meeting, Santiago, Chile.

ASPI (Australian Strategic Policy Institute) (2019) *Mapping China's Tech Giants*. International Cyber Policy Centre. Available at: https://www.aspi.org.au/report/mapping-chinas-tech-giants/ (accessed: 4 May 2026).

BCN (Biblioteca del Congreso Nacional de Chile) (2024) *Historia de la Ley 21.663 sobre Ciberseguridad*. Available at: https://www.bcn.cl/leychile/navegar?idNorma=1202434 (accessed: 4 May 2026).

Beresford, M. (2008) 'Doi Moi in Review: The Challenges of Building Market Socialism in Vietnam', *Journal of Contemporary Asia*, 38(2), pp. 221–243.

Bradford, A. (2023) *Digital Empires: The Global Battle to Regulate Technology*. New York, NY: Oxford University Press.

Brautigam, D. (2009) *The Dragon's Gift: The Real Story of China in Africa*. Oxford: Oxford University Press.

Brautigam, D. (2020) 'A Critical Look at Chinese "Debt-Trap Diplomacy"', *Area Development and Policy*, 5(1), pp. 1–14.

British Council (2024) *Booming Vietnamese Students Studying in China and South Korea*. Education Insight Brief. Available at: https://opportunities-insight.britishcouncil.org/short-articles/news/booming-vietnamese-students-studying-china-and-south-korea (accessed: 4 May 2026).

Bui, N. S. and Lee, J.-A. (2022) 'Comparative Cybersecurity Law in Socialist Asia', *Vanderbilt Journal of Transnational Law*, 55(3), pp. 631–693.

Butler, G. (2023) 'GDS Secures $270m Green Financing for Johor Data Center', *Data Center Dynamics*. Available at: https://www.datacenterdynamics.com/en/news/gds-secures-270m-green-financing-for-johor-data-center/ (accessed: 4 May 2026).

Cambero, F. (2021) 'Chile Fast-Tracking 5G Roll-Out, But with Tight Rules on Security, Official Says', *Reuters*. Available at: https://www.reuters.com/business/media-telecom/chile-fast-tracking-5g-roll-out-with-tight-rules-security-official-says-2021-03-22/ (accessed: 4 May 2026).

China Digital Times (2026) 'RightsCon 2026 in Zambia Cancelled Under Pressure from China', 2 May. Available at: https://chinadigitaltimes.net/2026/05/rightscon-2026-in-zambia-cancelled-under-pressure-from-china/ (accessed: 5 May 2026).

Chinese Consulate Los Angeles (2017) 'President Xi Jinping Meets with Chilean President Michelle Bachelet', May. Available at: https://losangeles.china-consulate.gov.cn/eng/topnews/201705/t20170522_4296078.htm (accessed: 4 May 2026).

Cochilco (Comisión Chilena del Cobre) (2024) *Mercado del cobre y la minería en Chile*. Santiago: Cochilco.

Cooley, A. (2012) *Great Games, Local Rules: The New Great Power Contest in Central Asia*. Oxford: Oxford University Press.

Custer, S. et al. (2021) *Tracking Chinese Development Finance: An Application of AidData's TUFF 2.0 Methodology*. Williamsburg, VA: AidData at William and Mary. Available at: https://china.aiddata.org (accessed: 4 May 2026).

EIAS (European Institute for Asian Studies) (2024) *Bamboo Diplomacy Meets 5G: Europe's High-Stakes Bid on Vietnam's Telecommunications Transformation*, July. Available at: https://eias.org/publications/op-ed/europes-high-stakes-bid-on-vietnams-telecommunications/ (accessed: 4 May 2026).

El Kadi, T. H. (2022) *How Huawei's Localization in North Africa Delivered Mixed Returns*. Carnegie Endowment for International Peace. https://carnegieendowment.org/research/2022/04/how-huaweis-localization-in-north-africa-delivered-mixed-returns

Ellis, R. E. (2020) *Chinese Advances in Chile*. Strategic Studies Institute, US Army War College. Available at: https://www.academia.edu/45313976/Chinese_Advances_in_Chile_R_Evan_Ellis (accessed: 4 May 2026).

Erie, M. S. and Streinz, T. (2021) 'The Beijing Effect: China's "Digital Silk Road" as Transnational Data Governance', *New York University Journal of International Law and Politics*, 54(1), pp. 1–91.

Government of Chile and Government of the People's Republic of China (2005) *Free Trade Agreement Between the Government of the People's Republic of China and the Government of the Republic of Chile*. Available at: https://edit.wti.org/document/show/36e4e8a8-416a-4389-a6b9-08c388a63562 (accessed: 4 May 2026).

Greenleaf, G. and Kaldani, T. (2025) 'Data Privacy Laws in Central Asia: Between ex-SSR and "Belt and Road"', *International Data Privacy Law*, 15(1), pp. 67–84. https://doi.org/10.1093/idpl/ipaf001

Greitens, S. C. (2020) *Dealing with Demand for China's Global Surveillance Exports*. Washington, DC: Brookings Institution, Global China Series.

Guarascio, F. (2025) 'Exclusive: Huawei, ZTE Seal 5G Deals in Vietnam After US Tariffs, as Ties with China Warm', *Reuters*, 28 November. Available at: https://www.reuters.com/world/china/huawei-zte-seal-5g-deals-vietnam-after-us-tariffs-ties-with-china-warm-2025-11-28/ (accessed: 4 May 2026).

Hanoi University of Science and Technology (HUST) (2025) 'HUST and Huawei Technologies Worked Together on Talent Development and Education', 5 December. Available at: https://hust.edu.vn/en/news/news/hust-and-huawei-technologies-worked-together-on-talent-development-and-education-654092.html (accessed: 4 May 2026).

Hoffman, S. (2019) *Engineering Global Consent: The Chinese Communist Party's Data-Driven Power Expansion*. Australian Strategic Policy Institute Policy Brief Report No. 21/2019.

Huang, Y. (2023) Egyptian Chinese University expansion. *Xinhua*. Available at: https://english.news.cn/ (accessed: 4 May 2026).

Huawei (2023) 'Chile's Puerto Williams: World Southernmost Town Now Has 5G'. Available at: https://www.huawei.com/en/media-center/our-value/puerto-williams (accessed: 4 May 2026).

Human Rights Watch (2026) 'Zambia: Summit on Human Rights, Technology Effectively Canceled', 1 May. Available at: https://www.hrw.org/news/2026/05/01/zambia-summit-on-human-rights-technology-effectively-canceled (accessed: 5 May 2026).

International Mining (2025) 'Huawei in South America: Unified Networks for the Life of Mine', 8 December. Available at: https://im-mining.com/2025/12/08/huawei-in-south-america-unified-networks-for-the-life-of-mine/ (accessed: 4 May 2026).

ITIDA (Information Technology Industry Development Agency) (2024) 'Egypt and China Sign Five Key Agreements at the Summit of Forum on China-Africa Cooperation', 6 September. Available at: https://itida.gov.eg/ (accessed: 4 May 2026).

Jili, B. (2022) 'The Spread of Chinese Surveillance Tools in Africa: A Focus on Ethiopia and Kenya', in Yayeh, F. A. (ed.) *Africa-China and an Evolving Global Order*. London: Routledge.

Jili, B. (2023) *Africa's Demand for and Adoption of Chinese Surveillance Technology*. Atlantic Council DFRLab and Africa Center Issue Brief, May. Available at: https://www.atlanticcouncil.org/in-depth-research-reports/issue-brief/what-is-driving-the-adoption-of-chinese-surveillance-technology-in-africa/ (accessed: 4 May 2026).

Kerkvliet, B. J. T. (2019) *Speaking Out in Vietnam: Public Political Criticism in a Communist Party–Ruled Nation*. Ithaca, NY: Cornell University Press.

Khasanova, L. and Tai, K. (2024) 'Shades of Authoritarian Digital Sovereignty: Divergences in Russian and Chinese Data Localisation Regimes', *Journal of Cyber Policy*, advance online publication. https://doi.org/10.1080/23738871.2024.2413938

Laruelle, M. (ed.) (2018) *China's Belt and Road Initiative and Its Impact in Central Asia*. Washington, DC: Central Asia Program, George Washington University.

Li, K. (2022) *Speech by H.E. Li Keqiang at the 25th China-ASEAN Summit*, Ministry of Foreign Affairs of the PRC, 11 November. Available at: https://www.fmprc.gov.cn/eng/gjhdq_665435/2675_665437/2696_663396/2699_663402/202211/t20221112_10973135.html (accessed: 4 May 2026).

Liang, J., Rohman, I. K. and Yuliatiningtyas, S. (2025) 'Digital Economy Cooperation Between China and ASEAN: Motivations, Current Status, and Challenges', in *9th*

International Conference on Strategic and Global Studies (ICSGS 2025). Paris: Atlantis Press, pp. 843–862.

London, J. D. (ed.) (2014) *Politics in Contemporary Vietnam: Party, State, and Authority Relations*. Basingstoke: Palgrave Macmillan.

Lusaka Times (2026) 'Government Postpones RightsCon 2026 Lusaka Summit', 29 April. Available at: https://www.lusakatimes.com/2026/04/29/government-postpones-rightscon-2026-lusaka-summit/ (accessed: 5 May 2026).

Meduza (2023) 'Yandex Agrees to Relocate Kazakhstan Branch Servers After Astana Briefly Blocks Site', 21 August. Available at: https://meduza.io/en/news/2023/08/21/yandex-agrees-to-relocate-kazakhstan-branch-servers-after-astana-briefly-blocks-site (accessed: 4 May 2026).

Morgan Lewis (2023) *Kazakhstan: Personal Data Protection Update*. Practitioner Briefing. Available at: https://www.morganlewis.com/ (accessed: 4 May 2026).

Morosini, F., Lucas T., and Marília M. (2024). Navigating the Digital Divide: Challenges and Strategies for Latin American Countries in E-commerce and Data Governance Regulation. LAPEG Paper No. 1. Washington, DC: Center for the Advancement of the Rule of Law in the Americas, Georgetown University Law Center, and Center for Law, Regulation, and Sustainable Economy. https://www.law.georgetown.edu/carola/wp-content/uploads/sites/29/2024/11/2024-LAPEG_1_Policy-Brief-Digital-Trade.pdf.

Net Rights Coalition (2026) 'Joint Statement on the Postponement of RightsCon 2026 in Lusaka', 30 April, Signed by More Than 130 Digital-Rights Stakeholders. Available at: https://www.accessnow.org/ (accessed: 5 May 2026).

Network World (2014) 'Zambia Pays Loan for Libya's LAP Green But Zamtel Case Continues', December. Available at: https://www.networkworld.com/article/2855613/zambia-pays-loan-for-libyas-lap-green-but-zamtel-case-continues.html (accessed: 4 May 2026).

Observatory of Economic Complexity (OEC) (2024) *Chile/China Bilateral Trade Data*. Available at: https://oec.world/en/profile/bilateral-country/chl/partner/chn (accessed: 4 May 2026).

Offshore Energy (2018) 'Huawei and CTR to Deliver FOA Subsea Cable Project in Chile', March. Available at: https://www.offshore-energy.biz/huawei-and-ctr-to-deliver-foa-subsea-cable-project-in-chile/ (accessed: 4 May 2026).

OHCHR (2026) 'Zambia's de facto Cancelation of RightsCon an Attack on Rights and Freedoms: Special Rapporteur', 4 May. Available at: https://www.ohchr.org/en/statements-and-speeches/2026/05/zambias-de-facto-cancelation-rightscon-attack-rights-and-freedoms (accessed: 5 May 2026).

Organization of American States (OAS) (2018) *The OAS and Chile Expand Cooperation in Cybersecurity*. Available at: https://www.oas.org/en/media_center/photonews.asp?sCodigo=FNE-95071 (accessed: 4 May 2026).

Potter, P. B. (2003) 'Globalization and Economic Regulation in China: Selective Adaptation of Globalized Norms and Practices', *Washington University Global Studies Law Review*, 2(1), pp. 119–150.

PowerChina (2023) 'PowerChina Supports Cultivation of Highly Skilled Talent in Zambia'. *PR Newswire*. Available at: https://www.prnewswire.co.uk/news-releases/powerchina-supports-cultivation-of-highly-skilled-talent-in-zambia-301714043.html (accessed: 4 May 2026).

Qu, T. (2023) 'Malaysia's Touch 'n Go Sees Payoff from Ant Group Joint Venture with E-wallet Service in World's Largest e-payments Market', *South China Morning Post*. Available at: https://www.scmp.com/tech/tech-trends/article/3226524/ (accessed: 4 May 2026).

RCR Wireless (2021) 'Chile Kicks Off 5G Era with Initial Deployments', 20 December. Available at: https://www.rcrwireless.com/20211220/5g/chile-kicks-off-5g-era-initial-deployments (accessed: 4 May 2026).

Republic of Kazakhstan (2013) *Law of the Republic of Kazakhstan No. 94-V of 21 May 2013 "On Personal Data and Their Protection"*. Astana: Adilet. Available at: https://adilet.zan.kz/eng/docs/Z1300000094 (accessed: 4 May 2026).

Republic of Kazakhstan (2015) *Law of the Republic of Kazakhstan No. 419-V of 24 November 2015 "On Amendments to Certain Legislative Acts on Informatization"*, published 26 November 2015, Entered into Force 1 January 2016. Available at: https://adilet.zan.kz/ (accessed: 4 May 2026).

Sekaran, R. (2025) 'Malaysia Signs MoU with China to Strengthen AI and Digital Economy', *The Star/Asia News Network*, 17 April. Available at: https://asianews.network/malaysia-signs-mou-with-china-to-strengthen-ai-and-digital-economy/ (accessed: 4 May 2026).

Semafor (2026) 'Zambia Cancels Digital Rights Summit Over China-Taiwan Tension', 1 May. Available at: https://www.semafor.com/article/05/01/2026/zambia-cancels-tech-and-rights-summit-over-taiwan-participation (accessed: 5 May 2026).

Sishuwa, S. (2026) Public Commentary on RightsCon Postponement and Pre-Electoral Civic-Space Restrictions in Zambia. Cited in Human Rights Watch, "Zambia: Summit on Human Rights, Technology Effectively Canceled, 1 May 1. https://www.hrw.org/news/2026/05/01/zambia-summit-on-human-rights-technology-effectively-canceled

Stuenkel, O. (2020) 'Latin American Governments Are Caught in the Middle of the U.S.-China Tech War', *Foreign Policy*. Available at: https://foreignpolicy.com/2021/02/26/latin-america-united-states-china-5g-technology-war/ (accessed: 4 May 2026).

Tech Policy Press (2026) 'RightsCon Canceled After Zambia Requires "Full Alignment" with National Values', 1 May. Available at: https://www.techpolicy.press/rightscon-canceled-after-zambia-requires-full-alignment-with-national-values/ (accessed: 5 May 2026).

Tran, M. (2025) 'Vietnam's Cautious Acceptance of Chinese 5G Technology', *The Diplomat*, 4 December. Available at: https://thediplomat.com/2025/12/vietnams-cautious-acceptance-of-chinese-5g-technology/ (accessed: 4 May 2026).

Universidad de Chile (2022) 'U. de Chile, Huawei Chile y Movistar desarrollarán Laboratorio 5G con tecnología de punta en Campus Carén'. Available at: https://uchile.cl/noticias/187345/u-de-chile-huawei-chile-y-movistar-desarrollaran-laboratorio-5g-(accessed: 4 May 2026).

Vu, T. (2010) *Paths to Development in Asia: South Korea, Vietnam, China, and Indonesia*. Cambridge: Cambridge University Press.

Vu, K. (2026) 'Huawei Signs Deal with Vietnamese Bank SHB to Expand Vietnam Footprint', *Reuters*, 20 April. Available at: https://www.reuters.com/world/asia-pacific/huawei-signs-deal-with-vietnamese-bank-shb-expand-vietnam-footprint-2026-04-20/ (accessed: 4 May 2026).

Wise, C. (2020) *Dragonomics: How Latin America Is Maximizing (or Missing Out on) China's International Development Strategy*. New Haven, CT: Yale University Press.

Wood, N. (2025) 'Malaysia Snubs the West as U Mobile Picks Huawei and ZTE to Build its 5G Network', *Telecoms.com*, 16 April. Available at: https://www.telecoms.com/5g-6g/malaysia-snubs-the-west-as-u-mobile-picks-huawei-and-zte-to-build-its-5g-network (accessed: 4 May 2026).

Xinhua (2022) 'Railway Industry Training Program Adds Value to Malaysia-China Joint Rail Project', 28 July. Available at: https://english.news.cn/20220728/f053dd83c3b04f789c7be4b0a22df02a/c.html (accessed: 4 May 2026).

Xinhua (2023) 'China, Vietnam Pledge to Strengthen Law Enforcement Cooperation', 14 September. Available at: https://english.news.cn/20230914/df28f92dafc849378758065850048f4d/c.html (accessed: 4 May 2026).

Zheng, S. (2020) 'China's Huawei Loses Out to Japan's NEC on Chile-Asia Trans-Pacific Cable Project', *South China Morning Post*, July. Available at: https://www.scmp.com/news/china/diplomacy/article/3095367/chinas-huawei-loses-out-japans-nec-chile-asia-trans-pacific (accessed: 4 May 2026).

ZTE (2013) *Sustainability Report 2012*. Shenzhen: ZTE Corporation.

4 Normative Power at the Regional Level

Mechanisms, Institutions and the Diffusion of China's Digital Governance Norms

1. Introduction

The theoretical framework developed in Chapter 2 established that normative power is evidenced through a two-stage method: first, identifying textual and structural similarity between China's governance framework and the choices of other actors; second, tracing that similarity through specific mechanisms to identifiable agency rather than to coincidental convergence. Following Chapter 3's bilateral analysis, this chapter applies that method at the regional level. As Chapter 2 set out, the regional level operates as both amplifier and filter for Chinese-origin governance preferences, and the recursive relationship between levels – bilateral experience feeding into regional positions, regional endorsements feeding into international forums – is most readily traced through regional institutional outputs. That makes this level a direct site of normative diffusion and, simultaneously, a multiplier of bilateral influence.

The four mechanisms specified in Chapter 2 – regional institutional anchoring (R1), declaratory legitimation through coalition construction (R2), regulatory contagion and peer diffusion (R3) and counter-mobilisation through alternative institutional frameworks (R4) – are operative at this level. Each leaves a distinct evidentiary trace, and the cases that follow show how the four interact in practice, with R1–R3 acting as push vectors and R4 as the principal pull constraint.

Four regional contexts are examined, with each case foregrounding a distinct mechanism while illustrating how the four interact. The Shanghai Cooperation Organisation (SCO) and the Regional Comprehensive Economic Partnership (RCEP) are analysed together as cases of regional institutional anchoring (R1) operating in different registers of international legal authority: the SCO through political and security cooperation frameworks, RCEP through binding trade law. BRICS is examined as the primary arena of declaratory legitimation and South–South coalition construction (R2), with attention to how the institutional vocabulary changes across successive presidencies and to the limits of attribution in a grouping where multiple states (notably Russia and India) hold their own distinctive positions on digital governance. ASEAN provides the most complex case, foregrounding normative influence through economic interdependence, institutional framing, and agenda-setting (R3) in a context where counter-mobilisation from European regulatory frameworks (R4) is most visible.

DOI: 10.4324/9781042023738-5

The chapter is careful, throughout, to distinguish what the documentary record establishes from what it does not. Where the evidence supports strong attribution claims, those claims are made; where it supports only correlation or multi-channel diffusion, the analysis is framed accordingly. This approach is consistent with the broader thesis of the dissertation, which argues that Chinese normative power at every level is real but bounded, and that overstating its reach is as analytically misleading as understating it.

2. The Chinese Normative Vocabulary: What Is Being Traced

Before examining the regional texts in which Chinese governance logic may appear, this section specifies the identifiable vocabulary and structural logic of China's digital governance promotion regionally – the external diplomatic expression of the domestic architecture analysed in Chapter 1 – whose presence, adaptation, or translation in regional documents constitutes the first stage of the attribution method developed in Chapter 2.

The connection between Chapter 1's domestic analysis and this chapter's regional tracing is substantive rather than incidental. Chapter 1 showed that China's cyber sovereignty framework is not primarily an international advocacy position but a domestically embedded governance architecture: operationalised through the Cybersecurity Law (2017), Data Security Law (2021) and Personal Information Protection Law (2021) legal stack, institutionalised through the Cyberspace Administration of China and enforced through a compliance regime that ties private actors to public governance objectives through licensing, security assessments and platform accountability mechanisms (Zeng, Stevens and Chen, 2017; Creemers, 2022). What this chapter traces internationally is the same governance logic – the same principles of state authority over cyberspace, the same security–development–control triad, the same jurisdictional framing of data as a sovereign asset – in its diplomatic rather than strictly legal form. The vocabulary changes across arenas: what is a compliance obligation in domestic law becomes a principle of sovereign equality in a multilateral declaration. But the underlying structural logic is what normative power analysis must track – not surface vocabulary but the operative assumptions about how digital governance should be organised and by whom.

Chapter 1 established three criteria for attaching a 'Chinese' label to a governance norm: Party-doctrinal centrality, legal and institutional embedding, and external promotion. The three terms identified below satisfy all three. They are articulated in authoritative Party and state discourse, operationalised in domestic law and institutional design, and actively promoted through bilateral and multilateral diplomatic channels. That conjunction – not any single criterion – is what justifies their characterisation as Chinese normative exports rather than as generic governance ideas that China happens to share with others (Finnemore and Sikkink, 1998; Manners, 2002). It bears emphasising that the 'Chinese' label refers to the particular ideational packaging, doctrinal status, and external promotion strategy associated with these terms in Chinese practice; it does not imply that the underlying principles (sovereign equality, territorial jurisdiction, security primacy) are exclusively Chinese in origin or that other states cannot independently arrive at similar positions.

Before identifying the specifically digital vocabulary, it is necessary to establish the broader diplomatic framework within which that vocabulary is nested. The concept of a 'Community of Shared Future for Mankind' (人类命运共同体) was adavanced by Xi Jinping in 2013 and subsequently formalised through successive Party congresses and UN General Assembly engagements (State Council Information Office, PRC, 2023). It functions as an overarching foreign-policy frame organised around sovereign equality, multilateral cooperation, shared development and opposition to what Chinese official discourse characterises as hegemonic approaches to international politics. For digital-governance analysis, its significance is that it supplies a pre-existing legitimacy framework within which more specific Chinese preferences can be presented as elements of a wider vision rather than as stand-alone demands.

The first specifically digital term – and the one that travels most visibly across regional texts – is 'Community of Shared Future in Cyberspace' (网络空间命运共同体), introduced by Xi Jinping at the Second World Internet Conference in Wuzhen in December 2015 (Xi, 2015). It is a domain-specific application of the parent concept, applied to internet governance. This genealogy matters analytically because the cyberspace concept is not introduced as a new Chinese proposal but as an extension of a framework already in circulation, making it arrive pre-legitimised in any forum where the parent concept has already found traction. Xi framed cyberspace as 'the common space of activities for mankind' and called on countries to 'jointly build a community of shared future in cyberspace', immediately pairing this cooperative framing with an explicit first principle of 'respect for cyber sovereignty' (Xi, 2015). The pairing is analytically important: the 'shared future' concept performs what the China Media Project (2025) describes as a softening function – presenting China's governance vision as cooperative, inclusive and mutually beneficial while encoding, beneath that surface, the state-centric logic that the sovereignty principle makes explicit.

The second identified term is 'respect for cyber sovereignty'. In the 2015 Wuzhen speech, Xi defined it as the right of individual countries 'to choose their own path of cyber development, model of cyber regulation and Internet public policies, and to participate in international cyberspace governance on an equal footing' (Xi, 2015). Grounding the claim in the UN Charter's principle of sovereign equality is strategically important: it connects the claim to an established principle of international law, although the application of territorial sovereignty to internet governance remains contested (Zürn, 2018). A note of analytic caution is warranted here. Sovereignty-based claims about cyberspace are not a Chinese invention; they have been advanced by Russia (in different and sometimes more absolutist form), by India (rooted in its own ITU engagement and post-colonial policy traditions), by Brazil (post-Snowden) and by multiple African and Latin American states for reasons internal to their own political and developmental trajectories (Drake, 2005; Mueller, 2010). What is distinctive about the Chinese articulation is its specific packaging – the linkage of sovereignty to the broader 'Community of Shared Future' frame, the explicit doctrinal status it holds in Party discourse, and the systematic effort to project it through bilateral, regional, and multilateral channels. The chapter therefore traces the *Chinese* expression of cyber sovereignty rather than the principle in general.

The third term is 'cyber security' deployed not as a technical concept but as a matter of state responsibility and international order. Xi's formulation – that all cyber crimes should be 'firmly combated in accordance with relevant laws and international conventions, with no double standards' – frames cybersecurity as requiring state-led legal mechanisms (Xi, 2015). This framing is the international expression of the comprehensive security conception that Chapter 1 identified as the organising premise of China's domestic legal architecture: the idea that security encompasses political stability and social order alongside infrastructure protection, justifying expansive state authority over the digital sphere (Zeng, 2020).

Taken together, these three terms constitute the identifiable vocabulary that can be traced in regional texts. Chapter 2 established that the analytical test is not whether specific Chinese terms appear verbatim – original research repeatedly documents their strategic absence from joint declarations – but whether the underlying governance logic is present as a structural feature: state authority over cyberspace and data flows, intergovernmental rather than multistakeholder coordination, security-centred justifications for regulatory intervention and conditionality of cross-border digital flows on state-determined requirements. This is the distinction between surface vocabulary and structural logic that Chapter 2 identified as methodologically essential, and that the H2 (selective adaptation) mechanism predicts: recipient states regularly domesticate Chinese-origin governance principles into their own legal vocabularies, producing texts that share the structural logic while employing entirely different terminology.

3. Regional Institutional Anchoring: SCO and RCEP

The first and most direct regional mechanism is the embedding of Chinese governance logic in formal institutional frameworks whose authority over member states is independent of China's bilateral relationships with those states. This mechanism operates in two analytically distinct registers that correspond to the two organisational contexts examined in this section. In the SCO, institutional anchoring operates through political and security cooperation frameworks – normatively binding in the sense of shared multilateral commitment but not legally enforceable through domestic courts. In RCEP, it operates through binding international trade law with dispute settlement mechanisms (though as Section 3.2 will show, the e-commerce chapter's specific architecture limits enforceability in important ways). The combination of these two registers – from political declaration to treaty obligation – illustrates how the same governance logic can be expressed across different forms of international legal authority, while also revealing the limits of each.

3.1 The SCO: Structural Position and Security Framework Embedding

The SCO is the regional context in which the Chinese institutional position is most pronounced. Established in Shanghai in June 2001 by China, Russia, Kazakhstan, Kyrgyzstan, Tajikistan and Uzbekistan – transformed from the Shanghai Five group formed in 1996 – the SCO was formalised as a full intergovernmental organisation through a Charter signed in 2002 (SCO Secretariat, 2002). The organisation subsequently expanded to include India and Pakistan in June 2017, with Iran joining in July 2023 and Belarus in July 2024, bringing total membership to ten states (RFE/RL, 2024). At the 25th Council of Heads of State meeting in Tianjin on 1 September 2025, member states issued the Tianjin Declaration and approved the *SCO Development Strategy for the Next Decade (2026–2035)*, reaffirming commitments to a multipolar international order and the 'Shanghai Spirit' of mutual trust, mutual benefit, equality, consultation, respect for cultural diversity and joint development (SCO, 2025). The SCO now encompasses more than forty per cent of the world's population and spans much of the Eurasian landmass.

China is the SCO's largest economy, its most technologically advanced member, and the largest single provider of digital infrastructure investment to several Central Asian member states. In the broader trajectory of Chinese capital flows to the region, China signed a record $213.5 billion in new Belt and Road agreements globally in 2025 – a 75 per cent increase over 2024 – with Central Asia among the top recipients, and investment into Central Asia rose by roughly 375 per cent year-on-year in 2025, building on a substantial increase in 2024 and concentrated in metals, mining and energy infrastructure in Kazakhstan (Nedopil Wang, 2026). This material weight is significant, but it does not translate into uniform alignment on digital governance: Russia retains its own distinct strategic doctrine, India's domestic constitutional and policy framework diverges in important respects and Central Asian member states maintain parallel engagements with European and other partners. Existing research describes a marked asymmetry in SCO digital cooperation, with China frequently supplying technology, training, and technical support; that asymmetry is evidence of channel capacity, not by itself proof of normative convergence (Zeng et al, 2017)

The SCO's most consequential normative contribution to date is the *International Code of Conduct for Information Security*, first proposed in 2011 and revised in 2015 (UN General Assembly, 2015a, A/69/723). The strategic significance of this instrument lies in its routing: the Code was submitted to the United Nations General Assembly not by China alone but by SCO member states collectively (China, Kazakhstan, Kyrgyzstan, the Russian Federation, Tajikistan and Uzbekistan in the 2015 revision). By advancing its preferred norms through a regional organisation rather than unilaterally, China was able to recast its governance preferences as the collective position of a significant multilateral grouping – the R1 mechanism in operation. The Code's stated purpose is 'to identify the rights and responsibilities of States in the information space, promote constructive and responsible behaviour on their part and enhance their cooperation in addressing common threats and challenges in the information space' (UN General Assembly, 2015a, Annex, para. 1).

Textually, the Code carries the structural logic identified in Section 2. It frames cyberspace as a domain where state sovereignty and non-interference apply; commits states to refrain from using ICTs to undermine each other's 'political, economic and social stability'; affirms sovereign rights to protect 'their information space and critical information infrastructure against damage resulting from threats, interference, attack and sabotage'; and calls for an enhanced 'leading role' of the United Nations in internet governance (UN General Assembly, 2015a, Annex, paras. 2–4). The provision that states have the right to choose their own 'models of internet development, internet governance and Internet public policies' tracks closely the formulation Xi Jinping used at Wuzhen later that year (Xi, 2015), showing continuity between the SCO proposal and the diplomatic vocabulary China articulated more fully at Wuzhen later in 2015. As the Citizen Lab analysis observed at the time, the Code's narrative 'emphasises state sovereignty and territoriality in the digital space above all else, and is dominated by intelligence, national security, and regime stability imperatives' (McKune, 2015).

It is worth noting that the Code has not been adopted by the General Assembly and remains a circulated proposal rather than a binding instrument. Its analytical importance lies less in its formal status than in its function as a reference text: it formalises a state-centred model of digital governance as an articulated alternative within UN discussions, and it has been cited in Chinese diplomatic communications as evidence of multilateral endorsement of the principles it contains. This recursive feedback between regional and international levels – a regional document used to evidence the breadth of support for positions advocated at the international level – is a defining feature of Chinese normative strategy and is examined further in Chapter 5.

The 2021 Joint Action Plan on Ensuring International Information Security for 2022–2023, adopted by the SCO Expert Group, marked a step from declaratory endorsement toward administrative routinisation (SCO Secretariat, 2021). The Plan emphasises state-led responses to cyber threats, information sharing between member-state security authorities, and coordinated action against what it frames as 'information terrorism' – a category that, as the Citizen Lab and other analysts have noted, encompasses political speech deemed threatening by member governments alongside technical attacks (McKune, 2015; SCO Secretariat, 2021). The framing is broadly consistent with the comprehensive security conception embedded in China's 2017 Cybersecurity Law and its predecessor 2015 National Security Law, though it also reflects pre-existing SCO commitments inherited from the 2001 Shanghai Convention's tripartite 'terrorism, separatism, and extremism' framework.

The Tianjin Declaration of 1 September 2025 extends the SCO's digital governance agenda into emerging-technology domains, like artifical intelligence. The summit approved the SCO Development Strategy through 2035, issued statements and action plans on the digital economy, artificial intelligence, and scientific and technological innovation, and took a political decision to establish an SCO Development Bank (SCO, 2025).

China also announced new SCO cooperation platforms and centres in fields including the digital economy and technological innovation. These steps demonstrate agenda expansion, but the public record does not yet establish how far the new initiatives will generate common regulatory rules rather than projects, coordination, and capacity-building. The consensus-based character of the organisation remains a significant constraint on the embedding of any single member's preferences (China Daily Hong Kong, 2025).

What the SCO achieves for China's normative strategy, then, is best characterised as a *normative floor* rather than full regulatory convergence. By 'normative floor' is meant a baseline of shared principles – sovereign equality in cyberspace, non-interference in internal affairs, state-centric governance – that member states treat as legitimate and non-objectionable, even where their domestic regulatory architectures diverge substantially. This is analytically distinct from two adjacent conditions. It is stronger than weaker forms of coordination, in which states align on specific issues without committing to an underlying normative vocabulary; the floor commits members to a shared discursive space in which sovereignty-grounded premises are accepted as default rather than contested. But it is substantially weaker than full convergence, in which shared principles translate into substantively aligned policy frameworks. The floor establishes the range of positions that SCO members recognise as acceptable; what lies above the floor – specific regulatory choices on platform oversight, content moderation, data localisation – remains a matter of sovereign discretion. In the terms of the norm diffusion literature (Finnemore and Sikkink, 1998; Acharya, 2004), this corresponds to a cascade-stage dynamic combined with localisation: the principle is internalised as a legitimate default across the organisation, but implementation is adapted to each adopting state's political and institutional context.

That full regulatory convergence does not obtain is empirically clear. Russia maintains its own sovereignty doctrine, embodied in domestic legislation including the 2019 'sovereign internet' law that reflects Russian state priorities and has at times diverged from Chinese positions even where the two states' broader strategic alignment is close. India's governance philosophy diverges from China's in structurally significant respects: New Delhi has engaged with multistakeholder internet governance forums, maintains a constitutional framework that – formally at least – constrains state surveillance more than the Chinese framework does, and has periodically banned Chinese applications on national security grounds in a manner that signals strategic competition rather than normative alignment (USIP, 2024). Central Asian member states continue to engage with European regulatory frameworks, Council of Europe advisory relationships, and Western development financing alongside Chinese-led initiatives, producing hybrid governance environments that cannot be characterised as Chinese-aligned in any straightforward sense.

What the SCO does institutionalise is a set of minimum standards of state authority over cyberspace as the baseline for regional digital cooperation, endorsed by all member states regardless of how their specific regulatory models differ from China's. Three such standards are observable across SCO texts. First is the legitimacy of state-defined security exceptions: the principle, embedded in the SCO's foundational security framework and reproduced in subsequent declarations on information security, that member states retain sovereign authority to determine what constitutes a threat in the digital domain. Second is the right to nationally determined content governance, repeatedly affirmed across SCO summit declarations: that states may regulate information flows within their territory according to domestically defined standards. Third is a stated preference for intergovernmental cooperation over multistakeholder mechanisms, reflected in the SCO's institutional design and consistently advanced by China and Russia in SCO-adjacent multilateral forums including the UN Group of Governmental Experts and the ITU (Zürn, 2018). What China achieves through the SCO, in short, is a multilateral legitimation of the proposition that state sovereignty in cyberspace is an appropriate organising principle for regional digital order – a proposition whose institutional inscription narrows the normative space available to alternatives without forcing any member state to adopt Chinese frameworks.

3.2 RCEP: Binding Trade Law and the Architecture of Data Governance

The Regional Comprehensive Economic Partnership – the free trade agreement linking fifteen Asia-Pacific economies, finalised on 15 November 2020 under ASEAN auspices after negotiations that formally launched at the 2012 ASEAN Summit in Cambodia – provides a case of institutional anchoring that is analytically distinct from the SCO in kind rather than merely in degree (RCEP Secretariat, 2020; MFAT, 2022). RCEP's membership encompasses the ten ASEAN states alongside China, Japan, South Korea, Australia and New Zealand, representing approximately thirty per cent of global GDP and around thirty per cent of the world's population (Swiss Re Institute, 2022). The agreement entered into force on 1 January 2022 for the initial ratifying states (DFAT, 2022). India participated in RCEP negotiations for seven years before withdrawing in November 2019, citing concerns about import surges from China and insufficient protections for its services sector (MFAT, 2022) – a withdrawal that left the agreement's membership without what would have been its most significant counterweight to Chinese economic preponderance within the grouping.

The cases discussed in this chapter – SCO, BRICS, ASEAN – involve the embedding of Chinese normative preferences in declarations, cooperation frameworks and institutional agendas. These instruments carry normative significance but are not legally enforceable in the sense that trade law is. RCEP is different in kind: a binding international treaty with formal dispute settlement machinery (though, importantly, that machinery does not extend to the e-commerce chapter, as discussed below). When governance preferences are embedded in its architecture, they acquire the authority of obligations that ratifying states have formally accepted as binding.

RCEP is also the first multilateral trade agreement China has joined that contains substantive digital economy disciplines. Chapter 12 sets commitments on cross-border data flows (Article 12.15), the location of computing facilities (Article

12.14) and provisions on paperless trading, electronic authentication, personal information protection and cybersecurity cooperation. This marks the first time China has accepted formal multilateral commitments on cross-border data flows and digital governance (Congressional Research Service, 2022).

To understand what RCEP's digital economy architecture represents, it is necessary to situate it against the alternative regional framework whose trajectory preceded it. The Comprehensive and Progressive Agreement for Trans-Pacific Partnership (CPTPP) – the agreement that became RCEP's primary structural counterpart – originated as the Trans-Pacific Partnership, a twelve-economy agreement whose roots lay in a smaller four-party accord signed in 2005 by New Zealand, Chile, Singapore and Brunei. The United States announced its intention to join the negotiations in February 2008 under President George W. Bush, a move that fundamentally transformed the agreement's ambition and scope; President Obama formalised American participation in November 2009, and the TPP became a centrepiece of his administration's strategic pivot to Asia (Congressional Research Service, 2022). The United States was the lead architect of the resulting agreement, which was designed to establish high-standard trade rules across the Asia-Pacific – including binding digital economy disciplines – that would shape regional economic integration ahead of, and in deliberate exclusion of, Chinese participation. When the United States withdrew from the TPP in January 2017, the remaining eleven signatories proceeded with the agreement, rebranding it as the CPTPP and suspending rather than permanently removing twenty-two provisions included primarily at United States insistence. The CPTPP entered into force in December 2018, and the core digital economy disciplines – including the prohibitions on data localisation and cross-border data flow restrictions – were retained in full rather than suspended (CPTPP Secretariat, 2018).

China has not joined the CPTPP. It submitted a formal accession application in September 2021 – a move analysts have read in different ways: as a genuine signal of interest in shaping accession criteria, as a strategic move to complicate the terms of future enlargement, or as a combination of both (Erie and Streinz, 2021). More than four years later, the application remains in process. China has not been formally rejected, but no accession working group has been established: CPTPP members have not reached the consensus required to open formal negotiations. The contrast with the United Kingdom – which applied in February 2021, seven months before China, concluded negotiations in March 2023 and entered into force as a CPTPP member on 15 December 2024 – and with Costa Rica, for which a working group was established in November 2024, is informative without being conclusive. The CPTPP membership has moved to process applications it has chosen to advance; Beijing's has not advanced. The CPTPP accession process requires prospective members to demonstrate compliance with existing obligations before entry, and China's domestic data governance architecture is structurally in tension with the agreement's data flow disciplines as currently written. China's domestic framework remains in tension with several CPTPP disciplines, although the 2024 Provisions on Facilitating and Regulating Cross-Border Data Flows relaxed some filing and security-assessment thresholds rather than uniformly tightening the regime. The pattern is consistent with the chapter's broader observation that China engages most intensively with frameworks where it can shape architecture and engages more cautiously with frameworks where it cannot.

RCEP's approach to cross-border data flows is more architecturally complex than a simple accommodation of Chinese preferences. The agreement's e-commerce chapter formally includes prohibitions on data localisation (Article 12.14) and on restrictions on cross-border data transfers (Article 12.15). Article 12.14(1) 'recognise[s] that each Party may have its own measures regarding the use or location of computing facilities, including requirements that seek to ensure the security and confidentiality of communications' but Article 12.14(2) provides that 'no Party shall require a covered person to use or locate computing facilities in that Party's territory as a condition for conducting business in that Party's territory' (RCEP Secretariat, 2020, Art. 12.14). Article 12.15(2) similarly provides that 'a Party shall not prevent cross-border transfer of information by electronic means where such activity is for the conduct of the business of a covered person'. On its face, these provisions appear to commit RCEP signatories – including China, for the first time multilaterally – to a liberalising data flow regime (Streinz, 2021).

Two structural features of the agreement, however, qualify the apparent liberalisation significantly. The first is the architecture of the exceptions. Both Articles 12.14(3) and 12.15(3) permit a Party to adopt 'any measure that it considers necessary to achieve a legitimate public policy objective' and 'any measure that it considers necessary for the protection of its essential security interests'. Footnote 12 to Article 12.14(3)(a) clarifies that 'the necessity behind the implementation of such legitimate public policy shall be decided by the implementing Party', and Article 12.14(3)(b) specifies, with respect to essential security measures, that 'such measures shall not be disputed by other Parties' (RCEP Secretariat, 2020, Art. 12.14(3); see also Bacchus, 2023). These exceptions are therefore self-judging: states determine for themselves whether a measure is necessary, and that determination is, in the security case, explicitly insulated from challenge. CPTPP's analogous provision (Article 14.13.3) contains a 'legitimate public policy' exception but does not include the same self-judging language for essential security measures, and CPTPP retains the e-commerce chapter within its dispute settlement system (CIGI, 2023; Bacchus, 2023). The self-judging architecture is therefore not unique to RCEP – variants appear across modern trade agreements – but RCEP combines it with the second structural feature in a way the CPTPP does not.

The second feature is the exclusion of the e-commerce chapter from RCEP's formal dispute settlement mechanism. Article 12.17(3) provides explicitly: 'No Party shall have recourse to dispute settlement under Chapter 19 (Dispute Settlement) for any matter arising under this Chapter' (RCEP Secretariat, 2020, Art. 12.17(3); Streinz, 2021). The combined effect is that a state maintaining data localisation measures within the RCEP framework faces no externally adjudicable consequence: the prohibitions exist in the text without reviewable enforceability. Trade analysts have therefore characterised RCEP's e-commerce chapter as embodying a 'progressive–cooperative' rather than a 'legally binding–actionable' model, with several describing the chapter's prohibitions as essentially hortatory in operative effect (Streinz, 2021; Mishra and Valencia, 2023; Bacchus, 2023; CIGI, 2023). It is worth noting that this characterisation is contested at the margins – some scholars argue that the formal commitments still create reputational and political costs even without dispute settlement – but the structural difference from CPTPP and similar agreements is widely accepted.

The relationship between RCEP's text and China's domestic data governance architecture deserves careful framing. The Cybersecurity Law of 2017 requires critical information infrastructure operators to store data domestically and mandates security assessments before any outbound transfer. The Data Security Law of 2021 classifies data according to its significance for national security and restricts outbound transfers of 'important data'. The Personal Information Protection Law, also enacted in 2021, imposes layered conditions on cross-border personal data transfers including government security assessments. Taken together, this legislative architecture constitutes a layered transfer-control regime that combines targeted localisation duties with security assessments, certification, standard contractual clauses, and consent-based requirements (Creemers, 2022; Bradford, 2023). RCEP's exception architecture is sufficiently broad that this regime can operate without modification under the agreement: the legitimate public policy and essential security exceptions can be invoked self-judgingly to cover the CSL's CIIO localisation, the DSL's controls on 'core' and 'important' data, and the PIPL's outbound transfer requirements. This is not a coincidence. As Streinz (2021) and Mishra and Valencia (2023) both argue, the structure of RCEP's e-commerce provisions reflects the negotiating pressure that follows from including a state with a comprehensive data sovereignty architecture as a treaty party. The chapter's claim is therefore correlational rather than directly causal: the agreement's architecture is consistent with, and explicable by, the participation of states with substantial domestic data localisation regimes (China being the largest, but Vietnam, Indonesia and Thailand also having significant localisation requirements of their own); the precise weighting of China's negotiating influence relative to other parties cannot be established from the public record alone.

China's negotiating position was not, in any case, isolated within the agreement. Several ASEAN members – Vietnam, Indonesia and Thailand – had independently enacted or were actively developing their own data localisation requirements, providing a constituency within the negotiations for weaker disciplines independent of China's preferences. The CPTPP members within RCEP's membership – Australia, Japan, New Zealand and Singapore – would have preferred tighter language, having already accepted more demanding disciplines in CPTPP. They calculated, on the available record, that securing a large regional trade framework that included China was a strategic priority that outweighed achieving CPTPP-equivalent digital disciplines (Congressional Research Service, 2022). The weakening of the data chapter was thus, plausibly, the price several CPTPP members were willing to pay for the agreement's conclusion – but it was a price that suited multiple parties' preferences, not China's alone.

The normative significance of RCEP's architecture extends beyond China's immediate regulatory interests. By embedding flexible data disciplines into an agreement covering fifteen economies and approximately thirty per cent of global GDP, RCEP has helped normalise the proposition that data localisation, when justified by public policy or national security, is a legitimate policy tool rather than a trade barrier – and has done so through the medium of treaty law rather than diplomatic declaration. As Streinz (2021) notes, RCEP's architecture makes available to all member states a legitimating reference point that did not previously exist in binding multilateral form. A government developing its own digital governance framework within the RCEP region can now point not to Chinese advocacy but to the treaty text itself – endorsed by Japan, South Korea, Australia and New Zealand alongside China and the ASEAN states – as evidence that restricting cross-border data flows in the name of public policy or national security is internationally recognised practice. The normative signal travels without requiring active Chinese promotion in each domestic context, which is precisely what distinguishes institutional anchoring as a mechanism from direct bilateral influence. Whether this signal will be invoked to justify localisation measures in the years ahead is an empirical question that the chapter notes but does not seek to settle.

Within the chapter's overall argument, the SCO and RCEP together illustrate how Chinese-aligned governance preferences can be embedded across different institutional registers – political and security cooperation, on one hand; binding international economic treaty, on the other. The two cases also illustrate the limits of each register: SCO declarations are normatively significant but not legally enforceable; RCEP's e-commerce chapter is part of a legally binding agreement but is excluded from its dispute settlement machinery and structured around self-judging exceptions. The combined effect is real but bounded: a regional architecture in which sovereignty-grounded digital governance is institutionally available and increasingly normalised, without being either uniformly adopted or fully enforceable.

4. Declaratory Legitimation and Coalition Construction: BRICS

BRICS offers a qualitatively different normative arena from either the SCO or RCEP. Where the SCO operates with a clear Chinese asymmetry of resources and where RCEP imposes binding obligations through treaty law, BRICS operates as a forum for declaratory politics among major economies of broadly comparable diplomatic weight. Its endorsements convert governance preferences into positions that can be claimed, rhetorically, to represent a broader Global South majority. The grouping's demographic and economic weight is substantial: its combined population exceeds forty per cent of the world's people, and its membership has expanded with Egypt, Ethiopia, Iran, and the United Arab Emirates joining in January 2024 and Indonesia formally joining in January 2025; Saudi Arabia's position following the 2023 invitation remained less clearly settled in official public descriptions

(BRICS, 2025; CFR, 2025). This is the R2 (declaratory legitimation) mechanism operating at scale, and its outputs feed back into UN General Assembly voting patterns, treaty negotiations and the Global South coalition politics that Chapter 5 examines at the international level.

The analytical characteristic that distinguishes BRICS from the SCO is the absence of a single dominant member's structural position. In the SCO, China's economic and technological asymmetry permits direct embedding of its normative vocabulary in declarations; in BRICS, where the grouping includes major economies with their own governance traditions – Russia, India, Brazil, South Africa – China operates as a coalition-builder rather than an institutional anchor (Finnemore and Sikkink, 1998). The result is a different embedding strategy in which Chinese governance logic is encoded in structural features of joint declarations while explicit Chinese vocabulary is often (though not always) withheld or substituted with broader formulations. It is important to note that this dynamic also reflects the preferences of other BRICS members: Russia, in particular, has its own well-developed sovereignty-first vocabulary and was the chair of BRICS in 2024, with significant influence over the Kazan Declaration's text. The 'Chineseness' of any particular BRICS formulation must therefore be read carefully, with attention to which member's chairship produced which text and to where the substantive ideas originated.

The 2022 Beijing Declaration, issued during the XIV BRICS Summit that China hosted and chaired, illustrates the indirect mode of normative embedding. Notably, the terms 'digital sovereignty' and 'cyber sovereignty' do not appear in the text. Yet the Declaration commits members to 'respect the sovereignty and territorial integrity of all States' and supports 'the leading role of the United Nations in promoting constructive dialogue on ensuring ICT-security… and developing a universal legal framework in this realm' (BRICS Summit Secretariat, 2022). Each element encodes a governance preference: the sovereignty and UN-centrism provisions specify the governance mechanism as intergovernmental rather than multistakeholder; 'universal legal framework' directs digital cooperation towards binding state-to-state instruments rather than the voluntary norms and private-sector standards that have dominated the multistakeholder tradition. The Declaration also advances BRICS digital economy cooperation through the Digital Economy Working Group and the Digital BRICS Task Force – institutional mechanisms that embed the orientation into administrative routines.

What makes the 2022 Declaration analytically significant is the indirection of the normative work. Sovereignty-grounded governance logic is embedded within broader multilateral language that emphasises state authority, security, and intergovernmental coordination, without the term 'cyber sovereignty' being deployed. This is a process of framing rather than labelling, in Finnemore and Sikkink's (1998) terms. A note of caution is warranted, however: similar formulations appear in non-BRICS texts produced under different institutional auspices, including (with somewhat different emphases) statements by the G77, the Non-Aligned Movement and the African Union. The Declaration's formulations should therefore be read as expressing a position broadly shared across multiple Global South coalitions, with China as one (significant) contributor to that shared position rather than as its sole architect.

The 2024 Kazan Declaration, issued under the Russian BRICS chairship at the sixteenth BRICS Summit in Kazan on 22–24 October 2024, articulates the sovereignty position more explicitly. Paragraph 54 of the Declaration provides: 'We are committed to promoting respect for States' sovereignty and sovereign equality in the ICT environment and oppose unilateral actions that could undermine international cooperation in this domain, including global supply chains sustainability' (BRICS Summit Secretariat, 2024, para. 54). The Declaration also commends 'the ongoing work of the UN OEWG on Security of and in the Use of ICTs 2021–2025 as a sole global and inclusive mechanism on this matter' and supports 'the establishment by consensus of a single-track, state-led permanent mechanism under the auspices of the United Nations, reporting to the First Committee of the UNGA' (BRICS Summit Secretariat, 2024, para. 54). Paragraph 55 records the BRICS Working Group on security in the use of ICTs and the Roadmap of Practical Cooperation as institutional manifestations of these commitments.

Two qualifications are important here. First, the Kazan Declaration was produced under Russian chairship, and its sovereignty-first framing reflects Russian as much as (or, on some readings, more than) Chinese preferences. Russia has been the more vocal advocate of explicit sovereignty-absolutist language in UN forums, and the Kazan formulation is consistent with Russian drafting style rather than Chinese diplomatic vocabulary, which more often softens such statements within 'shared future' or 'win–win' frames. Second, the same Declaration also commits BRICS members to 'the importance of information integrity and ensuring free flow of and public access to accurate fact-based information, including the freedom of opinion and expression' (BRICS Summit Secretariat, 2024, para. 56) – language that pulls in a different direction from the sovereignty-grounded framing of paragraph 54. BRICS declarations are negotiated documents, and the texts that emerge from successive presidencies reflect compromise among members with overlapping but distinct preferences.

The progression from 2022 to 2024 nonetheless illustrates one observable pattern: implicit structural encoding of sovereignty-grounded framings (2022) preceded their more explicit articulation (2024). This is consistent with what the chapter has called the gradual hardening of a shared vocabulary across institutional cycles, through which what began as embedded structural assumption becomes explicit collective commitment. The mechanism is most visible analytically when examined as a process – comparing declarations across time – rather than as a snapshot of any single text (Finnemore and Sikkink, 1998). It bears emphasising that this progression is not unidirectional: the Rio Declaration of 6 July 2025, issued under the Brazilian BRICS chairship, did not deepen the explicit sovereignty language and instead returned to a more balanced articulation, including stronger references to multistakeholder participation in AI governance – a movement that reflects the influence of the chairing state and of India (which has its own distinct AI governance positions) rather than a uniform trajectory toward more explicit sovereignty language.

The relationship between BRICS declaratory work and the international-level outcomes traced in Chapter 5 should be characterised with care. The trajectory of the UN Convention against Cybercrime – from UNGA Resolution 74/247 (December 2019, adopted on a divided 79–60–33 vote) to consensus adoption of the Convention by the General Assembly in December 2024 (UNODC, 2024; UN General Assembly, 2019) – is the most consequential international outcome of the period. BRICS endorsements were one element among several that shaped the diplomatic environment in which this trajectory unfolded; the Russia-led drafting effort, the Sino-Russian coalition, the broader G77 dynamics, the United States' relative disengagement from norm-setting forums during parts of the period and the operational pressures of cross-border cybercrime cooperation all contributed. The chapter therefore characterises BRICS declaratory work as part of the regional normative environment within which the consensus emerged, without claiming that BRICS endorsements were the proximate cause of the international outcome. Chapter 5 traces the substantive content of the Convention and the United States' subsequent non-signature in detail; the connection between BRICS declarations and that outcome is best read as one channel among several through which Global South coalition support was mobilised.

5. ASEAN, the EU Counter-Pull and the Limits of Influence

China's engagement with ASEAN on digital governance is qualitatively different from its SCO or BRICS engagement. China has been ASEAN's largest trading partner since 2009, accounting for 20.1 per cent of the region's total trade in 2024 – a structural economic asymmetry that creates leverage without the organisational dominance China enjoys in the SCO (ASEAN Secretariat, 2024). Chinese firms have deployed 5G networks, cloud infrastructure, data centres and surveillance systems across ASEAN member states under what is loosely termed the Digital Silk Road, embedding particular technical standards in ways that can create path dependencies (Mochinaga, 2021; Erie and Streinz, 2021). But ASEAN's foundational principle of 'centrality' – that ASEAN, rather than any external power, drives regional agenda-setting – provides an institutional counterweight, and member states engage with European and American governance frameworks alongside Chinese ones. The ASEAN context therefore provides a setting in which the most nuanced claim of the theoretical framework can be tested: that normative power can operate through the structural embedding of governance logic in development and connectivity language, without explicit sovereignty vocabulary and without the institutional leverage that China holds in other regional bodies.

5.1 Framing and Agenda-Setting in ASEAN Cooperation Documents

The *ASEAN-China Joint Statement on Facilitating Cooperation in Building a Sustainable and Inclusive Digital Ecosystem*, adopted at the 27th ASEAN-China Summit in Vientiane on 10 October 2024, is analytically significant for what it both includes and omits. The term 'sovereignty' is not explicitly used in the statement

– a finding that might initially appear to undercut the diffusion argument – but the document's structural logic places state actors at the centre of digital cooperation in ways that are consistent with the broader pattern this chapter has traced. The Statement promotes 'building an open, secure, inclusive and interoperable digital ecosystem' to accelerate 'the development of the digital economy, digital society, and digital government' (ASEAN Secretariat, 2024). The operative detail is in the modality of cooperation: member states commit to 'carry out exchanges and communication on digital development strategies, digital regulatory practices, policies and rules and standards' – placing governments as the primary subjects of digital governance exchange rather than firms, technical communities or civil society.

This structural choice repays close attention. The reference to 'digital government' treats digital infrastructure and governance as falling within national governmental jurisdiction, implying that states exercise authority over their domestic digital environments. Similarly, the emphasis on 'digital security, including... policies, standards... and capacity building' positions governments as the central actors in setting regulatory frameworks. This is the R2 (declaratory legitimation through framing) mechanism – the channel, developed in Chapter 2, through which Chinese normative preferences travel by becoming the vocabulary of the cooperation itself – operating at its most subtle: a state-authority orientation embedded within development and connectivity language, so that the structural assumption appears as the natural way to organise digital cooperation rather than as a specifically Chinese preference. The cooperative framing tends to make the orientation more broadly acceptable to ASEAN member states that would resist an explicit sovereignty-first framework.

It is important not to overstate the analytic significance of this finding, however. State-led approaches to digital cooperation are common across many international forums, including the OECD's Digital Economy Ministerial framework, the G20's digital track and various EU bilateral cooperation agreements. The presence of a state-authority orientation in an ASEAN-China document does not, on its own, establish a specifically Chinese imprint on the text. What makes the case more analytically interesting is the combination of: (a) the absence of multistakeholder language that would typically accompany an OECD or EU-influenced text, (b) the centrality of 'digital government' as an organising concept rather than, for example, 'digital society' or 'digital citizenship', and (c) the document's explicit alignment with subsequent Chinese-led initiatives on AI capacity-building and digital ecosystem development. Together, these features support the inference that Chinese drafting preferences shaped the document's structural logic, while not foreclosing the possibility that ASEAN preferences for state-led approaches independently aligned with this framing.

The Chairman's Statement of the 28th ASEAN-China Summit, held in Kuala Lumpur on 28 October 2025 under the chairship of Malaysian Prime Minister Anwar Ibrahim and attended by Chinese Premier Li Qiang, advances the normative embedding through more visible agenda-setting. The Statement records ASEAN's appreciation for Chinese initiatives across multiple domains: 'We note China's efforts to promote global AI governance including through the United Nations

General Assembly Resolution A/RES/78/311… We appreciated China's initiative to develop the ASEAN-China Action Plan on the Cooperation in Building a Sustainable and Inclusive Digital Ecosystem (2026–2030). We acknowledged China's commitment to advance cooperation in Science, Technology and Innovation' (ASEAN Secretariat, 2025). The same Summit also witnessed the signing of the ASEAN-China Free Trade Area (ACFTA) 3.0 Upgrade Protocol, which extends cooperation into digital and green economy domains (Wikipedia, 2026; ASEAN Secretariat, 2025). In each case, the statement attributes the initiative to China specifically and records ASEAN's endorsement – a positioning that institutionally acknowledges China as agenda-setter and ASEAN as endorser.

This positioning is not, however, equivalent to ASEAN's adoption of Chinese governance frameworks. The Chairman's Statement preserves ASEAN's centrality language throughout, references multiple non-Chinese frameworks alongside Chinese initiatives and embeds the digital cooperation provisions within ASEAN's own community-building agenda (the ASEAN Community Vision 2045). What the Statement establishes is that China has acquired a recognised agenda-setting role in ASEAN-China digital cooperation – a role that is significant but bounded by ASEAN's own institutional architecture and by member states' parallel engagements with non-Chinese frameworks.

5.2 The EU Counter-Pull: Counter-Mobilisation in Practice

The ASEAN evidence requires balance, and this is where the fourth mechanism – counter-mobilisation (R4) – becomes analytically essential. The pattern across ASEAN member states is one of selective adaptation and partial alignment, shaped by the simultaneous pull of European regulatory frameworks that create competing incentives for incompatible governance choices.

The EU's adequacy framework and its broader digital-trade and data-protection rules constitute an important counter-mechanism. They create incentives for GDPR-compatible safeguards among states and firms seeking low-friction data relations with the European market, although adequacy is a demanding legal determination and should not be treated as the automatic objective of every ASEAN state (Erie and Streinz, 2021). The EU–Singapore Digital Trade Agreement—signed on 7 May 2025 and in force from 1 February 2026—illustrates a related form of regulatory pull: it contains commitments supporting cross-border data flows while preserving public-policy space and restricting unjustified localisation requirements and forced source-code transfer (European Commission, 2026). Singapore has not simply imported the GDPR, and it does not hold an EU adequacy decision; rather, its Personal Data Protection Act supplies a distinct, rights-based framework that facilitates regulatory interoperability. Thailand's Personal Data Protection Act of 2019, fully effective from June 2022, draws substantially on GDPR concepts, including lawful bases, data-subject rights, and extraterritorial reach (Bradford, 2023). The result is a competitive normative landscape in which Chinese-origin structural logics and European regulatory frameworks exert different forms of influence over the same governance choices, while recipient states retain substantial agency.

The ASEAN Digital Masterplan 2025 and the ASEAN Digital Economy Framework Agreement (DEFA) negotiations reflect this competitive normative terrain (ASEAN Secretariat, 2020). Both documents reference multiple international frameworks without endorsing any single model, and both preserve space for member-state variation in governance architecture. This is consistent with the condition that Chapter 2 identified as partial alignment, which is the most common outcome when normative power operates in a contested field. The H2 (selective adaptation) mechanism is operative across ASEAN: member states draw on Chinese governance instruments in domains where Chinese supply is most available or cost-effective (especially infrastructure and surveillance technology) while maintaining European-compatible frameworks in domains where EU market access or international regulatory cooperation require compatibility (especially data protection for cross-border services). The result is governance hybridity in which no single external model is reproduced wholesale, but in which Chinese-origin structural features are present in specific regulatory choices that closer inspection reveals.

6. Conclusion: What the Regional Evidence Establishes, and What It Does Not

Setting the four organisational contexts together, the regional evidence supports a cumulative pattern that meets the three attribution conditions developed in Chapter 2 – though with the important qualifications that each case section has already specified. On *coherence*, the governance logic that circulates across SCO, BRICS, ASEAN and RCEP shares a recognisable set of structural features: state authority over cyberspace, intergovernmental rather than multistakeholder coordination as the preferred mode of digital cooperation, security-centred justifications for state authority over digital infrastructure and conditionality of cross-border data flows on state-determined requirements (Zeng, 2020; Erie and Streinz, 2021). That consistency across contexts operating through different mechanisms and in different institutional registers is the kind of coherence that attribution requires. But it is also a coherence that, in several cases, reflects independent convergence on these features by states with their own strategic and developmental reasons to favour them – not a uniform Chinese imprint.

On *channel specificity*, the pathways through which sovereignty-grounded digital governance becomes regionally available are identifiable in each case: China's structural position in the SCO; its role as summit host and norm entrepreneur in BRICS during specific chairships (notably 2022); the dense ASEAN–China cooperation network through which Chinese-proposed initiatives become regionally endorsed frameworks; and RCEP's negotiating process through which exception architectures compatible with several parties' (including China's) domestic regulatory regimes were embedded in binding trade law.

On *cumulativity*, the pattern holds across four organisational contexts and the primary documents examined in each, with each context contributing a different mechanism – direct institutional embedding, declaratory endorsement, implicit framing, agenda-setting and treaty-based exception architecture. The cumulative effect is a regional normative environment in which sovereignty-grounded digital governance is institutionally available as a legitimate option across multiple forums and registers – a broader regional repertoire than one organised predominantly around liberal multistakeholder vocabulary.

The evidence must, however, be clear about what it does *not* establish, and these limits are as important as the affirmative findings.

First, the regional pattern documents normative availability and partial institutional anchoring – not regulatory convergence. No regional organisation has replicated China's domestic regulatory apparatus. BRICS member states pursue divergent AI and data governance strategies despite endorsing sovereignty-grounded ICT declarations: India's AI governance discourse emphasises ethical and inclusive principles; Brazil maintains strong civil-libertarian protections; South Africa operates within a constitutional framework that constrains state surveillance more than the Chinese model does. ASEAN member states draw extensively on European and American frameworks alongside Chinese ones. The gap between declaratory endorsement and operational regulatory convergence is consistently large across all four contexts.

Second, the chapter is unable to demonstrate, on the public record, that Chinese normative effort is the dominant cause of the patterns observed. The same outcomes – sovereignty-grounded framings, intergovernmental coordination preferences, data localisation regimes – can be (and in many cases are) produced by states' own strategic and developmental considerations independent of Chinese influence. The Vietnam case, in particular, illustrates that textual convergence with the Chinese normative core does not entail causal derivation from it: Vietnamese policymakers have multiple reasons to favour sovereignty-grounded digital governance, including reasons rooted in defensive posture against Chinese cyber activity. Causal attribution must therefore proceed cautiously, distinguishing cases of probable channel-specific transmission from cases of structural convergence with multiple plausible sources (RCEP's broader membership).

Third, the chapter is not in a position to predict the future trajectory of these dynamics. Several variables identified in the analysis – the credibility of the developmental framing, the responsiveness of Western-led institutions to Global South representational concerns, the trajectory of US engagement with regional forums, the resilience of EU regulatory pull, and the future direction of Chinese strategic effort – will jointly shape whether the patterns documented here consolidate, fragment, or shift in new directions. The chapter establishes what the regional record looks like as of early 2026; it does not establish what it will look like in 2030 or beyond.

What China has plausibly contributed through regional channels, then, is the establishment of state-centric digital governance as a legitimate, available, and increasingly normalised reference point – not the displacement of alternative frameworks, the creation of a Chinese-led regional digital order or the regulatory convergence of the major Asian economies. The distinction matters both analytically and practically: it means that the regional normative infrastructure to which Chinese effort has contributed is genuinely consequential for how digital governance choices are framed across a wide range of jurisdictions, while stopping well short of comprehensive regulatory harmonisation.

The four mechanisms analysed in this chapter make non-redundant contributions to this infrastructure. Institutional anchoring in the SCO and RCEP provides forms of formal authority that declarations alone cannot supply. Declaratory legitimation through BRICS converts overlapping preferences into apparent collective positions available to member states as reference points for their own governance choices. Peer diffusion among ASEAN member states and between BRICS members can amplify Chinese influence without requiring active Chinese advocacy in each domestic context – but can also operate in ways that are difficult to disentangle from independent national choices. At the same time, counter-mobilisation – operating primarily through the EU's regulatory pull – constrains, redirects and hybridises what Chinese influence produces in the more contested terrain, ensuring that the outcomes documented in this chapter are partial alignments rather than wholesale adoptions. Together, these four mechanisms constitute the regional normative infrastructure through which the digital order's foundational assumptions are continuously reproduced, contested, and – in ways that the following chapter examines at the international level – gradually consolidated.

References

Acharya, A. (2004) 'How Ideas Spread: Whose Norms Matter? Norm Localization and Institutional Change in Asian Regionalism', *International Organization*, 58(2), pp. 239–275.

Asan Institute (2025) *The 2025 Tianjin SCO Summit: China's Intentions and Limits*. October. Seoul: Asan Institute for Policy Studies.

ASEAN Secretariat (2020) *ASEAN Digital Masterplan 2025*. Jakarta: ASEAN Secretariat.

ASEAN Secretariat (2024) *ASEAN-China Joint Statement on Facilitating Cooperation in Building a Sustainable and Inclusive Digital Ecosystem*, 10 October. Available at: https://asean.org/asean-china-joint-statement-on-facilitating-cooperation-in-building-a-sustainable-and-inclusive-digital-ecosystem/

ASEAN Secretariat (2025) *Chairman's Statement of the 28th ASEAN-China Summit*, 28 October. Available at: https://asean.org/chairmans-statement-of-the-28th-asean-china-summit/

Bacchus, J. (2023) *The Digital Decide: How to Agree on WTO Rules for Digital Trade*. Waterloo, ON: Centre for International Governance Innovation.

Bradford, A. (2023) *Digital Empires: The Global Battle to Regulate Technology*. New York, NY: Oxford University Press.

BRICS (2025) *About the BRICS*. Brazilian Presidency of BRICS 2025. Available at: https://brics.br/en/about-the-brics

BRICS Summit Secretariat (2022) *XIV BRICS Summit Beijing Declaration*. Available at: https://brics.br/en/documents/collection-of-previous-presidencies/leaders-declarations

BRICS Summit Secretariat (2024) *XVI BRICS Summit Kazan Declaration: Strengthening Multilateralism for Just Global Development and Security*, 22–24 October.

CFR (Council on Foreign Relations) (2025) *What Is the BRICS Group and Why Is It Expanding?* Available at: https://www.cfr.org/backgrounders/what-brics-group-and-why-it-expanding

China Daily Hong Kong (2025) 'sCO Summit 2025 in Tianjin: A Positive Reset for Global Governance', September. Available at: https://www.chinadailyhk.com/hk/article/619863

China Media Project (2025) 'Community of Shared Future in Cyberspace', 12 March. Available at: https://chinamediaproject.org/the_ccp_dictionary/community-of-shared-future-in-cyberspace/

CIGI (Centre for International Governance Innovation) (2023) *Digital Trade: Is RCEP the WTO's Future?* Available at: https://www.cigionline.org/articles/digital-trade-rcep-wtos-future/

ClearIAS (2025) *Tianjin Declaration: 25th SCO Summit 2025*. September. Available at: https://www.clearias.com/tianjin-declaration/

Congressional Research Service (2022) *Regional Comprehensive Economic Partnership (RCEP)*. Library of Congress. Available at: https://www.congress.gov/crs-product/IF11891

CPTPP Secretariat (2018) *Comprehensive and Progressive Agreement for Trans-Pacific Partnership*. Available at: https://www.mfat.govt.nz/en/trade/free-trade-agreements/free-trade-agreements-in-force/cptpp/

Creemers, R. (2022) 'China's Emerging Data Protection Framework', *Journal of Cybersecurity*, 8(1), p. tyac011. doi:10.1093/cybsec/tyac011.

Department of Foreign Affairs and Trade, Australia (DFAT) (2022) *Regional Comprehensive Economic Partnership Agreement (RCEP)*. Available at: https://www.dfat.gov.au/trade/agreements/in-force/rcep

Drake, W. J. (ed.) (2005) *Reforming Internet Governance: Perspectives from the Working Group on Internet Governance*. New York, NY: United Nations ICT Task Force.

Erie, M. S. and Streinz, T. (2021) 'The Beijing Effect: China's "Digital Silk Road" as Transnational Lawmaking', *New York University Journal of International Law and Politics*, 54(2), pp. 1–71.

European Commission (2026) *EU-Singapore Digital Trade Agreement enters into force*. Press Release, 2 February. Available at: https://policy.trade.ec.europa.eu/news/eu-singapore-digital-trade-agreement-enters-force-2026-02-02_en

Finnemore, M. and Sikkink, K. (1998) 'International Norm Dynamics and Political Change', *International Organization*, 52(4), pp. 887–917.

InsightsOnIndia (2025) 'Tianjin Declaration 2025: SCO and AI Cooperation', 17 December. Available at: https://www.insightsonindia.com/2025/12/17/the-tianjin-declaration/

Manners, I. (2002) 'Normative Power Europe: A contradiction in terms?', *Journal of Common Market Studies*, 40(2), pp. 235–258.

McKune, S. (2015) *An Analysis of the International Code of Conduct for Information Security*. Citizen Lab, Munk School of Global Affairs, University of Toronto. Available at: https://citizenlab.ca/2015/09/international-code-of-conduct/

Ministry of Foreign Affairs and Trade, New Zealand (MFAT) (2022) *RCEP Overview*. Available at: https://www.mfat.govt.nz/en/trade/free-trade-agreements/free-trade-agreements-in-force/regional-comprehensive-economic-partnership-rcep/rcep-overview

Mishra, N. and Valencia, A. M. P. (2023) 'Digital Services and Digital Trade in the Asia Pacific: An Alternative Model for Digital Integration?', *Asia Pacific Law Review*, 31(2), pp. 489–516.

Mochinaga, D. (2021) *The Digital Silk Road and China's technology Influence in Southeast Asia*. New York, NY: Council on Foreign Relations.

Mueller, M. L. (2010) *Networks and States: The Global Politics of Internet Governance*. Cambridge, MA: MIT Press.

Nedopil Wang, C. (2026) *China Belt and Road Initiative (BRI) Investment Report 2025*. Shanghai: Green Finance and Development Center, FISF Fudan University.

RCEP Secretariat (2020) *Regional Comprehensive Economic Partnership Agreement*, 15 November. Available at: https://rcepsec.org/legal-text/

RFE/RL (Radio Free Europe/Radio Liberty) (2024) 'sCO Quickly Absorbs Belarus on Final Day of Regional Grouping's Astana Summit', 4 July. Available at: https://www.rferl.org/a/sco-summit-kazakhstan-belarus-russia-china-guterres/33021480.html

SCO (2025) *Tianjin Declaration of the Council of Heads of State of the Shanghai Cooperation Organisation*, 1 September. Available at: https://www.diplomacy.edu/resource/tianjin-declaration-of-the-shanghai-cooperation-organization/

SCO Secretariat (2002) *Charter of the Shanghai Cooperation Organisation*. Shanghai: Shanghai Cooperation Organisation.

SCO Secretariat (2021) *Joint Action Plan on Ensuring International Information Security for 2022–2023*. Shanghai: Shanghai Cooperation Organisation.

State Council Information Office, PRC (2023) *A Global Community of Shared Future: China's Proposals and Actions*. Available at: https://english.scio.gov.cn/whitepapers/2023-09/26/content_97747958.htm

Streinz, T. (2021) 'The Evolution of the Digital Silk Road and Data Governance Regimes', *AJIL Unbound*, 115, pp. 390–395.

Swiss Re Institute (2022) *RCEP: A New Mega Trade Bloc for Asia*. Available at: https://www.swissre.com/institute/research/topics-and-risk-dialogues/economy-and-insurance-outlook/mega-trade-bloc-asia-rcep.html

UN General Assembly (2015a) *International Code of Conduct for Information Security: Letter Dated 9 January 2015 from the Permanent Representatives of China, Kazakhstan, Kyrgyzstan, the Russian Federation, Tajikistan and Uzbekistan to the United Nations addressed to the Secretary-General*, A/69/723, 13 January. Available at: https://digitallibrary.un.org/record/786846

UN General Assembly (2019) *Countering the Use of Information and Communications Technologies for Criminal Purposes (Resolution 74/247)*, 27 December. Available at: https://undocs.org/A/RES/74/247

UNODC (2024) *UN General Assembly* Adopts Landmark Convention *on Cybercrime*, Press Release, 24 December. Available at: https://www.unodc.org/unodc/en/press/releases/2024/December/un-general-assembly-adopts-landmark-convention-on-cybercrime.html

USIP (United States Institute of Peace) (2024) *What Does Further Expansion Mean for the Shanghai Cooperation Organization?*, 31 May. Available at: https://www.usip.org/publications/2024/05/what-does-further-expansion-mean-shanghai-cooperation-organization

Xi Jinping (2015) *Remarks at the Opening Ceremony of the Second World Internet Conference*, Wuzhen, 16 December. Ministry of Foreign Affairs, PRC. Available at: https://www.mfa.gov.cn/eng/xw/zyjh/202405/t20240530_11341037.html

Zeng, J. (2020) *Slogan Politics: Understanding Chinese Foreign Policy Concepts*. Singapore: Palgrave Macmillan.

Zeng, J., Stevens, T. and Chen, Y. (2017) 'China's Solution to Global Cyber Governance: Unpacking the Domestic Discourse of "nternet Sovereignty"', *Politics and Policy*, 45(3), pp. 432–464.

Zürn, M. (2018) *A Theory of Global Governance*. Oxford: Oxford University Press.

5 The International Arena

Contestation, Coalition and the Normative Transformation of Global Digital Governance

Introduction

Chapter 4 traced how China's digital governance norms travel through regional channels: the Shanghai Cooperation Organisation as a vehicle of structural dominance, BRICS as an arena of declaratory legitimation, ASEAN as a site of agenda-setting and counter-mobilisation. This chapter follows the same governance logic into the international arena, where the stakes are highest and where Chinese strategic effort is most self-conscious. Across the United Nations General Assembly, the Group of Governmental Experts (GGE), the Open-Ended Working Group (OEWG), the International Telecommunication Union, the Ad Hoc Committee that produced the 2024 Convention against Cybercrime, and the Summit of the Future, China has pursued a sustained effort to shift the terms of global debate: to legitimise cyber sovereignty as a recognised principle of international order, to institutionalise governance arrangements that privilege state authority over digital infrastructure and data flows, and to challenge the normative consensus that the United States and its allies built in the 1990s and early 2000s (Segal, 2020; Hulvey, 2022; Deibert, 2022).

The chapter argues that, across two decades, Chinese normative effort has produced a measurable shift in the terms of global digital governance. The shift is best characterised as expansion rather than substitution. The range of governance options that count as legitimate has widened to accommodate sovereignty-first instruments and intergovernmental processes that, in 2001, sat closer to the margins of liberal internet-governance debates. Liberal vocabulary, multistakeholder architecture and rights-protective instruments retain formal institutional standing alongside the sovereignty-first alternative. The result is a condition of institutionalised normative pluralism in which Chinese-aligned positions are no longer marginal but are not dominant either.

1. The Liberal Baseline: Budapest, Multistakeholderism and the Architecture China Inherited

The international digital order that took shape in the late 1990s and early 2000s rested on a set of liberal commitments inherited from the post-war Western political tradition and extended to cyberspace as its natural organising logic (Netanel,

DOI: 10.4324/9781042023738-6

2000). The early internet governance framework fused classical liberal commitments – individual rights, limited state power, the rule of law – with a transnational, non-territorial logic that Mueller (2010, pp. 4–8, 253–268) has termed 'denationalised liberalism'. Three commitments stood at the centre of this framework, and the magnitude of the shift this chapter will document is best measured against them.

The first commitment was to human rights as binding constraints on state authority, including online. Drawing on the International Covenant on Civil and Political Rights (1966) and regional instruments such as the European Convention on Human Rights, this commitment held that individual rights – to privacy, free expression, due process, and protection from arbitrary interference – applied in the digital domain no less than offline, and that state action affecting these rights required justification by reference to international standards rather than domestic political preference alone (ICCPR, 1966; UN HRC, 2012; La Rue, 2011; Jørgensen, 2013). Rights were not concessions granted by states to their citizens; they were prior limits on what states could legitimately do, including in the name of security (Land, 2013; Kaye, 2015).

The second commitment was the rule of law as the organising principle for state conduct in cyberspace. This entailed several interlocking propositions: that powers of surveillance, investigation, and cross-border enforcement must rest on prior legal authorisation; that they must be proportionate to legitimate aims; that they must be subject to independent judicial oversight; and that international cooperation should rest on shared substantive rules rather than untrammelled sovereign discretion (Council of Europe, 2001, Art. 15; Clough, 2014; Walden, 2007). Cybercrime, on this view, was primarily a legal and technical problem to be managed through ordinary mechanisms of criminal justice, not a security threat warranting unconditional executive authority (Brown and Korff, 2009; Kerr, 2014). The premise that legitimacy derived from conformity to law, rather than from sovereign authority itself, distinguished this tradition from older statist conceptions of international order (Schmitt, 2017; UN GGE, 2013, 2015).

The third commitment was a pluralist conception of governance authority. The internet's foundational institutions had been built not by states acting through intergovernmental bodies but through the collaborative work of technical communities, private actors, civil society and governments operating in their respective roles (WGIG, 2005; Mueller, 2010; DeNardis, 2014). This multistakeholder logic embedded a substantive proposition: legitimate governance of a global network depended on the structured participation of its many constituencies, and intergovernmental authority – the default mode of international order in other domains – was both unsuited to and inappropriate for the digital one (Hofmann, 2016; Raymond and DeNardis, 2015; Carr, 2015). Embedded in this proposition was a further commitment to the relatively free flow of information and data across borders, treated not as a security risk to be managed by states but as a precondition of the network's integrity and value (Aaronson, 2015; Chander and Lê, 2015).

These commitments – human rights conditionality, rule of law constraint and multistakeholder pluralism – were given operational form by two foundational instruments. Together they defined the normative terrain that China would subsequently challenge.

The first was the Budapest Convention on Cybercrime, concluded under Council of Europe auspices on 23 November 2001 (Council of Europe, 2001). Budapest was the first binding international treaty on cybercrime and the operational expression of the liberal rule-of-law tradition. It articulated three commitments that would prove central to the subsequent contest. Article 15 made human-rights conditionality a treaty-level obligation, requiring that procedural powers be exercised 'subject to conditions and safeguards as are provided for under its domestic law, which shall provide for the adequate protection of human rights and liberties', and that those conditions incorporate 'the principle of proportionality' – making rights-protection a treaty-level obligation rather than a matter of domestic discretion. Article 32(b) permitted trans-border access to stored computer data with the lawful and voluntary consent of the person with authority to disclose it, treating the data subject rather than the state as the source of authorisation – the clause Russia would cite for two decades as evidence that Budapest violated state sovereignty and that a replacement UN treaty was needed. The Convention's material scope was narrowly drawn around a closed list of cyber-dependent offences: illegal access, illegal interception, data interference, system interference, computer-related fraud, computer-related forgery, content-related offences (in carefully delimited form) and offences related to copyright. The drafting was led by established liberal democracies; accession was open to non-European states, and over eighty parties eventually joined from Latin America, Africa and Asia. China did not join. Each of these features represented a constraint on state authority that Beijing found unacceptable because it embedded a governance philosophy that subordinated state security interests to individual rights and judicial independence.

The second pillar was the multistakeholder model of internet governance. Its foundational institution, the Internet Corporation for Assigned Names and Numbers (ICANN), was established in 1998 through a United States Department of Commerce initiative to privatise management of the Domain Name System. Following the National Telecommunications and Information Administration's (NTIA) Green Paper of January 1998 and White Paper of June 1998, ICANN was incorporated as a private not-for-profit body initially operating under a Memorandum of Understanding with the United States government – a formal dependency that, through successive instruments and ultimately the Internet Assigned Numbers Authority (IANA) functions contract administered by the NTIA, persisted until the IANA stewardship transition of October 2016, when stewardship of the internet's core identifier functions passed formally to the global multistakeholder community (NTIA, 1998; ICANN, 2016; Mueller, 2010). The technical standards layer was anchored by the Internet Engineering Task Force (IETF) and the World Wide Web Consortium (W3C), both operating through rough consensus among technical experts drawn from the private sector and research community rather than governmental delegation – design principles that deliberately excluded intergovernmental authority from the foundational layer of internet infrastructure (DeNardis, 2014).

The political contest over governance architecture came to a head at the World Summit on the Information Society (WSIS), held in Geneva in December 2003 and Tunis in November 2005. Convened under UN auspices pursuant to General Assembly Resolution 56/183 (UN General Assembly, 2001), WSIS was organised with the ITU as lead agency in partnership with UNESCO and UNDP. The designation of the ITU – a treaty-based intergovernmental body with universal state membership – as lead agency was itself politically significant, foregrounding an institutional logic in tension with the privately incorporated ICANN (Mueller, 2010; Kleinwächter, 2007). A coalition comprising China, Russia, Brazil, Iran, Saudi Arabia and the broader G-77 pressed for substantial reform of the multistakeholder model in favour of greater intergovernmental control, arguing that unilateral American stewardship of the internet's core identifiers was incompatible with sovereign equality (MacLean, 2004; Drake and Wilson, 2008; Kleinwächter, 2004). The Working Group on Internet Governance (WGIG), established by Secretary-General Kofi Annan between the two phases (UN Secretary-General, 2004), produced a July 2005 report whose now-canonical definition of internet governance – 'the development and application by governments, the private sector and civil society, in their respective roles, of shared principles, norms, rules, decision-making procedures and programmes that shape the evolution and use of the internet' – was itself a diplomatic compromise that accommodated both camps without resolving their disagreement (WGIG, 2005, para. 10; Malcolm, 2008; Hofmann, 2016).

The 2005 Tunis Agenda formalised the compromise through three structural ambiguities. First, the Agenda's working definition of internet governance assigned segregated roles to governments, the private sector, and civil society, while paragraph 35 affirmed that policy authority over internet-related public policy was 'the sovereign right of States' – a formulation that allowed each side to read its preferred governance philosophy into the text. Second, the Internet Governance Forum (IGF), established in 2006 as a global multistakeholder platform for policy dialogue, was created as a deliberative space rather than a governance body, lacking binding decision-making authority precisely because the United States, the European Union and the technical community insisted that it not displace ICANN (Malcolm, 2008; Mueller, 2010). Third, the contested language of 'enhanced cooperation' on international public policy issues, introduced at paragraph 69 of the Tunis Agenda, allowed each side to read its preferred governance philosophy into the text. Two successive UN Commission on Science and Technology for Development working groups (2013–2014 and 2016–2018) failed to reach consensus on operationalising the term, and the dispute remained live at the WSIS+20 review in December 2025 – twenty years after Tunis (UNCTAD, 2018; Tunis Agenda, 2005; Thumfart, 2024). China and its developing-country allies accepted these outcomes as a tactical accommodation rather than a genuine endorsement, and would continue to seek institutional alternatives capable of delivering the substantive intergovernmental authority that the Tunis Agenda had rhetorically affirmed but procedurally withheld.

China opposed both pillars from the start. It did not join the Budapest Convention, objecting to both its substantive content and its process, which it characterised as a Western imposition with inadequate developing-country participation. It consistently opposed the multistakeholder model at WSIS and subsequent forums, advancing instead the principle that internet governance should be conducted primarily by states through the UN system (Sukumar and Basu, 2024). As Hulvey (2022) and others have documented, China's early approach centred on the framing move of characterising internet governance questions as matters of sovereign equality and national development rather than individual-rights questions. Its early architecture of preferred norms can be reconstructed from official documents and diplomatic submissions across the period, and rests on five mutually reinforcing commitments. First, *cyber sovereignty* – the principle that states hold supreme authority over digital infrastructure and information flows within their territory (State Council Information Office, 2010; Xi, 2015; Ministry of Foreign Affairs and Cyberspace Administration of China, 2017). Second, *non-interference* – the norm that no external actor has standing to challenge how a state governs its digital space. Third, *state-centric internet governance* – the replacement of the multistakeholder model with an intergovernmental framework centred on the UN. Fourth, *broad domestic discretion* over surveillance, data access and cross-border enforcement, with weaker emphasis on independent judicial oversight than in the Budapest model. Fifth, *security primacy over individual rights*. These five preferences form a normative architecture that directly inverts the foundational assumptions of the liberal framework China has spent two decades contesting. The next two sections trace the trajectory by which they moved from minority advocacy to formally embedded international instruments.

2. From Defensive Multilateralism to Norm Entrepreneurship (2001–19)

2.1 The Defensive Baseline (2001–14)

The pre-2015 UN record shows a consistent dominance of liberal vocabulary across digital-governance instruments – the baseline against which China's posture is here measured. By 'liberal' is meant the three commitments identified above: human rights as binding constraints on state authority online, rule of law as the organising principle for state conduct in cyberspace and pluralist multistakeholder governance with its attendant commitment to relatively unconstrained cross-border information flow. These commitments structured the substantive content of the period's UN instruments and defined the normative terrain on which China had to operate.

The 2007 and 2010 ICT-for-development resolutions (UN General Assembly Resolutions 62/182 and 65/141) embodied the liberal framework in vocabulary and in the structural assumptions visible across their texts. They treated the internet as a single global infrastructure whose integration was itself the development goal: A/RES/65/141 acknowledged the internet as 'a central element of the infrastructure of the information society' that had become 'a global facility available to the public', and committed to 'expedite the integration of all countries... into the global economy'. They consistently endorsed multistakeholder governance as the proper architecture, repeatedly invoking the Tunis Agenda formulation that 'the international management of the Internet should be multilateral, transparent and democratic, with the full involvement of Governments, the private sector, civil society and international organisations' (A/RES/65/141, preamble). And they treated cybersecurity as essentially a non-category, with the term 'security' appearing only in passing and no operative paragraph framing it as a question requiring independent attention. This absence is itself analytically significant: these resolutions treated digital governance as a development and access question rather than a security question, an ordering structurally incompatible with the Chinese-preferred framing in which information security is the precondition within which development takes place. The 2013 post-Snowden privacy resolution (A/RES/68/167) and its 2014 follow-up (A/RES/69/166) tightened the framework on the human-rights dimension, claiming privacy online as a human right, calling on states to ensure that surveillance practices complied with international human rights law and extending this concern to the collection of metadata – consolidating an individual civil-libertarian framing and reaffirming the rule-of-law premise that surveillance powers must be subject to international standards rather than domestic political preference.

Against this dominant vocabulary, Chinese-preferred terms – sovereignty, non-interference, state-led governance, information security as a content-inclusive concept – circulated through a parallel corpus of texts authored or co-authored by Beijing. The State Council Information Office's June 2010 white paper *The Internet in China* declared that 'within Chinese territory the Internet is under the jurisdiction of Chinese sovereignty', elevating a domestic regulatory premise to a claim about the proper structure of international order (State Council Information Office, 2010). The same logic moved into UN-circulated text the following year through the *International Code of Conduct for Information Security* submitted by China, Russia, Tajikistan and Uzbekistan (A/66/359, 2011), which asked states to affirm that 'policy authority for Internet-related public issues is the sovereign right of states' and committed signatories not to use ICTs to interfere in other states' internal affairs (A/66/359, annex). Introducing the Code in the First Committee, China's Ambassador for Disarmament Affairs Wang Qun framed it as an effort to launch a UN-anchored norm-development process for cyberspace – an explicit counter-positioning against the multistakeholder governance architecture endorsed in the parallel ICT-for-development resolutions (UN First Committee, 20 October 2011). These commitments rested on prior SCO-level instruments – most directly the 2009 Yekaterinburg Agreement on Cooperation in the Field of Ensuring International Information Security – and were reaffirmed at the SCO's Dushanbe Summit in September 2014 (SCO, 2014). Across these texts the Chinese-preferred lexicon was articulated with full clarity, but it remained marginal in mainstream ICT-for-development and digital-rights resolutions: it was the language of co-signed letters, sub-regional declarations and First Committee interventions – not of the General Assembly's operative texts.

China's posture during this period can therefore be characterised as defensive in three senses. First, its principal mode of engagement was resistance: pushing back against Western-led frameworks, insisting on sovereignty and non-interference language, and declining to accede to the Budapest Convention on grounds that it had not been consulted in the drafting and that cross-border evidence-collection provisions encroached on territorial sovereignty (Zhang and Creemers, 2024). Second, the venues in which it most consistently advanced positive alternatives – the SCO, BRICS and bilateral engagements – sat outside the UN system proper, reflecting the difficulty of inscribing such alternatives directly into mainstream UN texts. Third, even where Chinese vocabulary did circulate within UN venues, it did so as a minority position requiring constant defence rather than as the operating premise of the texts themselves; the 2011 Code was distributed but never tabled as a draft resolution, and its 2015 revision (A/69/723) carried only minor modifications, an indication that the underlying coalition had not yet broadened sufficiently to make a UNGA push viable. China and its partners had begun to articulate positive alternatives, but they did not yet command either the institutional position or the breadth of coalition necessary to displace the dominant liberal vocabulary of UN digital governance.

One UN body partially exceeded this pattern. The Group of Governmental Experts on Developments in the Field of Information and Telecommunications in the Context of International Security, established by UN GA Resolution 58/32 in 2003, became from 2009 onward the principal UN channel for negotiating norms of responsible state behaviour in cyberspace. The 2013 GGE report (A/68/98) was the first multilateral document to affirm that 'State sovereignty and international norms and principles that flow from sovereignty apply to the conduct by States of ICT-related activities, and to their jurisdiction over ICT infrastructure within their territory' (para. 20). For Beijing and Moscow, this formulation confirmed that the GGE could be made to ratify the conceptual ground on which the Code of Conduct stood. The 2015 GGE report (A/70/174) elaborated that, in their use of ICTs, states must observe sovereignty, sovereign equality, peaceful settlement of disputes and non-intervention in the internal affairs of other states (para. 28(b)), and articulated eleven voluntary norms of responsible state behaviour covering cooperation against ICT threats, prevention of misuse of ICTs from territory, respect for human rights and privacy, protection of critical infrastructure, supply chain integrity and the prohibition of harm to incident response teams [paras. 13(a)–(k)]. What the GGE had not done – and what Western states pushed harder for between 2016 and 2017 – was clarify the corresponding restraints: how international humanitarian law (IHL), the right of self-defence under Article 51 of the UN Charter and the law of state responsibility (including countermeasures) translate into cyberspace (Markoff, 2017; Schmitt and Vihul, 2017). The 2016–2017 group, chaired by Karsten Geier of Germany, failed to produce a consensus report on precisely these questions, with Russia, China and Cuba leading the opposition (Tikk and Kerttunen, 2017; Henriksen, 2019; Korzak, 2017; Grigsby, 2017). In the only publicly available explanation from a refusing state, Cuba's representative Miguel Rodríguez objected that the draft would 'convert cyberspace into a theatre of military operations' and rejected the equivalence it drew between the malicious use of ICTs and an armed attack under Article 51 (Rodríguez, 2017). The failure of consensus over those clauses was the proximate cause of the breakdown, but the deeper dynamic, as Tikk and Kerttunen (2017) argue, was that sovereignty-first states had accumulated enough confidence in the parallel architecture they were building outside the GGE to refuse compromise inside it.

2.2 The Pivot to Norm Entrepreneurship (2015–19)

The period from 2015 to 2019 registers the first observable shift in China's posture, from defensive resistance to proactive norm entrepreneurship. The pivot point was Xi Jinping's December 2015 address at the Second World Internet Conference (WIC) in Wuzhen. Delivered before foreign leaders, ministers, international organisations, and technology executives, the speech advanced an international claim that 'cyber sovereignty' should serve as a core organising principle of global internet governance, linking it to sovereign equality, non-interference, and each state's right to choose 'its own path of cyber development, model of cyber regulation and Internet public policies' (Xi, 2015; Creemers, 2020). The Wuzhen speech is also where the cyberspace variant of the 'community of common destiny' framing (网络空间命运共同体) was consolidated for international audiences. Wuzhen marked the transition from resisting Western frameworks to clearly articulating a Chinese alternative, and it formally consolidated the institutional architecture through which that alternative would be promoted.

The WIC itself, launched in 2014 and consolidated through annual Wuzhen meetings, became the most visible expression of China's parallel institutionalism: the construction of Chinese-hosted forums that compete with Western-associated governance platforms for normative authority (Creemers, 2020; Negro, 2020). Unlike the Internet Governance Forum, which is organised around a more open multistakeholder format, the WIC is better understood as a Chinese-hosted, state-centred forum that includes governments, companies, international organisations, and technical actors but operates under a strong Chinese agenda-setting. Its declarations and associated documents repeatedly deploy a sovereignty-first vocabulary – 'community of shared future in cyberspace', 'respect for cyber sovereignty', non-interference, development, security and state responsibility (Cyberspace Administration of China, 2015; Qiushi, 2016; Creemers, 2020). The WIC functions both as a rehearsal space, where Chinese governance vocabulary is normalised through annual repetition, and as a mechanism through which Chinese positions can be presented as part of a broader international conversation rather than as unilateral Chinese advocacy. Its claim to global authority was nevertheless contested from the outset: Russia, Central Asian states and other like-minded governments often sent high-level delegations, while the United States remained wary of legitimating what it viewed as a Chinese-led alternative to the multistakeholder model and frequently sent only lower-level officials (Triolo, 2018; Negro, 2020).

In parallel, the SCO submitted a revised *International Code of Conduct for Information Security* to the UN as document A/69/723 on 13 January 2015, co-sponsored by China, Kazakhstan, Kyrgyzstan, the Russian Federation, Tajikistan and Uzbekistan, all members of the Shanghai Cooperation Organisation (UN General Assembly, 2015). The Code was submitted under General Assembly agenda item 91, 'Developments in the field of information and telecommunications in the context of international security', explicitly intended 'to push forward the international debate on international norms on information security'. Its narrative emphasised state sovereignty and territoriality in the digital space and was dominated by intelligence, national security and regime-stability imperatives, raising significant concerns under international human rights law (McKune, 2015; Eichensehr, 2015). The 2015 revision retained measures directed at prohibiting cyber interference 'in the internal affairs of other States or with the aim of undermining their political, economic and social stability', and affirmed sovereign rights of states to protect 'their information space and critical information infrastructure against damage resulting from threats, interference, attack and sabotage' (Meyer, 2020). The choice of *information security* rather than *cybersecurity* was substantive: it implied that the content of information flowing through networks – not only the integrity of the systems carrying it – fell within the legitimate scope of state regulation, a framing rejected by most liberal democracies as a vehicle for legitimising online censorship (CCDCOE, 2015; Grigsby, 2015). Although the Code was not adopted, its introduction consolidated a state-centred model of digital governance as a formally articulated alternative within UN discussions and discourse.

These parallel moves – China's Wuzhen platform, the SCO-led Code of Conduct, and the entrenchment of 'cyber sovereignty' as a Chinese-spearheaded norm – ran alongside, and increasingly converged with, China's posture inside the GGE. Reading the WIC, the Code of Conduct and the GGE together makes visible a coordinated dual-track strategy: constructing parallel forums and tabling alternative texts on the outside, while shaping, and where necessary blocking, language on the inside. The collapse of the 2016–17 GGE was the moment at which the parallel tracks emerged as an operational pattern. Beyond the immediate impasse over self-defence, international humanitarian law and countermeasures, the breakdown demonstrated that sovereignty-first states could now operate simultaneously as architects of alternative forums and as gatekeepers within the established one (Henriksen, 2019).

Two further developments completed the institutional pivot. China issued its *International Strategy of Cooperation on Cyberspace* on 1 March 2017 (Ministry of Foreign Affairs and Cyberspace Administration of China, 2017), articulating cyber sovereignty as the first basic principle of its preferred international order and calling for a 'multilateral, democratic and transparent' governance system under UN auspices. And in December 2018, the General Assembly adopted two resolutions with overlapping mandates but different institutional logics. Resolution 73/27, tabled by Russia – the traditional sponsor of the annual First Committee resolution on ICTs since 1998 – and co-sponsored by China and 32 other states, established an Open-Ended Working Group (OEWG) open to all UN member states, by a recorded vote of 119 in favour, 46 against, and 14 abstentions (UN General Assembly, 2018a; Grigsby, 2018). Resolution 73/266, sponsored by the United

States with 35 co-sponsors, renewed the GGE in its smaller expert format, composed of 25 experts appointed on the basis of equitable geographical distribution, by a recorded vote of 138 in favour, 12 against and 16 abstentions (UN General Assembly, 2018b). The two processes reflected different preferences over how cyber norms should be made. The GGE preserved the responsible-state-behaviour framework developed in the 2010, 2013 and 2015 consensus reports, relying on expert deliberation among a limited group of states. The OEWG, by contrast, created a universal and explicitly intergovernmental forum in which all member states could participate.

The institutional initiative for the OEWG was unmistakably Russian. Moscow had long sought to break what its representatives publicly characterised as the 'exclusive club' of GGE deliberations, and at the First Committee debate the Russian delegation argued that the OEWG would render UN negotiations 'more democratic, inclusive and transparent' (UN General Assembly, 2018a; Grigsby, 2018). An earlier draft of the Russian resolution had imported language drawn directly from the SCO International Code of Conduct for Information Security; Moscow stripped this text after pushback from Western delegations, but the underlying ambition – to elevate sovereignty-oriented norms into a universal UN process – remained intact (Korzak, 2021; Hakmeh, 2020). China's role in this process was less procedurally driven but normatively decisive: Beijing co-sponsored 73/27 and voted against 73/266, but its more consequential contribution was substantive. It supplied the doctrinal content that gave the OEWG track its sovereigntist character, drawing on its 2017 *International Strategy*, on Xi's Wuzhen address and on the SCO Code of Conduct.

The dual-track architecture established in December 2018 is the structural inheritance of the period this section has covered. The OEWG was not, by design, a sovereignty-first instrument: its 2021 final substantive report (A/75/816, 18 March 2021) was adopted by consensus on 12 March 2021 and retained key elements of the GGE acquis, including the affirmation that international law applies to ICT activity (para. 25), the eleven voluntary norms (paras. 24–34), confidence-building measures, capacity-building and references to human rights. It is therefore better read as a hybrid venue: multilateral in form, partially liberal in substance, but reflecting a state-centred logic in its institutional design and procedural rules. What the OEWG marked was a durable shift in the UN record: multistakeholder and expert-led approaches no longer stood alone as the default architecture for cyber governance. They now coexisted with a universal, state-centred process that better reflected sovereignty-first preferences. The next section traces the consequences in the domain where the consequences are most consequential – binding treaty law.

3. The Cybercrime Trajectory (2019–25): A Treaty in the Sovereignty-First Image

The clearest single case in the international record of how Chinese-aligned normative effort can shape a potentially binding treaty runs from December 2019 to the Hanoi signing ceremony of October 2025. It is the most consequential instance in this two-decade record in which an initiative originating outside the Western-led order — initiated by Russia, supported by China, and enabled initially by a much broader and heterogeneous Global South majority — produced a treaty instrument that will bind states that ratify it once the entry-into-force threshold is met. The trajectory is also the cleanest demonstration of what changes when sovereignty-first preferences are translated into binding international law rather than into political declaration. This section consolidates the case in one continuous treatment.

3.1 Why Budapest Was the Contested Baseline

The negotiations that produced the 2024 Convention were structured throughout by the contrast between the new instrument and the Budapest Convention of 2001 (Council of Europe, 2001). Three differences run through the whole trajectory and explain why a separate UN treaty became politically possible.

The first difference concerns material scope. Budapest defined a comparatively bounded set of offences: core cyber-dependent offences targeting the confidentiality, integrity and availability of computer systems and data, together with specified computer-related fraud and forgery offences and narrowly delimited content- and copyright-related offences. The UN Convention, by contrast, extends cooperation obligations to any 'serious crime' punishable by four or more years' imprisonment when committed through information and communications technology (UN General Assembly, 2024c, A/RES/79/243, Annex, Art. 4). In jurisdictions where speech offences, 'spreading false information', 'insulting the state', or vaguely framed extremism and separatism statutes carry sentences above the four-year threshold, the treaty obliges other parties to assist in their investigation and prosecution. The substantive insulation that Budapest's narrow scope provided against political abuse is reduced in the UN treaty's open-ended formulation, although the final text adopts an offence-specific approach to criminalisation rather than a general definition of cybercrime, which restricts the broader content-based offences pushed by a sub-coalition during negotiations (Digital Watch Observatory, 2024; EFF, 2024).

The second difference concerns procedural safeguards. Budapest's Article 15 made human-rights conditionality a treaty-level obligation, binding signatories to subject every procedural power to the European Convention on Human Rights, the ICCPR and equivalent instruments, and to require proportionality and independent judicial oversight as a matter of treaty compliance. The UN Convention's analogous safeguards clause references human rights in more general terms, defers their substantive content to domestic law, and does not expressly require independent judicial supervision over surveillance powers. For states whose domestic legal orders place few effective limits on executive surveillance, this displacement of safeguards from international obligation to national discretion functions as a permission rather than a constraint: the treaty asks each state to apply its own human rights standards, whatever those happen to be.

The third difference concerns cross-border cooperation. Budapest's Article 32(b), which Russia condemned for two decades as an infringement on sovereignty, rested on the proposition that lawful access to data could proceed where the relevant individual consented, treating the data subject rather than the state as the source of authorisation. The UN Convention rejects that premise. Cross-border access is routed through state-to-state mutual legal assistance, with grounds for refusal that include broadly framed national-security and public-order exceptions. The result is a regime in which cooperation is filtered through sovereign discretion at every step.

3.2 The 2019 Vote and the Coalition behind It

UN General Assembly Resolution 74/247 was introduced by Russia, co-sponsored by China and a group including Belarus, Cambodia, Iran, Myanmar, Nicaragua, North Korea, Syria and Venezuela, and adopted by the General Assembly on 27 December 2019 by a recorded vote of 79 in favour, 60 against and 33 abstentions (UN General Assembly, 2019, A/RES/74/247; US Department of State, 2020). The 79 votes in favour came predominantly from a cross-regional grouping in Africa, Asia and the Middle East; the 60 against included the European bloc, Australia, New Zealand, Republic of Korea, Japan, the United States, Paraguay, Panama and Tonga; the 33 abstentions came mainly from Latin American states and a few others (OpenGlobalRights, 2024). The resolution did not itself draft a treaty. It established an Ad Hoc Committee tasked with elaborating 'a comprehensive international convention on countering the use of information and communications technologies for criminal purposes'. As an open subsidiary body of the General Assembly, the Ad Hoc Committee admitted all UN member states as full participants from the first session and accredited a structured but limited role for civil society and private-sector observers, in deliberate contrast to the Budapest Convention's drafting genealogy, which had been completed within the Council of Europe and offered to non-members only as a finished text.

The composition of the 2019 majority is decisive for understanding what followed. A core group of authoritarian and semi-authoritarian states voted in favour because they shared the governance philosophy the resolution embodied, but the larger share of the majority was a developing-country coalition drawn from Africa, Asia and the Middle East, supporting the resolution primarily because it promised a governance framework built around the UN system and Global South participation. The text of Resolution 74/247 itself was deliberately structured to absorb that developmental concern: its sixth preambular paragraph takes note of ECOSOC Resolution 2019/19 on 'promoting technical assistance and capacity-building to strengthen national measures and international cooperation to combat cybercrime' (UN General Assembly, 2001, A/RES/74/247, preamb. para. 6; ECOSOC, 2019, E/RES/2019/19), and operative paragraph 1 frames the future Convention as serving 'developing' states' needs alongside the cooperation interests of the wider membership. For these states the appeal was substantially representational and developmental – a UN-anchored process open to all member states, in contrast to a Council of Europe instrument they had had no role in drafting – and substantively oriented toward capacity-building flows that the Budapest framework had not delivered at scale on the African continent (Chatham House, 2025; DiploFoundation, 2024).

The 2019 shift, in other words, does not represent a consensus endorsement of cyber sovereignty as a governance philosophy; it represents a coalition between an ideological core and a much larger representational-and-developmental majority that the Russia–China sponsorship was able to mobilise but did not normatively command. The 33 abstentions – including Argentina, Brazil, Costa Rica, Ecuador, Morocco, Peru, the Philippines, Tunisia and Turkey – encode a third position: hedging between the procedural openness of the UN-led process and substantive concerns about its likely direction, without endorsing either pole.

That heterogeneity became visible immediately after the vote. The Brazilian amendment L.90, which sought to set the Ad Hoc Committee's decision-making threshold at a two-thirds majority – closer to the consensus practice favoured by the European Union than to the simple majority preferred by Russia – and the United Kingdom amendment L.92, which reduced states' ability to block external participants, both attracted support from a substantial portion of the original 79-vote bloc. The Brazilian amendment passed by 88 in favour, 42 against and 32 abstentions; the UK amendment passed by 82 in favour, 33 against and 43 abstentions (UN General Assembly, 2021, GA/12328). On the cumulative evidence, of the 79 states that supported Resolution 74/247, roughly 38 – about 48 per cent – subsequently changed position on procedural and modalities decisions, abstaining or absenting themselves rather than supporting the Russian and Sino-Russian line on decision-making thresholds and civil-society participation (DiploFoundation, 2023). India, the largest single state in the co-sponsorship pool, exemplifies the pattern: New Delhi has consistently emphasised supply-chain security, data localisation, capacity-building and technical cooperation, while explicitly declining to amplify cyber sovereignty arguments at the UN (Indian Council of World Affairs, 2024). A coalition that loses nearly half its strength on the first set of procedural votes after its founding decision is not, on any reasonable definition, cohesive.

3.3 The Ad Hoc Committee and the Negotiation

From January 2022 to August 2024, the Ad Hoc Committee held six negotiating sessions, followed by a concluding session that met in two parts before approving the final text on 8 August 2024 (UNODC, 2024a). The drafting was a site of sustained contestation, and the published session documents allow Chinese interventions to be traced with precision rather than inferred.

In April 2022, ahead of the Second Session, the Russian Federation tabled a joint submission on behalf of itself, Belarus, Burundi, China, Nicaragua and Tajikistan, proposing the criminalisation of an extensive list of content-related offences, including vaguely defined extremism-related acts (UNODC, 2022a; EFF, 2023b). In the consolidated negotiating document circulated for the Fourth Session in mid-January 2023, China formally proposed an offence criminalising the dissemination of 'false information' causing 'serious social disorder', explicitly extending to 'information relating to natural or human-caused disasters' (Ad Hoc Committee,

2023, Consolidated Negotiating Document, A/AC.291/16; Bannelier, 2023; EFF, 2023c). The proposal would have given states sweeping authority to criminalise online content under the cybercrime framework. Sustained opposition from Western states, several Latin American delegations, civil society organisations and the technology industry forced its removal from the body of the draft, although several authoritarian-aligned states sought its reintroduction at later stages (EFF, 2024; Human Rights Watch, 2024). The final Convention does not contain the provision, and the final text takes an offence-specific approach to criminalisation focused on cyber-dependent crimes rather than adopting a general definition of cybercrime (Digital Watch Observatory, 2024).

In the Sixth Session (August–September 2023), China – together with Pakistan, Iran and Mauritania – tabled an additional proposal on 'cooperation between national authorities and service providers' that would have obliged providers to render 'offensive and harmful content' inaccessible, a proposal rejected by the United States, Canada, Australia, the European Union and its member states, Georgia and others (DiploFoundation, 2023b).

China's positioning was not, however, identical to Russia's, and the divergence is itself analytically important. Where Moscow continued to push for the reintroduction of criminal provisions on critical information infrastructure (CII) in the final negotiating session, Beijing notably declined to support that proposal (Sukumar and Basu, 2024). The pattern across the negotiations therefore shows China as a decisive contributor to the content-control dimension of the draft – the 'false information' clause being the most consequential single proposal it tabled – while remaining selectively cautious where binding norms might constrain its own offensive cyber posture.

The substantive defeat of the most explicit Chinese content-control proposal is itself analytically informative. As Pavlova's analysis records, 'Russia, China, Iran, and even India insisted on a long list of additional offences', but 'their efforts to control the debate on what constitutes cybercrime fell short' and 'the final outcome of negotiations was largely determined by a coalition of democratic countries' working with substantial Latin American, Caribbean and African support (Pavlova, 2025). At the concluding session, the Caribbean Community delegation, speaking through Jamaica, joined Nigeria, Brazil, Morocco, Ecuador, Peru, Chile, Uruguay, Argentina, Algeria, Costa Rica, Uganda, Ghana, Mexico, South Africa, Colombia, Paraguay and Panama in supporting Articles 5 and 24 in their drafted form against Iranian-led attempts to weaken safeguards (Global Initiative Against Transnational Organized Crime, 2024). The cross-regional pattern of this coalition – Caribbean, Latin American, African and Asian states aligning with the EU bloc on substantive safeguards – is the clearest evidence that the 2019 majority did not translate into a stable preference structure on the actual content of the treaty.

The same pattern recurred on Article 6, the human-rights safeguard providing that nothing in the Convention 'shall be interpreted as permitting suppression of human rights or fundamental freedoms' (UN General Assembly, 2024c, art. 6). Iran's attempt to remove this clause, supported by Russia, India, Sudan, Venezuela, Syria, the DPRK, Libya and a small number of others, failed to attract the broader coalition that had backed Resolution 74/247 in 2019 (Article 19, 2024a; EFF, 2024; Hakmeh and Mansour, 2024). An Iranian proposal to remove the safeguard against cooperation requests motivated by political opinion or other protected characteristics received 25 votes in favour and was defeated (EFF, 2024). The ideological core voted as expected; the developmental majority did not follow.

3.4 The Final Text and What It Establishes

The final Convention retains substantive individual-rights language. Article 6 provides that 'nothing in this Convention shall be interpreted as permitting suppression of human rights or fundamental freedoms', covering expression, conscience, opinion, religion or belief, peaceful assembly and association. On the core governance principle and data control dimensions, however, the final text embeds language compatible with the sovereignty bloc's preferences. Article 5(1) requires States Parties to carry out their obligations 'in a manner consistent with the principles of sovereign equality and territorial integrity of States and that of non-intervention in the domestic affairs of other States', while Article 5(2) specifies that nothing in the Convention entitles a State Party to undertake 'the exercise of jurisdiction and performance of functions that are reserved exclusively for the authorities of [another] State by its domestic law' (UN General Assembly, 2024c, art. 5). This formulation is more explicit than Budapest's general sovereignty provisions and is compatible with the cyber sovereignty agenda Beijing has advanced since the 2015 Wuzhen address and the 2017 *International Strategy of Cooperation on Cyberspace* (FDD, 2025; Sukumar and Basu, 2024).

The shift from formal opposition in 2019 to consensus adoption on 24 December 2024 (UNGA Resolution 79/243) reflects a more complex diplomatic dynamic than a simple Western boycott. Russia's full-scale invasion of Ukraine in February 2022 – four days before the AHC's first negotiating session – significantly reduced Moscow's political capital in the negotiations (Christakis, 2023; Hakmeh and Mansour, 2024), and a coalition led by Western and Latin American states, with active engagement from Canada, Mexico, and several African Budapest signatories, redirected the drafting away from the most expansive Russian and Chinese proposals. Some Western and allied states then calculated that a second recorded negative vote would be more damaging to their multilateral standing than allowing the Convention to pass by consensus while preserving room for later signature and ratification debates (Walker, 2024; Atlantic Council, 2024). In its explanation of position, the United States Mission to the United Nations expressed concern that the Convention's broad scope and weaker safeguards relative to the Budapest standard could be used to harm individual rights, and noted that some states might seek to misuse the treaty (USUN, 2024). The United States declined to sign at the Hanoi opening ceremony.

The Convention opened for signature in Hanoi on 25–26 October 2025 (UNODC, 2025). The UNODC press release recorded 71 states and the European Union signing during the two-day ceremony, including 21 African states; UN News reported 65 states; the running totals shifted as the ceremony unfolded (UNODC, 2025;

Connecting Africa, 2025). At the time of writing, the Convention had attracted more than seventy signatures, while Azerbaijan, Qatar and Vietnam had deposited instruments of ratification; it therefore remained well short of the forty ratifications required for entry into force a prospective rather than realised outcome (UN Treaty Collection, 2026). The asymmetry between consensus adoption and limited ratification is itself diagnostic of how partial the coalition behind the Convention is. Several of the most-cited 2019 co-sponsors did not translate their initial vote into signature at Hanoi. India is the diagnostic case: a co-sponsor of L.11/Rev.1 in November 2019, repeatedly characterised in the cyber-norms literature as a Global South 'swing state' (Indian Council of World Affairs, 2024), India declined to sign the Convention at Hanoi, citing concerns over privacy, data sovereignty and governance compatibility with its domestic constitutional framework (Drishti IAS, 2025; Medianama, 2025). Indonesia, similarly, did not sign at Hanoi despite its 2019 co-sponsorship and despite holding the office of Rapporteur on the Committee's bureau. The pattern fits the analytical claim of Section 3.2 – that for many states in the 2019 majority, the appeal of the resolution was the procedural openness of a UN-anchored process, not the substantive sovereignty-first content the negotiation eventually attempted to load into it.

4. The Global Digital Compact (2024): Revisionism from Within

If the cybercrime trajectory is the cleanest case of Chinese-aligned normative effort succeeding in binding treaty form, the 2024 Global Digital Compact (GDC) is the cleanest case of the strategic posture that distinguishes Chinese engagement from Russian rejectionism within the same coalition. Adopted on 22 September 2024 as Annex I to the Pact for the Future (UN General Assembly, 2024a, A/79/L.2), the GDC is the first UN framework instrument to span the full range of digital governance dimensions in a single negotiated text – internet governance model, data flows, human rights online, AI governance and capacity-building. It was co-facilitated by the Permanent Representatives of Sweden and Zambia under General Assembly decision 77/568 (UN Office for Digital and Emerging Technologies, 2024). Read against the trajectory traced in earlier sections of this chapter, the GDC is best understood not as an open contest between symmetrical positions, but as a text in which a sovereignty-inflected vocabulary – built up across two decades of Chinese norm entrepreneurship – has acquired formal institutional standing alongside, and sometimes in place of, the liberal multistakeholder vocabulary that previously held the field.

The substantive content that China brought into the GDC negotiations did not originate in those negotiations. It is the cumulative output of a sustained campaign that began with the SCO-led *International Code of Conduct for Information Security* of 2011 and 2015 (UN General Assembly, 2011, A/66/359; UN General Assembly, 2015, A/69/723) and was progressively elaborated through three Chinese-authored vehicles in the consolidation phase: the *Global Initiative on Data Security* (GIDS) launched by Foreign Minister Wang Yi in September 2020, the *Global Initiative for AI Governance* (GIAIG) launched in October 2023, and the *Global Cross-Border Data Flow Cooperation Initiative* announced by Xi Jinping at APEC in November 2024 and released in full at the World Internet Conference Wuzhen Summit (Ministry of Foreign Affairs of the People's Republic of China, 2020; Ministry of Foreign Affairs of the People's Republic of China, 2024c). Across these vehicles, a stable conceptual core is observable: cyber sovereignty (网络主权) and its application to data – that 'states should respect the sovereignty, jurisdiction and governance of data of other states' – coupled with three operative principles that recur almost verbatim across Chinese texts: a 'balance' between security and development, the demand that the digital environment be 'open, fair and non-discriminatory', and the framing of standard-setting as an intergovernmental task pursued through 'extensive consultation, joint contribution and shared benefits' (共商共建共享) (Ministry of Foreign Affairs of the People's Republic of China, 2020). This is not a residual or defensive position. It is a positive normative offer, articulated in idiomatic Chinese diplomatic vocabulary, and pitched explicitly as 'a basis for international rules-making on data security'.

The GDC's textual outcomes track this offer closely on three of the dimensions where Chinese effort has been most concentrated. First, on data governance, the final text endorses 'interoperable' approaches without specifying a substantive regulatory model and without reproducing the EU-style adequacy logic or the US-style cross-border-flows-with-narrow-exceptions logic – leaving operational space precisely where the GIDS asks states to 'respect the sovereignty, jurisdiction and governance of data' of others (UN General Assembly, 2024a, A/79/L.2 Annex I; Ministry of Foreign Affairs of the People's Republic of China, 2020). Second, on AI governance, the GDC commits to establishing an Independent International Scientific Panel on AI and a Global Dialogue on AI Governance under the auspices of the UN – an intergovernmental architecture that aligns with the GIAIG's call for AI governance 'with the UN as the main channel' and that gives China terrain in which its leadership in capacity-building diplomacy is structurally easier to leverage than in OECD- or G7-led venues. The Chinese Foreign Ministry made the alignment explicit two days after adoption: the Compact's measures on data security and AI, spokesperson Lin Jian observed, were 'consistent with what needs to be done to deliver on China's Global Initiative for AI Governance and Global Initiative on Data Security' (Ministry of Foreign Affairs of the People's Republic of China, 2024b). Third, on the rights register, the human-rights vocabulary of the Compact has been embedded inside a broader framework of 'inclusion', 'development', 'non-discrimination', and 'cultural diversity' – a vocabulary that closely parallels the language of the Global Development Initiative and the Global Civilisation Initiative and that, as Morrell (2025) shows, was the locus of sustained negotiating contestation during the GDC drafting process.

The one dimension on which Chinese-aligned content did not displace the prior vocabulary is internet governance proper, where the final text reaffirms that 'Internet governance must continue to be global and multistakeholder in nature' and reiterates the role of the Internet Governance Forum (UN General Assembly,

2024a, A/79/L.2 Annex I, paras. 28–29). The asymmetry is itself analytically informative: the multistakeholder formula was retained where Chinese capacity to shift it remained limited (the technical-coordination layer governed by ICANN, the IETF and the regional internet registries), while sovereignty-compatible language gained ground precisely in those domains – data, AI, capacity-building and the architecture of follow-up – where the relevant authority lies with states meeting under intergovernmental auspices, and where China has spent two decades building both bilateral coalitions and institutional position. The GDC is, in this sense, not a hybrid produced by accident. It is the imprint of a deliberate division of labour in Beijing's strategy: accept liberal architecture where it cannot yet be moved, and concentrate normative push where intergovernmental authority is the operative variable.

The GDC's adoption also clarified, by contrast, what non-revisionist Chinese normative engagement looks like. At the opening of the Summit of the Future, Russia tabled amendment A/79/L.3, co-sponsored by Belarus, the DPRK, Iran, Nicaragua, Syria, and Venezuela, seeking to insert a paragraph reaffirming that 'the United Nations and its system shall not intervene in matters which are essentially within the domestic jurisdiction of any State as provided in Article 2 (7) of the Charter of the United Nations' (UN General Assembly, 2024d, A/79/L.3; IISD, 2024). The Republic of the Congo, on behalf of the African Group, introduced a no-action motion that carried by 143 votes to 7, with 15 abstentions; the Pact and its annexes were then adopted without a vote (UN Department of Global Communications, 2024, GA/12627). On the available primary record, China voted in favour of the no-action motion rather than with the Russia-led grouping (Friedrich Naumann Foundation, 2024). China's affirmative vote on the no-action motion is more than a procedural curiosity. A blanket reassertion of Article 2(7) as a brake on UN action would have foreclosed precisely the forum authority – over AI governance, data governance, capacity-building and digital cooperation – that the GDC was extending to the General Assembly system, and that Beijing has spent two decades positioning itself to shape. Russia's last-minute, recorded-vote, sovereignty-absolutist intervention is the model of what Beijing's mode of engagement is not: in Beijing's strategy, the legitimacy of the UN-centred order is the asset, not the target. Foreign Minister Wang Yi, speaking at the Summit on 23 September, framed China's approach in exactly these terms – 'uphold[ing] the UN-centred international system' and pursuing 'true multilateralism' through extensive consultation rather than through a procedural assertion of non-interference (Ministry of Foreign Affairs of the People's Republic of China, 2024a). The same week, China and Zambia co-hosted the High-Level Meeting on International Cooperation on Capacity-Building of Artificial Intelligence and launched the *AI Capacity-Building Action Plan for Good and for All*, with high-level participation from more than eighty countries – a textbook display of the coalition-building style that the Russia-led amendment would have been incompatible with (Ministry of Foreign Affairs of the People's Republic of China, 2024a).

5. Standards as Structural Norm Power: The International Telecommunication Union (I2)

Alongside the UN political arena, the International Telecommunication Union (ITU) has been the primary site of China's technical standard-setting strategy and the principal expression of the I2 mechanism, technical standard-setting as structural norm power. The ITU's significance derives from its specific institutional architecture. As a treaty organisation in which member-state governments hold formal voting rights, it is the intergovernmental standard-setting body most compatible with China's preference for state-led governance arrangements. Where the IETF, W3C and IEEE operate through rough consensus among technical experts drawn from multiple sectors, the ITU gives states formal decision-making authority through a voting structure that privileges governmental representation (DeNardis, 2014; Russell, 2014). For China, which has consistently argued that digital governance should be conducted through intergovernmental rather than purely multistakeholder institutions, the ITU is the standards body whose architecture most closely matches its governance philosophy, and it is the institution where China has invested most heavily in positional capacity. This section reconstructs that engagement from primary sources – ITU plenipotentiary records, study-group documentation and contemporaneous expert analyses – and is careful to distinguish what is documented (proposals submitted, positions held, voting outcomes) from what is inferred (downstream normative effects).

5.1 Positional Capacity at the ITU

China's ITU engagement has been both quantitatively significant and qualitatively strategic. Houlin Zhao, the most prominent example, served three consecutive elected senior posts at the ITU: Director of the Telecommunication Standardisation Bureau (TSB) from 1999 to 2006, Deputy Secretary-General from 2007 to 2014 and Secretary-General from 1 January 2015 to 31 December 2022 (ITU, 2014; Broadband Commission, n.d.). He was first elected Secretary-General at the 2014 Plenipotentiary Conference in Busan, receiving 152 of 156 ballot papers as the sole candidate and re-elected at the 2018 Plenipotentiary Conference in Dubai with 176 of 178 ballot papers (ITU, 2014; CSIS, 2022). Zhao was the first Chinese national to hold the Secretary-Generalship in the ITU's 150-year history. The Chinese delegation to the ITU has also grown in size and proposal activity over the same period, with industry participation from Huawei, ZTE, China Mobile, China Unicom and the China Academy of Information and Communications Technology (CAICT) operating alongside the state delegation (Hoffmann, Lazanski and Taylor, 2020; Hulvey, 2022). The quantitative presence translates into qualitative influence through standard procedures, since states and firms that submit more proposals, hold more rapporteurship positions and participate more actively in drafting groups exercise disproportionate influence over final standards regardless of formal voting rules (Mattli and Büthe, 2003).

Two earlier pieces of context bear noting. The ITU's role as a UN-level cybersecurity convener was established at WSIS in 2003 and 2005, which entrusted the ITU with cybersecurity facilitation (Stimson Center, 2024). On 17 May 2007, then-Secretary-General Hamadoun Touré launched the Global Cybersecurity Agenda (GCA) as a 'framework for international cooperation' built on five pillars: legal measures, technical and procedural measures, organisational structures, capacity-building and international cooperation (ITU, 2007). The GCA is best characterised as a cooperation framework rather than as a normative instrument; it does not prescribe substantive cybercrime offences or evidentiary procedures in the manner of the 2001 Budapest Convention. The International Multilateral Partnership Against Cyber Threats (IMPACT), originally announced by the Government of Malaysia in 2006, was named the operational home of the GCA through a 2008 Bangkok Memorandum of Understanding, with its global headquarters in Cyberjaya formally opened on 20 May 2009 (IMPACT, 2009; CCDCOE, 2024). The GCA-IMPACT architecture provided a UN-affiliated capacity-building channel through which developing states could receive cybersecurity assistance without acceding to a Council of Europe instrument, and that channel pre-dated the most active phase of Chinese ITU engagement.

The 2012 World Conference on International Telecommunications (WCIT-12) in Dubai produced the most visible early marker of the normative divide that Chinese ITU engagement was working to expand. After two weeks of intensive negotiation, the conference adopted revised International Telecommunication Regulations (ITRs) that included, alongside their core technical telecommunications provisions, a non-binding resolution on the 'Internet' and a preambular reference to the right of states to access international telecommunications services (EDRi, 2012; ITU, 2012). 89 member states signed the revised ITRs on 14 December 2012; 55 – including the United States, the United Kingdom, Canada, Australia, Germany, France, Japan, India and Kenya – declined to sign (ITU, 2012; Mueller, 2012; Telefónica, 2012). The signatories' coalition was largely composed of African and Arab states, China, Russia and states within Russia's sphere of influence (Telefónica, 2012; Internet Governance Project, 2012). Hulvey's (2022) analysis of the ITR negotiations using ITU archival data concludes that the framing of the revisions as questions of sovereignty rather than as questions of technical telecommunications management – a framing she argues was advanced by the Chinese delegation and ultimately championed by the African Group – was central to the coalition that produced the 89-vote majority. Content analysis of the negotiations documents that 'China's position was ultimately taken up and championed by the African Group' (Hulvey, 2022, p. ii). At WCIT-12, the WCIT Chair Mohamed Nasser Al Ghanim of the UAE described the final text as a 'package' intended to achieve a 'delicate balance' between competing interests; the Iranian delegate's call for a vote on inclusion of the 'right of access of Member States to access international telecommunications services' in the preamble passed by 77 to 33 with 8 abstentions, a vote that crossed a 'red line' for several Western states amid concerns over the proposed Internet Resolution (EDRi, 2012). The 89–55 split documented in 2012 showed that the ITU's intergovernmental structure could be made to ratify positions that the multistakeholder architecture would have absorbed differently, and that the framing of internet governance questions as sovereignty questions was capable of mobilising a cross-regional coalition.

5.2 The 'New IP' Proposal: A Documented Case, Not a Successful One

The case that most clearly demonstrates the I2 mechanism in operation is the 'New IP' proposal, submitted to ITU-T's Telecommunications Standardisation Advisory Group (TSAG) in September 2019 by Huawei, China Mobile, China Unicom and the Ministry of Industry and Information Technology of China in document TSAG-C83 (ITU-T TSAG, 2019; Internet Society, 2020). A follow-up submission was made in January 2020 to the Focus Group on Technologies for Network 2030 (FG NET-2030), which had been established under Study Group 13 in 2018 (Internet Society, 2020). The proposal called for a 'top-down design for the future network' through a 'new information and communications network with new protocol system', which the proponents argued was needed to address heterogeneous network interconnection, 'islanding' risks and security and trust limitations of the existing TCP/IP architecture (Huawei Technologies, 2019, TSAG TD-598; Sharp and Kolkman, 2020). Critics – including the Internet Society in an April 2020 discussion paper, the IETF in a March 2020 liaison statement, RIPE NCC in April 2020 and the IEEE in a September 2020 contribution to TSAG – argued that the proposal would risk fragmenting the internet into less interoperable networks, that the architectural questions it raised were already being addressed in existing standards bodies under different frameworks, and that the appropriate forum for this work was the IETF rather than the ITU-T (Internet Society, 2020; IETF, 2020; RIPE NCC, 2020; Hoffmann, Lazanski and Taylor, 2020). The *Financial Times* reported in March 2020 that early presentation slides for the proposal included references to a 'shut-up command' capable of stopping packet transmission to or from a target address; the framing of this feature was contested by Huawei, which described 'New IP' as a research initiative rather than an operational architecture (Gross and Murgia, 2020; Huawei response cited in Hoffmann, Lazanski and Taylor, 2020).

In July 2020, Huawei reframed the proposal under the label 'Future Vertical Communication Networks' (FVCN). The Internet Society's analysis concluded that the substantive content was largely unchanged; Huawei contested this characterisation (Internet Society, 2020). At the December 2020 plenary meetings of Study Groups 13 and 11, the relevant ITU-T bodies decided not to accept 'New IP' – related items as new work items and to suspend further discussion until the World Telecommunication Standardisation Assembly (originally scheduled for March 2022) (Internet Society, 2022; Hoffmann, Lazanski and Taylor, 2020). Elements of the original proposal continued to surface in subsequent SG13 work items – including proposals on 'Polymorphic Networking', 'Immersive real-time communications', and '6G Networking Technologies' – which the Internet Society flagged as conceptually related (Internet Society, 2022).

The proposal therefore did not achieve adoption in its original form, and this matters for how its analytical significance is described. Its submission and the negotiation it generated did normalise debate on protocol-level architectural redesign within ITU-T forums – the question entered the agenda, was discussed and required formal procedural disposition. Whether this constitutes 'legitimation' of state-accessible control architectures or simply the normal operation of an open standards process is contested. What can be said carefully is that 'New IP' demonstrates the channel logic the chapter has been describing: Chinese-led submissions tend to be routed through institutional venues – in this case, ITU-T's TSAG and Focus Group on Network 2030 – where intergovernmental authority is structurally stronger than at the IETF. The case illustrates that channel logic regardless of whether the specific proposal succeeded. The case also illustrates the I2–I3 interaction: Chinese and Huawei delegations presented the proposal as addressing quality-of-service and connectivity needs for developing states, using the same developmental framing that grounds the South–South coalition examined in Section 6 (ICANN, 2020). The coalition provides the political support; the technical proposal provides the institutional vehicle.

5.3 Identifier Resolution, Lawful Interception, AI Standards and 5G via 3GPP

Four further sites of Chinese engagement deserve more careful description than the chapter's earlier draft provided, because each illustrates a different aspect of the I2 mechanism and each requires different evidentiary handling.

First, in Study Group 17 (security), Chinese-authored proposals have included a 2019 contribution titled 'A Decentralised Framework for Object Identifier Resolution', which proposed an object-identifier resolution system as an alternative to the Domain Name System (Hoffmann, Lazanski and Taylor, 2020). The proposal generated concerns within Western technical communities that alternative identifier architectures could reduce predictability in cyberspace and create new governance questions, though it did not result in the adoption of a substitute identifier infrastructure. A more general claim – that ITU-T standards developed under Chinese leadership in SG17 systematically embed real-name verification as a baseline design feature – is harder to substantiate from the public record. China's domestic real-name registration regime is well-documented (Creemers, 2016), but the chapter distinguishes between domestic regulatory practice and specific ITU-T Recommendations, and treats any claim about the latter as requiring direct citation of the relevant Recommendation text.

Second, in Study Group 11 (signalling and protocols), ITU-T has published a body of standards on traffic identification and management (the Y.2770 series on deep packet inspection, originally approved in 2012) and on lawful interception interfaces. These standards exist and have been the subject of expert critique (Hoffmann, Lazanski and Taylor, 2020), but they predate the most active period of Chinese standards engagement and were developed under leadership and editorship that included contributors from multiple states. The defensible claim is therefore that Chinese contributions in SG11 have built on and extended an existing line of work whose governance implications were already debated when the work began, rather than that DPI and lawful-interception standards exist specifically because of Chinese influence.

Third, on AI standards, Chinese-authored contributions to ITU-T Focus Group work on AI for health (FG-AI4H), AI for autonomous and assisted driving, and to Study Group 16 have been substantial in volume (ITU-T records). At the FOCAC 2024 summit and in the lead-up to the GDC, China announced the *AI Capacity-Building Action Plan for Good and for All* and co-hosted the High-Level Meeting on International Cooperation on Capacity-Building of Artificial Intelligence with Zambia (Ministry of Foreign Affairs of the People's Republic of China, 2024a; see Section 6.3). Whether ITU-T AI standards will embed sovereignty-compatible governance assumptions in ways that produce path-dependent effects on developing-state regulatory frameworks is a forward-looking claim that the available evidence cannot yet adjudicate; this chapter treats it as a hypothesis worth tracking rather than as a documented outcome (cf. Cihon et al., 2020).

6. South–South Coalition Construction (I3)

The institutional moves documented in Sections 2 through 5 required a coalition: a durable, cross-regional alignment of states willing to vote, sponsor and rhetorically support Chinese-preferred institutional designs in forums where China's formal weight is one vote among 193. The construction and maintenance of that coalition is the I3 mechanism. Where I1 operates through the choice of institutional venue and procedural positioning, and I2 operates through the embedding of governance assumptions in technical architecture, I3 operates through the assembly of political relationships that convert latent governance preferences among developing states into coordinated normative outcomes.

6.1 The Pre-Assembly Architecture

The South–South coalition that operates in international digital governance forums is not assembled from scratch at each negotiation. It is pre-assembled through the regional and bilateral channels documented in Chapter 4, then activated in multilateral settings. Analysis that examines only what happens in UN rooms misses where coalition-building actually occurs. The pre-assembly proceeds through four interlocking layers.

The first layer is material infrastructure, the physical and operational substrate that the so-called Digital Silk Road has built across Africa, Central Asia, Southeast Asia, the Middle East and parts of Latin America. Fibre-optic backbones, submarine cables, 5G deployments, data centres, e-commerce platforms and Safe City surveillance packages delivered through Huawei, ZTE, China Mobile, China Telecom and Alibaba Cloud tend to foster infrastructural affinity for governance frameworks that legitimise state authority over digital systems (Erie and Streinz, 2021). The second layer is high-level diplomatic engagement, in which Xi Jinping's state visits and major foreign-policy speeches – the 2015 Wuzhen address, the

2016 G20 Hangzhou digital economy agenda, successive Forum on China-Africa Cooperation (FOCAC) summits, the China-CELAC Forum, the China-Arab States Cooperation Forum and the China-Pacific Island Countries dialogues – systematically fold digital-governance language into broader development and security partnerships. Ministerial engagement through the Cyberspace Administration of China, the Ministry of Foreign Affairs, and the Ministry of Industry and Information Technology translates this framing into operational cooperation: bilateral cybersecurity and data-governance memoranda of understanding, training programmes for foreign officials at Chinese institutions, seminars for foreign regulators and journalists and scholarships cycling mid-career officials from Global South administrations through Chinese universities (Gagliardone, 2019; Repnikova, 2022).

The third layer is China's set of declaratory initiatives, which aggregate bilateral and regional engagements into coherent normative packages that can be carried into SCO or BRICS, and from there into UN forums as cross-regional positions rather than unilateral Chinese advocacy: the *Global Initiative on Data Security* of September 2020, the *Global Development Initiative* of 2021, the *Global Security Initiative* of 2022, and the *Global AI Governance Initiative* of October 2023 (Ministry of Foreign Affairs of the People's Republic of China, 2020, 2021, 2022, 2023). These initiatives are designed to be carriable: they are vocabulary that partner states can adopt in regional declarations without committing to the full Chinese governance architecture, and they are reference points China can invoke when seeking support in UN forums. The fourth layer is the regional frameworks examined in Chapter 4. The SCO's successive iterations of the *International Code of Conduct for Information Security* (UN General Assembly, 2011, A/66/359; UN General Assembly, 2015, A/69/723) gave Chinese and Russian language on cyber sovereignty, non-interference and state authority over information flows its first multilateral institutional expression – a text developed among SCO members that was subsequently circulated as UN document A/69/723 and used as a reference point in First Committee debates (McKune, 2015; Rõigas, 2015). BRICS communiqués from the 2015 Ufa Declaration forward have consistently included digital-governance language – on data sovereignty, on UN centrality, on reform of international digital governance architecture – that tracks the Chinese normative vocabulary and that BRICS partners then carry into UN deliberations (BRICS, 2015, 2021; Belli, 2021, 2022). ASEAN-China digital cooperation, institutionalised through the ASEAN-China Information Harbor in Guangxi, the ASEAN Digital Ministers Meeting engagement track and the 2020 ASEAN-China Partnership on Digital Economy Cooperation, performs a similar function in Southeast Asia (Ministry of Foreign Affairs of the People's Republic of China, 2021).

6.2 Infrastructure Proximity and the Limits of Attribution

The relationship between Chinese digital investments and the coalition requires careful treatment. Chinese firms – Huawei, ZTE, China Telecom, Hikvision and others – have invested heavily in infrastructure across a substantial portion of the states that voted in favour of the 2019 cybercrime resolution (e.g., Egypt, Ethiopia,

Kazakhstan, Malaysia, Myanmar, Nigeria, Pakistan, Serbia, the UAE, Venezuela and Zimbabwe) or abstained (e.g., Ecuador, Saudi Arabia, Turkey and Zambia) (UN General Assembly, 2019). Two qualifications apply. First, what is sometimes called the Digital Silk Road is better understood as an aggregation of commercially driven firm-level decisions and bilaterally negotiated project agreements than as a coherent, centrally directed state strategy. Second, the overlap between infrastructure presence and pro-Chinese voting is suggestive but does not establish direct causation: many of the same states have infrastructure relationships with Western firms and multilateral institutions, and several countries with substantial Chinese infrastructure presence abstained or hedged rather than voting straightforwardly in alignment with Chinese preferences (see Chapter 3; on UN voting-pattern scholarship more generally, Flores-Macías and Kreps, 2013; Strüver, 2016; Kastner and Pearson, 2021).

What infrastructure relationships plausibly contribute is something more diffuse than conditionality. States operating Chinese-supplied telecommunications, e-government or surveillance systems work within a technical environment where Chinese governance assumptions – lawful interception interfaces, data localisation requirements, network management architectures – are practically embedded. This does not compel any particular UN vote, but it creates a context in which governance frameworks compatible with the installed technical base are more administratively natural than frameworks requiring significant technical reconfiguration. Senegal's National Data Centre, inaugurated in 2021 and built by Huawei with a USD 79 million Chinese government loan, illustrates the dynamic: government data and digital platforms previously hosted on US and European servers were repatriated to a Huawei-engineered facility in Diamniadio, and the move was framed by Senegalese officials as a step toward digital sovereignty (Nyabiage, 2021; Hawkins, 2022; Article 19, 2024b). Once the physical, software and operational layers of state digital infrastructure run on Chinese-built systems, regulatory frameworks oriented toward data localisation, state-managed cross-border transfers and security-led oversight align with the installed base, while frameworks built around free cross-border data flows and multistakeholder oversight require reconfiguration the recipient state has neither the fiscal nor the technical capacity to undertake (Gravett, 2020; Feldstein, 2020). The infrastructure relationship may lower the practical cost of governance alignment without determining it – a structural facilitation rather than a constraint. The coalition is better explained by the developmental framing examined below than by infrastructure dependency, an explanation that accounts for why the coalition includes democratic developing states with limited Chinese infrastructure exposure alongside infrastructure-integrated cases.

6.3 The Developmental Framing: Coalition-Widening through Shared Grievance, Not Necessarily Authoritarian Alignment

The 79-country majority on the 2019 cybercrime resolution included states – across sub-Saharan Africa, South and Southeast Asia, Latin America and the Middle East – whose relationship with China was too limited to be explained by infrastructure dependency or organisational pre-commitment. Reading those votes as the product of an 'authoritarian bloc' misses what is empirically observable in the developing-state record itself: a long-standing, independently articulated Global South position on digital governance that emphasises sovereignty over digital environments, intergovernmental rule-making through the UN, capacity-building, and the redress of structural exclusion from the institutions that built the existing baseline. Where Chinese-aligned positions have gained majorities, it is generally because that position overlaps with this developing-state position on substantive content – not because developing states have endorsed Chinese-style internet censorship or domestic governance practices.

The most direct evidence for this lies in what Global South states say in their own voice, in their own forums. The Group of 77 and China statement on data and cross-border data flows, delivered to the GDC informal consultations in April 2023, sets out the developing-country position without reference to Chinese diplomatic vehicles or terminology: that 'the rules cannot be unilaterally defined', that 'the United Nations needs to play a key role in advancing a more balanced global data governance', and that the existing data economy risks reducing developing countries to 'mere raw data providers to... global digital platforms' (Group of 77 and China, 2023). The 2025 G77 Ministerial Declaration goes further, reiterating 'the need to uphold the principles of digital sovereignty, equity, and the right to development in the digital era' and welcoming GDC implementation 'respecting national policies and priorities and applicable legal frameworks' (Group of 77 and China, 2025, paras. 70–71). These formulations are not borrowed from Beijing; they articulate a developmental and representational case that predates the period in which China became an active norm entrepreneur, and that is voiced collectively by 134 states whose domestic regimes range across the full political spectrum.

The independence of this position is also visible in the architecture of the negotiations themselves. The Ad Hoc Committee that produced the UN Convention against Cybercrime was chaired by Algeria and vice-chaired by Nigeria and Egypt, with a coordinated African Group present in every session and with substantive interventions on capacity-building, technical assistance and international cooperation framed in explicitly developmental terms (African Union, 2024a; UNODC, 2022a). Egypt's opening statement at the first substantive session in February 2022 framed the convention as an instrument 'for the Global South, including the African continent' and as a vehicle for international cooperation in light of the asymmetry between developing-country exposure to cybercrime losses and developing-country capacity to respond (Permanent Mission of the Arab Republic of Egypt in Vienna, 2022). The African Union's *Common African Position on the Application of International Law to the Use of Information and Communication Technologies in the Cyberspace*, adopted by the Peace and Security Council in January 2024 and endorsed by the Assembly the following month, articulates a sovereignty-grounded reading of cyber norms, insists that 'capacity-building and technical assistance must respect State sovereignty', and emphasises 'expanding international cooperation and capacity building' to 'empower and enable the full participation of developing countries in policy making forums related to the governance of cyberspace' (African Union, 2024b, paras. 32, 67). The position is African, drafted by African states, and it converges on sovereignty-grounded vocabulary because that vocabulary tracks what these states are actually arguing for – territorial protection against extraterritorial cyber operations by more capable states, control over their own digital infrastructure and a seat at the table in rules they are expected to comply with.

The credibility of the developmental framing therefore rests on a structural condition that is not of China's making: the genuine exclusion of developing states from the institutions that built the existing governance baseline. The Budapest Convention was drafted in 2001 under Council of Europe auspices with no African, Southeast Asian or Middle Eastern states in the drafting group; eventual accession did not alter the foundational design choices made without their input (Council of Europe, 2001; Gercke, 2012). ICANN operated under a Memorandum of Understanding with the US Department of Commerce from 1998 until the IANA transition of 2016, a structural dependency Global South governments consistently cited as evidence that the multistakeholder model's neutrality claims were substantively misleading (Malcolm, 2008; Mueller, 2010). The IETF and W3C have historically been dominated by engineers from North American and European technology firms, with developing-country participation structurally limited by cost, language and capacity barriers (DeNardis, 2014; Russell, 2014). The UN Secretary-General's High-Level Panel on Digital Cooperation documented this gap explicitly in 2019: developing countries were underrepresented across virtually every major internet-governance institution relative to their share of the global internet user population (UN Secretary-General's High-Level Panel on Digital Cooperation, 2019). The point is not that developing states find sovereignty-first vocabulary attractive in the abstract; it is that they encountered an existing order whose claim to neutrality their own representational experience contradicted. From inside that experience, the choice between a multistakeholder model in which they had no meaningful voice and an intergovernmental model in which they at least had a seat is not a choice between freedom and authoritarianism. It is a choice between two unequal forms of inequality, in which intergovernmental procedure offers the more legible path to representation.

That conceptual independence is observable in the behaviour of states whose support for sovereignty-first multilateral positions cannot be reduced to pro-China orientation. Several of the most consistent supporters of intergovernmental and sovereignty-grounded outcomes – Ethiopia, Pakistan, Nigeria, Saudi Arabia, India in the 2010s – have governance interests and bilateral relationships with Western states that would make ideological alignment with China costly, and several have voted against Chinese or Russian positions on other digital files (notably the Pact for the Future no-action motion, where the African Group, Mexico and most G77 states voted against the Russia-led amendment). Their support for sovereignty-grounded multilateral positions on cybercrime, data and AI governance is better explained by the developmental argument – articulated in their own forums and on their own terms – than by any general pro-China orientation (Gagliardone, 2019; Kurlantzick, 2022; Ifeanyi-Ajufo, 2024). The analytic implication for Chinese normative power is therefore precise rather than expansive. Beijing's contribution to the consolidation phase has not been to convert developing states into supporters of authoritarian governance; it has been to frame, package and procedurally sponsor an intergovernmental and sovereignty-grounded reading of digital governance whose substantive content overlaps with the developmental case that the Global South has been making, in its own voice, since the early 2000s. Chinese normative power is leveraged on, not creator of, that overlap – and the distinction matters because it explains both the reach of the framing and its limits.

6.4 Capacity-Building: Documented Programmes, Official Voices and the Limits of Attribution

Capacity-building has expanded substantially in scope and visibility during the consolidation phase, and any account of Chinese normative power has to engage with it. The empirical record, however, supports a more careful claim than the language of 'socialisation' sometimes invites: that Chinese state and firm-led capacity programmes provide concrete material benefits to recipient countries, generate sustained working relationships between Chinese practitioners and their counterparts elsewhere, and circulate a recognisable governance vocabulary in those settings. What the record does not, on its own, establish is a causal pathway from training receipt to delegation behaviour at the UN. The argument advanced here is therefore correlational and mechanism-based: there is a documented infrastructure, there is a documented vocabulary that travels through it and there are public statements by officials from recipient countries indicating how they perceive the relationship. The combination is consistent with the broader pattern this chapter has traced, but it is not a clean attribution of votes or normative outcomes to training participation.

The infrastructure itself is now substantial and well-documented at the firm level. Huawei's ICT Academy programme, established in 2013, had partnered with more than 3,500 universities in over 110 countries by 2025, training over 1.8 million students cumulatively (Huawei, 2025). The company's LEAP programme – Leadership, Employability, Advancement and Possibility – was launched in cooperation with the African Telecommunications Union and announced an expanded target of training an additional 150,000 people in sub-Saharan Africa over three years at the LEAP Summit in Shanghai in 2024 (Ventureburn, 2024). Programmes operate alongside infrastructure deployment in Senegal, Egypt, Algeria, Morocco, Ethiopia, Cameroon and elsewhere; in Senegal, the Huawei-built infrastructure has been described by local researchers as constituting the 'backbone of network infrastructure' of the state's digital administration (Niang, 2024). At the intergovernmental level, China and Zambia co-hosted the High-Level Meeting on International Cooperation on Capacity-Building of Artificial Intelligence on the margins of the 79th UN General Assembly in September 2024 and launched the *AI Capacity-Building Action Plan for Good and for All*, with high-level participation from more than eighty countries and international organisations (Ministry of Foreign Affairs of the People's Republic of China, 2024a). The ITU's Telecommunication Development Bureau has coordinated capacity-building activities in which Chinese government and firm representatives participate as instructors, alongside delivery channels associated with the World Internet Conference and bilateral programmes run through the Ministry of Commerce and Ministry of Foreign Affairs (Rolland, 2020; Hackenesch and Bader, 2020; Repnikova, 2022).

These programmes are accompanied by a public discourse, generated by officials in recipient countries themselves, in which China is framed not as an authoritarian model to emulate but as a partner whose engagement is valued for its terms – speed of delivery, willingness to invest in infrastructure others have declined to fund, and political treatment of recipient states as equals rather than as objects of conditionality. The 2024 China–Rwanda joint statement, signed at the FOCAC Beijing Summit, records that 'the Rwandan side highly appreciates and actively supports the GDI, the GSI and the GCI proposed by President Xi Jinping, which provide new opportunities for the development of the Global South and draw a new vision for international progress' (Ministry of Foreign Affairs of the People's Republic of China, 2024d). The 2025 China–Kenya joint statement, signed during President Ruto's state visit to Beijing, records that 'Kenya commends and actively supports the GSI proposed by President Xi Jinping' and reaffirms the parties' commitment 'to respecting the sovereignty and territorial integrity of all countries' and to 'abiding by the purposes and principles of the U.N' (Ministry of Foreign Affairs of the People's Republic of China, 2025). These are bilateral instruments rather than independent endorsements – joint statements are jointly drafted, and the language reflects what both sides agreed to accept – but they nonetheless place sovereignty-grounded vocabulary in the mouths of African heads of state acting in their official capacity, in the context of substantive cooperation packages on infrastructure, training and digital development rather than as ideological pronouncements.

The same vocabulary surfaces in the speeches of officials from recipient countries at multilateral negotiations on digital governance. In the OEWG on ICT security, twenty African countries participated in the 2021–2025 cycle, with Algeria, Egypt, Ghana, Kenya, Morocco, Nigeria, South Africa, Uganda and Zimbabwe most actively contributing; their interventions emphasised capacity-building, the implementation of existing GGE norms and the application of international law to cyberspace (Diplo, 2024). African states have not simply been recipients of Chinese normative content; they have been authors of overlapping content of their own, often in negotiations chaired or co-chaired by them.

6.5 The Limits of the Coalition

The first limit appeared at the very first procedural moment after the 2019 vote: of the 79 states that supported Resolution 74/247, roughly 38 – about 48 per cent – subsequently changed position on procedural and modalities decisions, abstaining or absenting themselves rather than supporting the Russian and Sino-Russian line on decision-making thresholds and civil-society participation (DiploFoundation, 2023). The second limit appeared at the most ideologically loaded substantive moment: China's false information' proposal did not survive contact with the broader negotiating membership, and Iran's attempt to remove Article 6 (the human-rights safeguard) failed to attract the broader coalition that had backed Resolution 74/247 in 2019 (Article 19, 2024a; Hakmeh and Mansour, 2024). The third limit appeared at the ratification threshold: India and Indonesia, both 2019 co-sponsors, declined to sign the Convention at Hanoi in October 2025 (Drishti IAS, 2025; Medianama, 2025). The Indian Council of World Affairs' own review of the trajectory observes that New Delhi has 'projected the need to secure supply chains, localize data, capacity building, technical support' while 'refrain[ing] from amplifying on issue of cyber sovereignty at UN' (Indian Council of World Affairs, 2024) – a posture analytically incompatible with the Sino-Russian framing the original 2019 vote was supposed to entail.

A cautious reader might point to the 2025 BRICS Leaders' Statement on the Global Governance of Artificial Intelligence (BRICS, 2025) as evidence that the coalition holds in adjacent governance domains. The text was indeed adopted unanimously by all eleven BRICS members, including India, and it contains language compatible with the Chinese vocabulary of 'digital sovereignty', 'the right to development', and AI governance 'with the United Nations at its core'. But the same text simultaneously commits to 'multistakeholder' participation, 'transparency and accountability', and 'rights-based regulation' – the precise Western-liberal vocabulary the sovereignty-first framing was supposed to displace. As one analytical review of the Rio Declaration observes, its substantive content is a 'synthesis' rather than a Chinese-vocabulary outcome (Diplomatist, 2025; Science & Diplomacy, 2025). The BRICS AI text is therefore not evidence that the coalition is cohesive on substance; it is evidence that the coalition can produce a unanimous declaration only by writing the textual ambiguity into its founding document, a move structurally identical to the 2005 Tunis Agenda's accommodation of both governance philosophies in paragraph 35. Apparent unity in such texts is the product of constructive ambiguity, not of substantive convergence.

These limits reframe the conclusion that the I3 mechanism actually supports. The mechanism is good at producing votes that initiate processes; it is much less effective at translating those votes into negotiated text that retains the substantive content most aligned with Chinese preferences. The coalition is broadest at the level of grievance (against the perceived exclusivity of Western-led frameworks) and procedural form (UN-anchored, all-state participation). It narrows sharply when specific content provisions are negotiated and narrows further when binding commitments through ratification are required. The width of Beijing's coalition at the moment of the 2019 vote was not a function of substantive normative convergence but of a successful framing operation that aligned a sovereignty-first ideological core with a much larger representational-and-developmental majority. That alignment was always conditional, and the negotiating record of 2022–25 is the trace of the coalition shedding members at each successive decision point. The I3 mechanism's limits are, on the documentary record, more substantial than the chapter's earlier sections might suggest; the consolidation phase represents a meaningful but partial institutional gain rather than a stable transfer of normative authority. The structural feature that emerges is that the coalition's breadth is conditional on the credibility of the developmental framing itself. Substantial reform of the institutions through which developing states experience the existing baseline as excluding would erode that framing and narrow the coalition toward its core of states with direct Chinese institutional and infrastructure alignments. The current breadth is partly a function of the Western governance establishment's own credibility deficit, and maintaining it depends on that deficit persisting.

7. Conclusion: Influence, Not Dominance

What the evidence supports is the attribution of Chinese normative *influence* – that is, a documented capacity to shift what is legitimate, sayable and institutionally available within UN digital-governance forums. The range of acceptable governance options has expanded across two decades to include instruments and principles that, in the early 2000s, sat closer to the margins of liberal Internet-governance debates: stronger assertions of state authority over cyber policy, security-centred justifications for digital regulation, state-conditioned cross-border cooperation on access to electronic evidence, capacity-building as a substantive treaty obligation rather than a residual category and intergovernmental rather than purely multistakeholder forum authority over data, AI and digital cooperation. Each of these elements is now present in formally adopted international instruments – the UN Convention against Cybercrime (Hanoi Convention) adopted by UNGA Resolution 79/243 on 24 December 2024 and opened for signature in Hanoi on 25 October 2025 (UNODC, 2024b); the 2021–2025 Open-Ended Working Group on ICT security and the Global Mechanism agreed in its July 2025 final report as the successor framework; and the Global Digital Compact adopted as Annex I to the Pact for the Future on 22 September 2024. What the chapter has shown is that this expansion is consistent with – and substantially traceable through – a recognisable Chinese normative core, articulated across two decades in Chinese-authored vehicles (the SCO Code of Conduct drafts of 2011 and 2015, the Global Initiative on Data Security of 2020, the Global Initiative for AI Governance of 2023, the Global Cross-Border Data Flow Cooperation Initiative of 2024) and now visible in idiomatic form within UN texts. The chapter has been careful, throughout, to treat this as documentation of *influence on the available menu of legitimate options*, not of dominance over outcomes.

What the evidence does not support is the attribution of Chinese normative *dominance*, and the chapter has tried to be explicit about the boundary. Across all major substantive dimensions examined, liberal vocabulary retains formal institutional standing in parallel with its sovereignty-grounded counterpart. The Budapest Convention remains in force with broad ratification. The 2025 OEWG final report established a single Global Mechanism, incorporating elements previously associated with the proposed Programme of Action while preserving the universal intergovernmental format. The 2024 Cybercrime Convention was adopted by consensus, but the negotiation pattern that produced it indicates contestation rather than capture: proposals from Russia, China, Iran, Egypt, Nigeria and Pakistan to include broader content-based offences were resisted by the EU, the United States, Costa Rica and others, and the final text takes an offence-specific approach focused on cyber-dependent crimes rather than adopting a general definition of cybercrime (Digital Watch Observatory, 2024; EFF, 2024). At the AHC's concluding session, several Iranian proposals to delete human rights and procedural safeguards – including Article 6(2) on the non-suppression of human rights and Article 24's conditions on surveillance powers – failed; an Iranian proposal to remove the safeguard against cooperation requests motivated by political opinion or other protected characteristics received 25 votes in favour and was defeated (EFF, 2024). The Global Digital Compact preserved the multistakeholder formula on internet governance proper, reaffirming that 'Internet governance must continue to be global and multistakeholder in nature' and reiterating the role of the Internet Governance Forum (UN General Assembly, 2024a, A/79/L.2 Annex I). At the same Summit, the Russia-led amendment that would have inserted absolutist sovereignty language under Article 2(7) of the UN Charter was blocked through a no-action motion carried by 143 votes to 7, with China supporting the motion rather than voting with the Russia-led grouping (UN Department of Global Communications, 2024, GA/12627). The liberal framework has been contested, constrained and required to coexist with a sovereignty-grounded alternative – but it has not been displaced.

The distinction between influence and dominance matters analytically because conflating the two would overstate Chinese achievement and understate the persistence of liberal vocabulary in UN digital-governance forums. It matters politically because the conditions that have enabled Chinese normative influence are domain-specific and structurally contingent rather than universal. Three conditions appear to have been jointly necessary across the cases this chapter has examined: governance questions that can be framed in sovereignty-versus-multistakeholder terms; existing Western-led institutions that carry a credible legitimacy deficit among developing states; and institutional venues – the General Assembly, the ITU, the AHC – where Chinese strategic effort can interact productively with the procedural authority of state-led decision-making. The cybercrime trajectory satisfied all three. The originating resolution, A/RES/74/247, was adopted by the General Assembly on 27 December 2019 by a recorded vote of 79 in favour to 60 against, with 33 abstentions (UN General Assembly, 2019; US Department of State, 2020); five years later the Convention it produced was adopted by consensus. The shift between those two votes is the clearest indication in the record that the legibility of sovereignty-grounded vocabulary has changed, even where the substantive content of the final instrument was significantly modified by negotiating coalitions that included many Global South states and that produced outcomes more rights-protective and more narrowly framed than the Russia-led drafting position originally advanced. The decisive coalition was not assembled by Chinese coercion, and the Global South positions documented in Section 6 are best read as developmental and representational claims voiced by their authors, not as derivative of Chinese preference. This is a problem that cannot be solved through better advocacy of the liberal model alone. It requires addressing the substantive governance concerns – representation in international institutions, protection from external digital surveillance, support for domestic regulatory capacity – that the sovereignty-first framework claims to address (Aaronson, 2019; UN Secretary-General's High-Level Panel on Digital Cooperation, 2019).

What the twenty-year record allows the chapter to establish, with the level of certainty the primary sources support, is more limited than a thesis of normative dominance and more substantial than a thesis of marginal influence. It is that the baseline against which UN digital-governance outcomes are now measured is no longer the baseline of 2005; that the menu of legitimate governance options in UN forums has demonstrably expanded to include sovereignty-grounded and intergovernmental alternatives; that this expansion is substantially traceable, through documented Chinese-authored vehicles and documented Chinese institutional engagement, to a sustained mode of revisionism from within the UN-centred order; and that this mode of engagement is empirically distinguishable both from Russian sovereignty absolutism and from the developmental-representational claims that Global South states have articulated in their own voice and on their own terms across the same period. The condition of institutionalised normative pluralism characteristic of the present moment is itself a product of these distinct inputs operating together. Disentangling them – analytically, and in any successor research – is the task that the chapter has tried to begin rather than to complete.

References

Aaronson, S. A. (2015) 'Why Trade Agreements Are Not Setting Information Free: The Lost History and Reinvigorated Debate over Cross-Border Data Flows, Human Rights, and National Security', *World Trade Review*, 14(4), pp. 671–700.

Aaronson, S. A. (2019) 'Data is Different: Why the World Needs a New Approach to Governing Cross-Border Data Flows', *Digital Policy, Regulation and Governance*, 21(5), pp. 464–476.

Ad Hoc Committee (2023) *Consolidated Negotiating Document on a Comprehensive International Convention on Countering the Use of Information and Communications Technologies for Criminal Purposes*, A/AC.291/16, January.

African Union (2024a) *Statements at the Ad Hoc Committee on the Cybercrime Convention, Sessions 2022–2024*. Addis Ababa: African Union.

African Union (2024b) *Common African Position on the Application of International Law to the Use of Information and Communication Technologies in the Cyberspace*. Addis Ababa: African Union, January.

Article 19 (2024a) *UN Cybercrime Treaty: A Threat to Free Expression*. London: Article 19.

Article 19 (2024b) *Senegal's Digital Sovereignty: Promises and Risks of the National Data Center*. London: Article 19.

Atlantic Council (2024) *The UN Cybercrime Convention Is a Flawed Instrument; The United States Should Not Sign It*. Washington, DC: Atlantic Council.

Bannelier, K. (2023) 'The "False Information" Offence in the Draft UN Cybercrime Convention: A Critical Assessment', *Journal of International Criminal Justice*, 21(4), 771–789.

Belli, L. (2021) *CyberBRICS: Cybersecurity Regulations in the BRICS Countries*. Cham: Springer.

Belli, L. (2022) 'Cyber Sovereignty in the BRICS', *Computer Law and Security Review*, 47, p. 105689.

BRICS (2015) *Ufa Declaration*, 9 July. https://brics.utoronto.ca/docs/150709-declaration-en.html

BRICS (2021) *Joint Statement on Strengthening and Reforming the Multilateral System*. BRICS Foreign Ministers Meeting. https://brics2021.gov.in/

BRICS (2025) *BRICS Leaders' Statement on the Global Governance of Artificial Intelligence*. Rio de Janeiro, 6 July.

Brown, I. and Korff, D. (2009) 'Terrorism and the Proportionality of Internet Surveillance', *European Journal of Criminology*, 6(2), pp. 119–134.

Carr, M. (2015) 'Power Plays in Global Internet Governance', *Millennium*, 43(2), pp. 640–659.

CCDCOE (2015) *Updated Draft of the Code of Conduct Distributed in the United Nations*. Tallinn: NATO Cooperative Cyber Defence Centre of Excellence.

CCDCOE (2024) *International Telecommunication Union (ITU)*. Tallinn: NATO Cooperative Cyber Defence Centre of Excellence. Available at: https://ccdcoe.org/organisations/itu/ (accessed: 4 May 2026).

Chander, A. and Lê, U. P. (2015) 'Data Nationalism', *Emory Law Journal*, 64(3), pp. 677–739.

Chatham House (2025) *The UN Cybercrime Convention: Implementation Challenges*. London: Chatham House.

Christakis, T. (2023) *Russia's War on Ukraine and the Cybercrime Negotiations*. CEPS Policy Insights.

Cihon, P., Maas, M. M. and Floridi, L. (2020) 'should Artificial Intelligence Governance Be Centralised? Design Lessons from History', *Minds and Machines*, 30, pp. 197–228.

Clough, J. (2014) 'A World of Difference: The Budapest Convention on Cybercrime and the Challenges of Harmonisation', *Monash University Law Review*, 40(3), pp. 698–736.

Connecting Africa (2025) 'African states sign UN Cybercrime Convention at Hanoi Ceremony', 27 October.

Council of Europe (2001) *Convention on Cybercrime* (ETS No. 185). Strasbourg: Council of Europe.

Creemers, R. (2016) 'Cyber China: Upgrading Propaganda, Public Opinion Work and Social Management for the Twenty-first Century', *Journal of Contemporary China*, 26(103), pp. 85–100.

Creemers, R. (2020) 'China's Conception of Cyber Sovereignty: Rhetoric and Realization', in Broeders, D. and van den Berg, B. (eds.) *Governing Cyberspace: Behavior, Power, and Diplomacy*. Lanham, MD: Rowman and Littlefield, pp. 107–142.

CSIS (2022) *How to Win at the International Telecommunication Union*. Washington, DC: Center for Strategic and International Studies.

Cyberspace Administration of China (2015) *Wuzhen Initiative on Cyberspace Sovereignty and a Community of Common Future*. Wuzhen, China.

Deibert, R. J. (2022) *Reset: Reclaiming the Internet for Civil Society*. Toronto: House of Anansi Press.

DeNardis, L. (2014) *The Global War for Internet Governance*. New Haven, CT: Yale University Press.

Digital Watch Observatory (2024) *Ad Hoc Committee on Cybercrime: Final Report*. Geneva: DiploFoundation.

Diplo (2024) *Stronger Digital Voices from Africa: African Participation in the OEWG on ICT Security*. Geneva: DiploFoundation.

DiploFoundation (2023) *Tracking UN Voting Patterns on Cybercrime*. Geneva: DiploFoundation.

DiploFoundation (2023b) *Sixth Session of the Ad Hoc Committee: Negotiating Document Analysis*. Geneva: DiploFoundation.

DiploFoundation (2024) *The UN Cybercrime Convention and African Cybercrime Capacity*. Geneva: DiploFoundation.

Diplomatist (2025) 'BRICS AI Declaration: Synthesis or Substance?', *The Diplomatist*, July.

Drake, W. J. and Wilson, E. J. (eds.) (2008) *Governing Global Electronic Networks: International Perspectives on Policy and Power*. Cambridge, MA: MIT Press.

Drishti IAS (2025) *India and the UN Cybercrime Convention*. New Delhi: Drishti IAS.
ECOSOC (2019) *Resolution 2019/19: Promoting Technical Assistance and Capacity-Building to Strengthen National Measures and International Cooperation to Combat Cybercrime*, E/RES/2019/19.
EDRi (2012) *WCIT: What Happened and What It Means for the Internet*', *EDRigram*. Brussels: European Digital Rights.
EFF (2023b) *UN Cybercrime Treaty: Russian-Led Proposals on Content-Related Offences*. San Francisco, CA: Electronic Frontier Foundation.
EFF (2023c) *Why the UN Cybercrime Treaty's "False Information" Provision Threatens Free Expression*. San Francisco, CA: Electronic Frontier Foundation.
EFF (2024) *The UN General Assembly and the Fight Against the Cybercrime Treaty*, August. San Francisco, CA: Electronic Frontier Foundation.
Eichensehr, K. E. (2015) 'The Cyber-Law of Nations', *Georgetown Law Journal*, 103, pp. 317–380.
Erie, M. S. and Streinz, T. (2021) 'The Beijing Effect: China's "Digital Silk Road" as Transnational Lawmaking', *New York University Journal of International Law and Politics*, 54(2), pp. 1–71.
FDD (2025) *The UN Cybercrime Treaty: A Trojan Horse for Suppressing Dissent*. Washington, DC: Foundation for Defense of Democracies.
Feldstein, S. (2020) *The Rise of Digital Repression: How Technology is Reshaping Power, Politics, and Resistance*. Oxford: Oxford University Press.
Flores-Macías, G. A. and Kreps, S. E. (2013) 'The Foreign Policy Consequences of Trade: China's Commercial Relations with Africa and Latin America, 1992–2006', *Journal of Politics*, 75(2), pp. 357–371.
Friedrich Naumann Foundation (2024) *The Pact for the Future and the Russian Amendment*. Berlin: Friedrich Naumann Foundation for Freedom.
Gagliardone, I. (2019) *China, Africa, and the Future of the Internet*. London: Zed Books.
Gercke, M. (2012) *Understanding Cybercrime: Phenomena, Challenges and Legal Response*. Geneva: ITU Telecommunication Development Bureau.
Global Initiative Against Transnational Organized Crime (2024) *Cyber Convention Check-in: A Brief Review of the UN Cybercrime Convention*. Geneva: GI-TOC.
Gravett, W. (2020) 'Digital Neo-Colonialism: The Chinese Model of Internet Sovereignty in Africa', *African Human Rights Law Journal*, 20(1), pp. 125–146.
Grigsby, A. (2015) 'A New UN Code of Conduct for Information Security', *Council on Foreign Relations*, 28 January.
Grigsby, A. (2017) 'The End of Cyber Norms', *Survival*, 59(6), pp. 109–122.
Grigsby, A. (2018) 'The United Nations Doubles Its Workload on Cyber Norms', *Council on Foreign Relations*, 15 November.
Gross, A. and Murgia, M. (2020) 'China and Huawei Propose Reinvention of the Internet', *Financial Times*, 27 March.
Group of 77 and China (2023) *Statement on Data and Cross-Border Data Flows*, GDC Informal Consultations, April.
Group of 77 and China (2025) *Ministerial Declaration*, paragraphs 70–71.
Hackenesch, C. and Bader, J. (2020) 'The Struggle for Minds and Influence: The Chinese Communist Party's Global Outreach', *International Studies Quarterly*, 64(3), pp. 723–733.
Hakmeh, J. (2020) *Building a Cybersecurity Norms Framework: Coalition-Building in the OEWG*. London: Chatham House.
Hakmeh, J. and Mansour, K. (2024) 'The UN Cybercrime Convention: Implications for Human Rights and Cross-Border Cooperation', *International Affairs*.
Hawkins, A. (2022) 'Senegal Opens Huawei-Built Data Centre as African Digital Sovereignty Debate Grows', *The Guardian*, 24 June.
Henriksen, A. (2019) 'The End of the Road for the UN GGE Process: The Future Regulation of Cyberspace', *Journal of Cybersecurity*, 5(1), p. tyy009.

Hoffmann, S., Lazanski, D. and Taylor, E. (2020) 'standardising the Splinternet: How China's Technical Standards Could Fragment the Internet', *Journal of Cyber Policy*, 5(2), pp. 239–264.
Hofmann, J. (2016) 'Multi-stakeholderism in Internet Governance: Putting a Fiction into Practice', *Journal of Cyber Policy*, 1(1), pp. 29–49.
Huawei (2025) *Huawei ICT Academy: Annual Report 2025*. Shenzhen: Huawei Technologies.
Huawei Technologies (2019) *New IP, Shaping Future Network: Propose to Initiate the Discussion of Strategy Transformation for ITU-T*, ITU-T TSAG TD-598.
Hulvey, R. A. (2022) *Mobilizing for Sovereignty: China's Social Strategy to Write New Rules of the Game in Cyberspace*. IGCC Working Paper No. 2. La Jolla, CA: UC Institute on Global Conflict and Cooperation.
Human Rights Watch (2024) *UN Cybercrime Treaty: Concluding Session Outcomes*. New York, NY: Human Rights Watch.
ICANN (2016) *Stewardship Transition Coordination*. Los Angeles, CA: ICANN.
ICANN (2020) *ICANN Comments on ITU-T New IP Proposal*. Los Angeles, CA: ICANN.
IETF (2020) *Liaison Statement to ITU-T TSAG on the New IP Proposal*, 31 March. Internet Engineering Task Force.
Ifeanyi-Ajufo, N. (2024) 'African Agency in Global Cyber Governance', *Journal of Cyber Policy*, 9(1), pp. 1–21.
IISD (2024) 'summit of the Future: Russian Amendment Defeated', *Earth Negotiations Bulletin*, 22 September. International Institute for Sustainable Development.
IMPACT (2009) *IMPACT Global Headquarters Inauguration*, Cyberjaya, 20 May.
Indian Council of World Affairs (2024) *India and the UN Cybercrime Convention: A Critical Assessment*. New Delhi: ICWA.
Internet Governance Project (2012) 'ITU Phobia: Why WCIT Was Derailed', 18 December.
Internet Society (2020) *Discussion Paper: An Analysis of the "New IP" Proposal to the ITU-T*. Reston, VA: Internet Society.
Internet Society (2022) *Huawei's "New IP" Proposal: Frequently Asked Questions*. Reston, VA: Internet Society.
ITU (2007) *Global Cybersecurity Agenda (GCA): A Framework for International Cooperation in Cybersecurity*. Geneva: International Telecommunication Union.
ITU (2012) *Final Acts of the World Conference on International Telecommunications, Dubai 2012*. Geneva: International Telecommunication Union.
ITU (2014) *ITU Plenipotentiary Conference Elects Houlin Zhao as Next Secretary-General*, Press Release, 23 October. Geneva: International Telecommunication Union.
ITU-T TSAG (2019) *New IP, Shaping Future Network: Propose to Initiate the Discussion of Strategy Transformation for ITU-T*, TSAG-C83, September.
Jørgensen, R. F. (ed.) (2013) *Human Rights in the Global Information Society*. Cambridge, MA: MIT Press.
Kastner, S. L. and Pearson, M. M. (2021) 'Exploring the Parameters of China's Economic Influence', *Studies in Comparative International Development*, 56(1), pp. 18–44.
Kaye, D. (2015) *Report of the Special Rapporteur on the Promotion and Protection of the Right to Freedom of Opinion and Expression*, A/HRC/29/32. Geneva: UN Human Rights Council.
Kerr, O. S. (2014) 'The Next Generation Communications Privacy Act', *University of Pennsylvania Law Review*, 162, pp. 373–419.
Kleinwächter, W. (2004) 'WSIS: A New Diplomacy? Multi-Stakeholder Approach and Bottom Up Policy in Global Internet Governance', *Information Technologies and International Development*, 1(3–4), pp. 1–13.
Kleinwächter, W. (2007) 'The History of Internet Governance', in OSCE (ed.) *Governing the Internet: Freedom and Regulation in the OSCE Region*. Vienna: OSCE, pp. 41–64.
Korzak, E. (2017) 'UN GGE on Cybersecurity: The End of an Era?', *The Diplomat*, 31 July.
Korzak, E. (2021) 'The UN Cybersecurity Negotiations: Russia, Sovereignty, and the OEWG', *Cyber Defense Review*, 6(2).

Kurlantzick, J. (2022) *Beijing's Global Media Offensive*. Oxford: Oxford University Press.
La Rue, F. (2011) *Report of the Special Rapporteur on the Promotion and Protection of the Right to Freedom of Opinion and Expression*, A/HRC/17/27. Geneva: UN Human Rights Council.
Land, M. (2013) 'Toward an International Law of the Internet', *Harvard International Law Journal*, 54(2), pp. 393–458.
MacLean, D. (2004) 'Herding Schrödinger's Cats: Some Conceptual Tools for Thinking about Internet Governance', in MacLean, D. (ed.) *Internet Governance: A Grand Collaboration*. New York, NY: UN ICT Task Force, pp. 73–99.
Malcolm, J. (2008) *Multi-stakeholder Governance and the Internet Governance Forum*. Perth: Terminus Press.
Markoff, M. (2017) 'Explanation of Position at the Conclusion of the 2016–2017 UN GGE', US Department of State, 23 June.
Mattli, W. and Büthe, T. (2003) 'setting International Standards: Technological Rationality or Primacy of Power?', *World Politics*, 56(1), pp. 1–42.
McKune, S. (2015) *An Analysis of the International Code of Conduct for Information Security, Citizen Lab Research Brief*, September. Toronto: Citizen Lab.
Medianama (2025) 'India Declines to Sign UN Cybercrime Convention at Hanoi', 27 October. https://www.medianama.com/2025/10/223-72-nations-un-first-cybercrime-treaty-india-abstains-privacy/
Meyer, P. (2020) 'Norms of Responsible State Behaviour in Cyberspace', in Christen, M., Gordijn, B. and Loi, M. (eds.) *The Ethics of Cybersecurity*. Cham: Springer, pp. 347–360.
Ministry of Foreign Affairs and Cyberspace Administration of China (2017) *International Strategy of Cooperation on Cyberspace*, 1 March.
Ministry of Foreign Affairs of the People's Republic of China (2020) *Global Initiative on Data Security*, 8 September.
Ministry of Foreign Affairs of the People's Republic of China (2021) *Global Development Initiative*.
Ministry of Foreign Affairs of the People's Republic of China (2022) *Global Security Initiative Concept Paper*.
Ministry of Foreign Affairs of the People's Republic of China (2023) *Global AI Governance Initiative*, 18 October.
Ministry of Foreign Affairs of the People's Republic of China (2024a) *Wang Yi Speech at Summit of the Future*, 23 September.
Ministry of Foreign Affairs of the People's Republic of China (2024b) *Lin Jian Press Conference Remarks on the Global Digital Compact*, 24 September.
Ministry of Foreign Affairs of the People's Republic of China (2024c) *Global Cross-Border Data Flow Cooperation Initiative*. Presented at World Internet Conference Wuzhen Summit, November.
Ministry of Foreign Affairs of the People's Republic of China (2024d) *China–Rwanda Joint Statement*, FOCAC Beijing Summit, 5 September.
Ministry of Foreign Affairs of the People's Republic of China (2025) *China–Kenya Joint Statement*, April.
Morrell, T. (2025) 'Negotiating the Global Digital Compact: A Process Analysis', *Global Policy*.
Mueller, M. L. (2010) *Networks and States: The Global Politics of Internet Governance*. Cambridge, MA: MIT Press.
Mueller, M. L. (2012) 'ITU Phobia: Why WCIT was Derailed', *Internet Governance Project*, 18 December.
Negro, G. (2020) 'A History of Chinese Global Internet Governance and Its Relations with ITU and ICANN', *Chinese Journal of Communication*, 13(1), pp. 104–121.
Netanel, N. W. (2000) 'Cyberspace Self-Governance: A Skeptical View from Liberal Democratic Theory', *California Law Review*, 88(2), pp. 395–498.

Niang, I. (2025), 'Chinese Huawei Group and the Building of Senegalese Digital Grammar from 2006 to 2024,' U.S.–China Dialogue on Global Issues, Georgetown University, 20 October 2025.

NTIA (1998) *Statement of Policy on the Management of Internet Names and Addresses*, 5 June.

Nyabiage, J. (2021) 'senegal Launches Chinese-Funded Data Centre as African States Embrace Digital Sovereignty', *South China Morning Post*, 25 June.

OpenGlobalRights (2024) 'The UN Cybercrime Convention Is on Pause for Now – But Its Threat to Human Rights Remains'. https://www.openglobalrights.org/un-cybercrime-convention-pause-threat-human-rights-remains/

Pavlova, P. (2025) 'The UN Cybercrime Convention: Negotiations and Outcomes', *International Affairs*.

Permanent Mission of the Arab Republic of Egypt in Vienna (2022) *Statement at the First Substantive Session of the Ad Hoc Committee on Cybercrime*, February.

Qiushi (2016) 'Xi Jinping's Strategic Thought on Network Power'. http://www.qstheory.cn/

Raymond, M. and DeNardis, L. (2015) 'Multistakeholderism: Anatomy of an Inchoate Global Institution', *International Theory*, 7(3), pp. 572–616.

Repnikova, M. (2022) *Chinese Soft Power*. Cambridge: Cambridge University Press.

RIPE NCC (2020) *RIPE NCC Position on the New IP Proposal*. Amsterdam: RIPE NCC.

Rodríguez, M. (2017) 'Cuba's Position on the 2016–2017 UN GGE Report', Permanent Mission of Cuba to the United Nations.

Rolland, N. (2020) *China's Vision for a New World Order*, NBR Special Report 83. Seattle: National Bureau of Asian Research.

Russell, A. L. (2014) *Open Standards and the Digital Age: History, Ideology, and Networks*. Cambridge: Cambridge University Press.

Rõigas, H. (2015) 'An Updated Draft of the Code of Conduct Distributed in the United Nations', *NATO CCDCOE Incyder Article*.

Schmitt, M. N. and Vihul, L. (eds.) (2017) *Tallinn Manual 2.0 on the International Law Applicable to Cyber Operations*. Cambridge: Cambridge University Press.

Schmitt, C. (2017) *Political Theology: Four Chapters on the Concept of Sovereignty*. Chicago, IL: University of Chicago Press.

Science and Diplomacy (2025) 'BRICS and AI Governance: A Synthesis Document', September.

SCO (2014) *Dushanbe Declaration of Heads of SCO Member States*, September.

Segal, A. (2020) *China's Vision for Cyber Sovereignty and the Global Governance of Cyberspace*. Washington, DC: National Bureau of Asian Research.

Sharp, R. and Kolkman, O. (2020) *The New IP Proposal: A Technical Analysis*. Internet Society Working Paper.

State Council Information Office of the People's Republic of China (2010) *The Internet in China*, June.

Stimson Center (2024) *The International Telecommunications Union (ITU) and Cyber Accountability*. Washington, DC: Stimson Center.

Strüver, G. (2016) 'What Friends Are Made Of: Bilateral Linkages and Domestic Drivers of Foreign Policy Alignment with China', *Foreign Policy Analysis*, 12(2), pp. 170–191.

Sukumar, A. and Basu, A. (2024) 'India and the UN Cybercrime Convention', *India in Global Affairs*.

Telefónica (2012) *WCIT 2012: A Digital Divide Instead of a Digital Dividend*. Madrid: Telefónica.

Thumfart, J. (2024) *Power and Authority in Internet Governance: Return of the State?* London: Routledge.

Tikk, E. and Kerttunen, M. (2017) *The Alleged Demise of the UN GGE: An Autopsy and Eulogy*. Geneva: ICT4Peace Foundation.

Triolo, P. (2018) 'China's World Internet Conference: A Stage for Cyber Sovereignty', *DigiChina*, Stanford University.

Tunis Agenda (2005) *Tunis Agenda for the Information Society*, WSIS-05/TUNIS/DOC/6(Rev. 1)-E, 18 November.

UN Department of Global Communications (2024) *Press Release GA/12627: General Assembly Adopts Pact for the Future, Including Global Digital Compact*, 22 September.

UN First Committee (2011) *Statement of China's Ambassador for Disarmament Affairs Wang Qun on the International Code of Conduct for Information Security*, 20 October.

UN General Assembly (2001) *Resolution 56/183: World Summit on the Information Society*, A/RES/56/183, 21 December.

UN General Assembly (2011) *International Code of Conduct for Information Security*, A/66/359, 12 September.

UN General Assembly (2015) *International Code of Conduct for Information Security*, A/69/723, 13 January.

UN General Assembly (2018a) *Resolution 73/27: Developments in the Field of Information and Telecommunications in the Context of International Security*, A/RES/73/27, 5 December.

UN General Assembly (2018b) *Resolution 73/266: Advancing Responsible State Behaviour in Cyberspace*, A/RES/73/266, 22 December.

UN General Assembly (2019) *Resolution 74/247: Countering the Use of Information and Communications Technologies for Criminal Purposes*, A/RES/74/247, 27 December.

UN General Assembly (2021) *Final Substantive Report of the Open-Ended Working Group on Developments in the Field of Information and Telecommunications in the Context of International Security*, A/75/816, 18 March.

UN General Assembly (2024a) *Pact for the Future, Global Digital Compact and Declaration on Future Generations*, A/79/L.2, 22 September.

UN General Assembly (2024c) *Resolution 79/243: United Nations Convention against Cybercrime*, A/RES/79/243, 24 December.

UN General Assembly (2024d) *Russian Federation Amendment to the Pact for the Future*, A/79/L.3, 22 September.

UN GGE (2013) *Report of the Group of Governmental Experts on Developments in the Field of Information and Telecommunications in the Context of International Security*, A/68/98, 24 June.

UN GGE (2015) *Report of the Group of Governmental Experts on Developments in the Field of Information and Telecommunications in the Context of International Security*, A/70/174, 22 July.

UN HRC (2012) *Resolution 20/8: The Promotion, Protection and Enjoyment of Human Rights on the Internet*, A/HRC/RES/20/8, 16 July.

United Nations General Assembly. 1966. International Covenant on Civil and Political Rights. Adopted 16 December 1966, entered into force 23 March 1976. United Nations, Treaty Series, vol. 999, p. 171. Office of the United Nations High Commissioner for Human Rights. https://www.ohchr.org/en/instruments-mechanisms/instruments/international-covenant-civil-and-political-rights.

UN Office for Digital and Emerging Technologies (2024) *Global Digital Compact: Co-facilitators' Background Note*. New York: United Nations.

UN Office on Drugs and Crime (UNODC) (2022a) *First Substantive Session of the Ad Hoc Committee*. Vienna: UNODC.

UN Office on Drugs and Crime (UNODC) (2024a) *Member States Finalize a New Cybercrime Convention*, Press Release, 9 August.

UN Office on Drugs and Crime (UNODC) (2024b) *UN General Assembly Adopts Landmark Convention on Cybercrime*, Press Release, 24 December.

UN Office on Drugs and Crime (UNODC) (2025) *UN Convention against Cybercrime Opens for Signature in Hanoi*, Press Release, 26 October.

UN Secretary-General (2004) *Letter on the Establishment of the Working Group on Internet Governance*, A/59/580, 18 November.

UN Secretary-General's High-Level Panel on Digital Cooperation (2019) *The Age of Digital Interdependence*. New York, NY: United Nations.

UN Treaty Collection (2026) *Status of the United Nations Convention against Cybercrime*. New York, NY: UN Office of Legal Affairs.

UNCTAD (2018) *Final Report of the Working Group on Enhanced Cooperation*. Geneva: UNCTAD.

US Department of State (2020) *Voting Practices in the United Nations 2019: Report to Congress*. Washington, DC: US Department of State.

USUN (2024) *Explanation of Position of the United States on the Adoption of the Resolution on the UN Convention against Cybercrime*. New York, NY: US Mission to the United Nations.

Ventureburn (2024) 'Huawei LEAP Programme: 150,000 New Skills Targets in Sub-Saharan Africa', September.

Walden, I. (2007) *Computer Crimes and Digital Investigations*. Oxford: Oxford University Press.

Walker, A. (2024) 'The UN Cybercrime Convention: Why Western States Allowed Consensus Adoption', *Just Security*.

WGIG (2005) *Report of the Working Group on Internet Governance*, Château de Bossey, July.

Xi, J. (2015) *Remarks at the Opening Ceremony of the Second World Internet Conference*, Wuzhen, 16 December.

Zhang, E. S. and Creemers, R. (2024) Towards a UN-Centric Cybercrime Treaty: Chinese Positions and Interests at the UN Ad Hoc Committee for a Cybercrime Convention. Leiden: LeidenAsiaCentre. https://leidenasiacentre.nl/wp-content/uploads/2025/12/24-02-01-Towards-a-UN-Centric-Cybercrime-Treaty.pdf

Conclusion

After the Patchwork – AI and the Next Layer of Contested Cyberspace

A book that maps a moving target finishes in an awkward position. The empirical record assembled across the preceding chapters – eight bilateral cases, three regional institutional contexts, and roughly two decades of UN-level documentation – describes a configuration of global digital governance that was already shifting as the analysis was being written, and that appears to be shifting more rapidly now than at any point during the period the book examines. The push–pull, multi-level mechanism framework was developed to capture the dynamics through which Chinese normative preferences travel, are filtered through recipient agency, and combine with other inputs to produce hybrid governance outcomes. It has, I hope, done useful analytical work across the cybersecurity, data governance and platform-regulation domains where the book's evidentiary base is densest. But the framework is a description of a moment, and not a forecast of where the moment is going. This conclusion is concerned less with what the book has shown than with what its argument leaves us prepared, and unprepared, to see in the period ahead.

The patchwork the introduction announced and the chapters traced is best understood not as a steady state but as a transitional configuration whose continuation depends on conditions that may not hold. The institutional balance documented at the international level in Chapter 5 – liberal vocabulary surviving in formal architecture alongside a sovereignty-first alternative that has acquired durable institutional standing through the OEWG–GGE dual-track settlement, the 2024 Cybercrime Convention and the Global Digital Compact – was assembled against a particular technological backdrop: a digital order in which the principal objects of regulation were data flows, communications infrastructure and platform conduct. That backdrop is no longer the only one, and may not even be the dominant one, by the time the contests this book has tracked reach their next institutional decision points. The implementation of the 2025 WSIS+20 outcome, the ratification and implementation trajectory of the UN Convention against Cybercrime, and the follow-up mechanisms established under the Global Digital Compact will all unfold in an environment that artificial intelligence is already restructuring.

1. AI as Continuation, or as Break

It is tempting, and partially defensible, to read AI governance as a continuation of the contests Chapter 5 documented. Many of the same actors are at the table;

DOI: 10.4324/9781042023738-7

many of the same institutional venues are in use; many of the same vocabularies are in circulation. China's Global AI Governance Initiative of 2023 carries familiar sovereignty- and development-oriented themes into the AI domain: it affirms states' right to develop and govern AI in accordance with their national conditions, criticises technological monopolies and exclusive blocs, and emphasises developing countries' representation and access to AI capabilities (Roberts et al., 2021; Hine and Floridi, 2023). The UN-level pattern is recognisable. The Chinese-initiated capacity-building resolution A/RES/78/311, adopted without a vote on 1 July 2024 after attracting broad developing-country sponsorship, carried into the AI domain a familiar emphasis on capacity disparities, development, and the risk that poorer states would be left behind. The earlier US-led resolution A/RES/78/265 emphasised safe, secure and trustworthy AI, human rights, inclusion, and sustainable development. Their coexistence reflects differentiated emphases within an overlapping consensus rather than two fully opposed tracks. The 2025 General Assembly resolution A/RES/79/325, which established the Independent International Scientific Panel on AI and the Global Dialogue on AI Governance, added a differentiated institutional architecture based on complementary scientific and intergovernmental functions, rather than reproducing the politically contested dual-track structure found in cybersecurity governance.

There are reasons, however, to suspect that AI governance will not simply continue the patterns the book has traced (Tallberg et al., 2023; Schmitt, 2022). Three sources of likely discontinuity deserve mention, each of them tentative and each of them subject to revision as the empirical record fills in.

The first is technical. AI systems are not, in the legal sense, reducible to data flows. They are composed of training corpora, model weights, fine-tuning artefacts and deployment pipelines whose movement between jurisdictions is governed by principles that data-protection regimes were not designed to handle (Smuha, 2021). Cross-border data-transfer rules — — – identified in the regional analysis as a principal terrain on which Chinese-aligned and GDPR-aligned templates compete — apply most clearly to personal data contained in training and deployment pipelines. Their application to model weights is less settled and may depend on whether personal information can reasonably be extracted, inferred, or reconstructed from the model. The EU AI Act gives parts of its regulatory framework extraterritorial reach, recalling the jurisdictional ambition of the GDPR while applying it to different regulated actors, risks, and governance objects. Its long-run consequences for non-European jurisdictions remain underspecified (Veale and Zuiderveen Borgesius, 2021). Where governance objects shift, the mechanisms through which influence travels may shift with them.

The second source of likely discontinuity is infrastructural. The compute layer on which frontier AI depends is concentrated at several critical chokepoints, particularly advanced-semiconductor fabrication, accelerator design, hyperscale cloud provision, and large computing clusters (Crawford, 2021; Sastry et al., 2024). These dependencies are not identical to those of the network layer examined in this book and are increasingly shaped by export controls that have restructured trade in advanced chips and related equipment. Chapter 3 traced how Chinese vendors' provision of network and cybersecurity infrastructure in the 2010s – most clearly in the 4G build-out in Vietnam – translated equipment supply into governance influence without requiring explicit doctrinal alignment from the recipient state. The September 2024 Egyptian MOUs noted in that chapter — — – including proposed cooperation involving an Arabic-language large language model and chip-design research — — – suggest the possible emergence of a broader Chinese AI cooperation package. Because these were framework agreements rather than evidence of completed implementation, they should be treated as indicators of ambition rather than established infrastructure effects. Whether such bundling produces governance influence comparable to what the 4G build-out appears to have produced for Vietnam is a question this book cannot resolve, but it seems the right question to ask. The dual-use considerations that have shaped the literature on military AI (Maas, 2019; Kania, 2019) are likely to feature prominently in how compute-layer access is negotiated, with implications that cut across the political alignments organising the cybersecurity contests of the previous decade.

The third source of likely discontinuity is what might be called the cognitive turn. The contests the book has documented have concerned, principally, the movement and storage of information. AI governance contests are increasingly concerned with the production of information, with the alignment of generative systems to particular conceptions of acceptable output, and with the cultural and political assumptions encoded in training data (Webster et al., 2017; Hine and Floridi, 2023). Sovereignty-first frames adapt to this terrain with what may turn out to be uncomfortable ease: the same vocabulary that authorises state authority over data flows can be extended, with relatively minor adjustment, to authorise state authority over the model behaviours that produce content. China's administrative framework — — – including the algorithm-recommendation and deep-synthesis rules, the 2023 Interim Measures for Generative AI Services, filing mechanisms for algorithms and generative-AI services, and the AI-generated-content labelling measures effective from September 2025 — — – provides a comparatively developed regulatory repertoire. Other governments may selectively borrow from that repertoire, although evidence of direct emulation remains limited (Sheehan, 2023).

There is a further point worth mentioning, which the AI literature has begun to articulate but which the international relations literature on cyberspace governance has been slower to absorb. The cross-border externalities of frontier AI systems may be larger than the externalities of the data and platform-governance objects whose contestation Chapter 5 traced. A frontier model trained in one jurisdiction may be deployed across many others, directly or through cloud-based interfaces, open-weight releases, licensing arrangements, or downstream applications. The harms it may produce — — – from synthetic-media manipulation to autonomous decision-making in critical infrastructure — — – are not necessarily contained by the regulatory architecture of the training jurisdiction. (Tallberg et al., 2023; Truby, 2020). This may, paradoxically, generate stronger pressures toward substantive international coordination than any of the cybersecurity domains the book has examined, and it may do so along axes that cut across the political alignments organising the existing contests. The bilateral US–China consultations on AI risk initiated in 2024 provide preliminary evidence that shared concerns about advanced systems can produce limited functional engagement even amid broader strategic competition. They do not yet establish a durable coalition, but they suggest that AI governance may generate forms of engagement that the existing patchwork does not fully predict.

2. Three Possible Trajectories

This book does not try to predict the future. It is, however, possible to specify the conditions under which different trajectories would obtain, and to suggest, with appropriate caution, which seem more plausible at the present writing. Three trajectories deserve articulation, and the most likely near-term picture is probably some combination of all of them.

A first trajectory – consolidation – would see the structural logic of digital sovereignty extend from the data layer to the model and compute layers, with the regional and multilateral institutions documented in Chapters 4 and 5 carrying the same vocabulary across the new domain. On this trajectory, the standards processes for AI in the ITU, ISO/IEC and IEEE would yield technical baselines compatible with the sovereignty-first architecture; recipient states with existing Chinese-aligned cybersecurity frameworks would adopt complementary AI governance frameworks; and the institutional ceiling that has so far appeared to constrain Chinese normative dominance would weaken as Western counter-mobilisation, distracted by domestic AI policy contests, struggled to maintain the multi-mechanism counter-pressure observed in Chapter 5. The conditions for this trajectory are not absent: Chinese push capacity in AI standards is substantial (Sheehan, 2023; Webster et al., 2017), and the receptive ground in much of the developing world is broadly the same ground that supported the 2019 cybercrime resolution and that produced the supportive coalition behind A/RES/78/311 on AI capacity-building. The trajectory is not, however, the most probable. AI governance may multiply entry points for competing firms, standards organisations, scientific bodies, regulators, and technical communities, making uniform normative consolidation more difficult. The architecture established by A/RES/79/325 ——– with the Independent International Scientific Panel on AI and the Global Dialogue operating through complementary functions ——– also distributes governance activity across more than one institutional mechanism.

A second trajectory – refraction – would see AI governance break the alignments documented in this book and produce new coalitions that do not map onto the existing patchwork. The European Union's AI Act, with its extraterritorial reach modelled on the GDPR, may exercise a Brussels-style effect that constrains Chinese influence in domains where data governance contests have produced hybridity (Veale and Zuiderveen Borgesius, 2021; Bradford, 2023). The US export control regime on advanced semiconductors and the associated diplomacy with allied producers may consolidate a compute-layer bloc whose membership cuts across the cybersecurity governance camps (Heim et al., 2024). Indian, Brazilian and Indonesian AI sovereignty discourse may yield frameworks that draw selectively from Chinese, European and American templates without resolving cleanly into any of them, extending into the AI domain the hybrid pattern the book documented for these countries in cybersecurity. Proposals for a BRICS AI study mechanism and Chinese initiatives for a China–BRICS AI cooperation platform signal an ambition to extend South–South technology cooperation into the AI domain, although their institutional status and practical scope remain emergent. The heterogeneity of AI-governance preferences within BRICS — — – including differences between India's development-and-inclusion framing and Chinese formulations — — – suggests that these initiatives are more likely to produce overlapping coalitions than a unified bloc. On this trajectory, the very terms of the contest would shift: what currently reads as 'Chinese-aligned versus liberal' would be reorganised around new dimensions, with new actors moving toward the centre and older dichotomies losing some of their explanatory traction (Roberts et al., 2021).

A third trajectory – saturation – would see governance capacity simply fail to keep pace with technical change, leaving the patchwork to thicken rather than to resolve. The implementation of the Cybercrime Convention, the 2025 WSIS+20 outcome, and the Global Digital Compact may yield governance instruments that remain addressed primarily to an earlier configuration of the digital order. Standards processes for next-generation network protocols, post-quantum cryptography and synthetic media authentication may settle technical baselines on timelines disconnected from the political processes that, in earlier decades, would have aligned the two. The result would not be Chinese dominance, nor liberal restoration, but a sustained mismatch between governance instruments and the systems they are intended to govern – a condition that would tend to advantage actors with the capacity to act across jurisdictional boundaries, whether those are large firms or state agencies with substantial extraterritorial reach, at the expense of actors operating within them.

These trajectories are not mutually exclusive, and the most plausible near-term picture probably combines elements of all three: refraction in domains where the EU's regulatory leverage and the US compute-layer architecture exercise effective counter-mobilisation, consolidation in domains and regions where the receptive ground has not changed and saturation in the technical layers where the pace of change exceeds the cycle time of multilateral negotiation. Mapping which combination obtains in which domain is the work a successor study would need to undertake, and the framework developed in this book is, I believe, transferable to that work – provided its mechanism categories are extended to register the specificities of the AI domain (training-data sourcing, compute access, model weights and licensing, content-generation governance) rather than imposed wholesale on a domain whose materiality differs from the data-flow domain in which they were originally developed.

While AI is the most legible of the next-layer governance contests, it is not the only one. There are at least three further layers of cyberspace in motion at the time of writing, each of them carrying governance implications that the existing institutional architecture is not well equipped to manage.

Post-quantum cryptography is the most technically mature and the least politically discussed. The standards processes through which quantum-resistant primitives are being selected – within NIST in the United States, in the relevant ITU-T and ISO/IEC working groups and in the related Chinese, European and Russian processes that may or may not converge with them – will set the cryptographic baseline on which the next several decades of digital infrastructure depend. The selection of those primitives is being made under conditions in which the assumptions of the 1990s and 2000s, when global cryptographic standards consolidated around a small number of widely shared algorithms, no longer obviously hold. Divergent national requirements, implementation profiles, certification regimes, or migration timelines in post-quantum cryptography could fragment interoperability and raise switching costs, even where the underlying algorithms remain technically compatible.

Spatial and immersive computing constitutes another emerging layer, more uncertain in its institutional contours but increasingly visible in policy attention. The governance questions that arise around persistent virtual environments – identity verification, conduct standards, jurisdictional reach over actions taken in shared synthetic spaces, the data infrastructures that underpin them – do not map cleanly onto either the platform regulation literature or the cybersecurity literature. The relational dynamics this book has tried to specify can be expected to operate in this layer too, but the specific instruments through which they will travel are not yet legible enough to model with any confidence.

Another layer is synthetic media and content. Here is where the cognitive turn discussed above is most acute. The institutional architecture for content authentication, deepfake disclosure and the legal status of AI-generated material is being built simultaneously across multiple jurisdictions and multiple standards bodies, and the templates that emerge from each of these processes are likely to encode different assumptions about the proper relationship between users, platforms, and the state. China's mandatory AI-content labelling regime, the EU AI Act's transparency provisions, evolving US federal and state-level approaches, and industry-led provenance initiatives such as C2PA are not currently organised within a common governance framework, and there is no obvious institutional venue in which they would be coordinated even if the political will to do so existed. The patchwork at the content layer may, accordingly, be denser than at any layer the book has so far examined.

3. Possible Implications

A few orientations follow from the foregoing, each tentative and each subject to revision as the contests now underway resolve.

For the scholarly literature, the principal implication is that the analytical infrastructure built up around digital authoritarianism and the export of Chinese governance models is approaching the limits of its usefulness. The framework developed in this book has tried to do justice to the relational and hybridised character of the patterns it traces; the next generation of work in this field will need to go further, examining how the AI-era expansion of governance objects – compute, models, training data, generated content – interacts with the institutional architectures Chapter 5 mapped (Tallberg et al., 2023; Schmitt, 2022). The case-study method that produced the bilateral analysis here remains valuable, but its evidentiary base will need to expand to include the procurement decisions, model licensing arrangements and standards-body voting records that the AI-era contest is generating in real time. There is also a methodological question about the unit of analysis: where the cybersecurity domain made the state a defensible primary unit, the AI domain may require that firms, standards consortia, and technical communities be elevated from background condition to object of study in their own right (DeNardis, 2014; Mueller, 2020; Crawford, 2021).

For policy practitioners, the implications are harder to specify, because they depend on which trajectory obtains. Under conditions of consolidation, the priority would be sustaining the institutional ceiling that has so far appeared to constrain Chinese normative dominance, which would require sustained Western counter-mobilisation in the AI standards venues, alongside the substantive reforms in multilateral institutions that the book has argued are the precondition for credible engagement with Global South governance demands. Under conditions of refraction, the work would shift toward managing new alignments productively rather than forcing them into the existing camps; the dual-track patterns exhibited by India, Brazil, Indonesia and South Africa offer a template that other middle powers may find usable, and that the international system may need to learn to accommodate rather than to discipline. Under conditions of saturation, the priority would shift again, toward developing governance instruments capable of operating at the speed of technical change, which may require institutional designs the existing multilateral system is not well placed to produce.

For recipient states, the considerations developed in Chapter 4 retain much of their force in the AI domain, with one addition. The capacity required for selective adaptation in AI governance appears more demanding than in data governance, because the technical specifications matter more, the implementation details are denser and the speed at which the underlying systems change is faster. States that lacked the capacity for selective adaptation in cybersecurity governance are unlikely to acquire it in AI governance through the same routes. The question of how external partners might support the requisite capacity-building, without bundling the support to the adoption of particular templates, is one this book has identified but cannot resolve.

4. The Patchwork's Afterlife

If the patchwork internet is the present condition, what comes after the patchwork is probably not a different condition but the same one with new objects in it. The relational push–pull dynamics this book has tried to specify can be expected to continue to operate, because the conditions that produce them – heterogeneous state preferences, asymmetric capacities for normative entrepreneurship, multiple institutional venues with overlapping jurisdictions and recipient agency that varies with domestic political economy – appear to be structural features of the present international system rather than transient features of the cybersecurity domain. What changes is the substance: new technologies, new governance objects, new instruments and the new fault-lines those instruments will produce. Whether the institutional pluralism the book has documented consolidates into a stable settlement, breaks apart under the pressures the AI era will exert, or persists in a more textured form across additional governance layers, is a question whose answer is being decided in venues whose deliberations are not yet fully visible.

The book has tried to map the terrain as it has been. It would be a mistake to read the map as a forecast. The patterns documented here describe one configuration in a longer sequence whose next configuration is being assembled now – in compute clusters, in model registries, in standards committees and in the negotiations that will set the terms under which the next generation of digital infrastructure is built and the next generation of digital governance is contested. The framework developed here is, I hope, transferable to that work. The conclusions reached are not. What the analysis can offer, in the end, is a cautious heuristic: that whatever the next layer of cyberspace looks like, it is unlikely to be governed by a single power, and unlikely to settle into a single architecture; that the actors who will matter are more various than the dominant framings suggest; and that the work of understanding what is happening, and of acting on that understanding with appropriate humility, has only become more urgent as the scope of what is being governed has widened.

The export of digital authoritarianism remains the wrong frame. The clash of civilisations remains the wrong frame. The end of the open internet remains the wrong frame. What is happening looks, on the evidence assembled here and on the evidence likely to accumulate in the years immediately ahead, more prosaic, more contested and ultimately more open than any of these formulations allows. The patchwork is not the failure of a more coherent order; it is the order. Understanding it on those terms – as the working condition of an interactively produced, multipolar normative environment whose objects are now expanding from data into models, from networks into compute and from infrastructure into the cognitive and content layers downstream of it – is the precondition for any policy or scholarly engagement that hopes to make sense of where digital governance goes next. The question is not who wins. The question is what kind of digital order the joint product of so many distributed efforts will sustain, and whether the principles embedded in that order can be made strong enough to address the challenges that gave rise to the contest in the first place. The book has tried to map the terrain. The work of building shared principles strong enough to govern what comes next remains.

References

Bradford, A. (2023) *Digital Empires: The Global Battle to Regulate Technology*. Oxford: Oxford University Press.

Crawford, K. (2021) *Atlas of AI: Power, Politics, and the Planetary Costs of Artificial Intelligence*. New Haven: Yale University Press.

DeNardis, L. (2014) *The Global War for Internet Governance*. New Haven: Yale University Press.
Hine, E. and Floridi, L. (2023) 'Artificial Intelligence with American Values and Chinese Characteristics: A Comparative Analysis of American and Chinese Governmental AI Policies', *AI and Society*, advance online publication.
Kania, E. B. (2019) 'Chinese Military Innovation in the AI Revolution', *The RUSI Journal*, 164(5–6), pp. 26–34.
Maas, M. M. (2019) 'How Viable Is International Arms Control for Military Artificial Intelligence? Three Lessons from Nuclear Weapons', *Contemporary Security Policy*, 40(3), pp. 285–311.
Mueller, M. L. (2020) 'Against Sovereignty in Cyberspace', *International Studies Review*, 22(4), pp. 779–801.
Roberts, H., Cowls, J., Morley, J., Taddeo, M., Wang, V. and Floridi, L. (2021) 'The Chinese Approach to Artificial Intelligence: An Analysis of Policy, Ethics, and Regulation', *AI and Society*, 36, pp. 59–77.
Sastry, G., Heim, L., Belfield, H., Anderljung, M., Brundage, M., Hazell, J., O'Keefe, C., Hadfield, G. K., Ngo, R., Pilz, K., Gor, G., Bluemke, E., Shoker, S., Egan, J., Trager, R. F., Avin, S., Weller, A., Bengio, Y. and Coyle, D. (2024) 'Computing Power and the Governance of Artificial Intelligence', arXiv, 2402.08797. https://doi.org/10.48550/arXiv.2402.08797.
Schmitt, L. (2022) 'Mapping Global AI Governance: A Nascent Regime in a Fragmented Landscape', *AI and Ethics*, 2(2), pp. 303–314.
Sheehan, M. (2023) *China's AI Regulations and How They Get Made*. Carnegie Endowment for International Peace, Working Paper, July.
Smuha, N. A. (2021) 'From a "Race to AI" to a "Race to AI Regulation": Regulatory Competition for Artificial Intelligence', *Law, Innovation and Technology*, 13(1), pp. 57–84.
Tallberg, J., Erman, E., Furendal, M., Geith, J., Klamberg, M. and Lundgren, M. (2023) 'The Global Governance of Artificial Intelligence: Next Steps for Empirical and Normative Research', *International Studies Review*, 25(3), p. viad040.
Truby, J. (2020) 'Governing Artificial Intelligence to Benefit the UN Sustainable Development Goals', *Sustainable Development*, 28(4), pp. 946–959.
Veale, M. and Zuiderveen Borgesius, F. (2021) 'Demystifying the Draft EU Artificial Intelligence Act', *Computer Law Review International*, 22(4), pp. 97–112.
Webster, G., Creemers, R., Triolo, P. and Kania, E. (2017) *Full Translation: China's 'New Generation Artificial Intelligence Development Plan' (2017)*. DigiChina, New America. https://digichina.stanford.edu/work/full-translation-chinas-new-generation-artificial-intelligence-development-plan-2017/

Appendix

Appendix A

1. Interview Corpus

This appendix documents the full corpus of semi-structured interviews on which Chapter 3 of this book draws. Interviews were conducted via Zoom or in person between March 2024 and July 2025 with regional experts on data protection, cybersecurity law and digital infrastructure across Southeast Asia, Central Asia, sub-Saharan Africa, North Africa and the United States. Interviewees were selected on the basis of demonstrated subject-matter expertise, including academic publication, regulatory practice or senior civil-service experience in data protection or cybersecurity, and willingness to speak on the record about regulatory drafting, implementation or commercial environment in their case country or region. Interviews were recorded with consent and partially transcribed. Quotations cited in Chapter 3 and elsewhere in the manuscript are taken from those transcriptions, lightly edited for readability and verified against the recording.

Interviewees are referred to throughout the manuscript by interview code (Interview-XX-N, where XX is the country code) rather than by name. Names, institutional affiliations and other potentially identifying information have been withheld at the request of interviewees who agreed to speak on a not-for-attribution basis, or as a uniform protocol across the corpus to ensure consistency. Full transcripts are retained on file by the author and may be made available for verification by editors or qualified scholars on request, subject to interviewee consent.

The relationship between the interview corpus and the chapter is one of triangulation rather than statistical inference. Interview testimony is used to confirm, complicate, or contextualise patterns visible in the quantitative and documentary streams, not to substitute for them. Where a claim rests substantially on interview testimony, this is noted in the case study, and the claim is supported by reference to the secondary literature where comparable empirical evidence is available.

2. *Interview Roster*

Code	*Country/region*	*Role*	*Date*	*Format*
Interview-VN-1	Vietnam	Personal-data-protection researcher; comparative perspective on East Asian regimes.	9 July 2025	Zoom
Interview-KZ-1	Kazakhstan	Academic specialist in cybersecurity policy; previously senior civil servant.	13 June 2025	Zoom
Interview-MY-1	Malaysia	Privacy practitioner working in regulatory compliance.	4 July 2025	Zoom
Interview-ZM-1	Zambia	Compliance lawyer at a national risk advisory; in contact with the Data Protection Commissioner.	12 March 2024	Zoom
Interview-ET-1	Ethiopia	Academic specialist in digital protection law.	10 March 2024	Zoom
Interview-KE-1	Kenya/United States	Academic researcher on Africa-China digital relations, US-based.	21 April 2024	Zoom
Interview-MW-1	Malawi	Practitioner specialising in data protection law.	24 April 2024	Zoom
Interview-NG-1	Nigeria	Academic specialist in data protection law.	18 March 2024	Zoom
Interview-NG-2	Nigeria	Academic researcher on AI governance in Africa, US-based.	8 April 2024	Zoom
Interview-NG-3	Nigeria	Academic specialist in data protection law.	1 April 2024	Zoom

(*Continued*)

Code	*Country/region*	*Role*	*Date*	*Format*
Interview-ZA-1	South Africa	Academic specialist in China-Africa digital relations.	24 April 2024	Zoom
Interview-US-1	United States	Practitioner at a major US law firm; comparative perspective on Africa-China.	26 April 2024	Zoom
Interview-ZW-1	Zimbabwe	Academic and practitioner specialising in digital rights.	11 April 2024	Zoom

3. Topics Covered and Representative Observations

The summaries below indicate the topics each interview covered and provide representative observations bearing on the manuscript's argument. Direct quotations in italics are taken from the transcript. Where an interview's content is partially or wholly reproduced as quotations in Chapter 3, this is indicated.

3.1 Interview-VN-1 (Vietnam)

Topics: Vietnam's 2018 Cybersecurity Law and 2023 Personal Data Protection Decree; relationship to Chinese regulatory architecture; Vietnamese civil society and private sector attitudes toward Chinese technology; data localisation provisions and their evolution; the role of the Ministry of Public Security in cybersecurity enforcement.

Representative observations. The interviewee insisted that direct Chinese influence on Vietnam's legal drafting cannot be evidenced from the public record. Vietnamese lawmakers do not cite China as a model, and there is no documented exchange of drafts between Vietnamese and Chinese counterparts. Yet the same interview characterised the underlying logic of Vietnamese cyber and data legislation as ideologically continuous with the Chinese model: a state-dominant regime in which the state acts as the ultimate protector of data, in which national security takes priority over the freedom of data flows, and in which enforcement is centralised in a single security ministry. The interviewee characterised the underlying logic of Chinese law as 'very similar to Vietnam's' on the dimensions of state dominance, centralised power and national security focus. On data localisation, the interviewee reported that Vietnamese civil society and the private sector view Chinese technology with pronounced scepticism, driven by nationalism and security concerns, but oriented toward economic protectionism ('Buy Vietnamese' campaigns) rather than direct contestation of regulatory borrowing.

Used in Chapter 3, §2.1 (Vietnam case).

3.2 Interview-KZ-1 (Kazakhstan)

Topics: the 2013 Law on Personal Data and Their Protection; data localisation policy; Russian platform compliance; Kazakhstan's pragmatic learning from Estonian, EU and Chinese frameworks; the Digital Silk Road relationship; Chinese commercial presence in Kazakhstan's telecommunications sector.

Representative observations. The interviewee was unambiguous in attributing Kazakhstan's data-localisation requirement to Chinese practice:

> After studying Chinese policy in terms of cyber security, we took experience that all personal data of Kazakhstan should be saved in the location of Kazakhstan territory. In the local, I mean, server... This policy was applied from Chinese experience, from Chinese policy. We applied it in Kazakhstan'.

On the broader regulatory environment, Kazakhstan was characterised as pragmatically learning from multiple foreign experiences without ideological alignment to any particular bloc. The stated normative orientation was integrationist: 'Kazakhstan is all the time open for other countries... we have to collaborate and communicate and build our networking with other countries'. On Chinese commercial presence: 'We don't have Chinese companies in Kazakhstan... I personally, I haven't heard anything about Chinese companies in the mobile networking industry', a finding consistent with the AidData record showing Huawei as an upstream equipment supplier rather than a consumer-facing operator.

Used in Chapter 3, §2.4 (Kazakhstan case).

3.3 Interview-MY-1 (Malaysia)

Topics: 2024 amendments to Malaysia's Personal Data Protection Act; the 2024 Cybersecurity Act; relationship between Malaysian, EU GDPR and Chinese PIPL frameworks; transfer impact assessments; Malaysia's hybrid regulatory architecture; the 'privacy paradox' in Malaysian society.

Representative observations. The interviewee framed Malaysia's approach as deliberately hybrid: aligning with EU GDPR-style regulation as the primary template while drawing practical lessons from Chinese frameworks. On data localisation, Malaysia did not impose direct localisation requirements but instead adopted transfer impact assessments to evaluate whether the recipient country provides equivalent protection. On cyber sovereignty, the interviewee observed that Malaysia's 2024 Cybersecurity Act reflects a growing emphasis on cyber sovereignty defined territorially and extended to the protection of cyberspace, echoing China's expanded conception of sovereignty without adopting Chinese terminology wholesale. The interviewee described privacy professionals and multinational companies as facing genuine dilemmas navigating between China's stricter data governance frameworks and looser regulations elsewhere, indicating that the regulatory environment is treated as plural rather than aligned with any single foreign reference.

Used in Chapter 3, §2.3 (Malaysia case).

3.4 Interview-ZM-1 (Zambia)

Topics: Zambia's 2024 data-protection regulation; relationship between the regulation, Chinese frameworks and the EU GDPR; Smart Zambia and the National Data Center; absence of public political controversy over Chinese influence; the trigger role of Google fines in regulatory awareness.

Representative observations. 'In terms of China's influence, China has been very helpful actually in terms of the African landscape of data protection', with Huawei and ZTE specifically named as platforms that have helped to increase data-protection awareness and provided technology now used in Zambia's data-protection efforts. Reading of regulatory borrowing: 'Our new Zambian regulation has borrowed a little bit from your regulation in China as well as the GDPR, except my observation is that your regulations in China are a little bit more stringent in terms of the penalties'. On legislative independence: 'Zambian legislators have still been independent despite growing influence', framing the Zambian regulatory development as driven by perceived necessity in a globalising data-protection environment rather than alignment to any external bloc. On public mobilisation: 'I haven't seen any uproar in terms of Chinese influence at this point, no'.

Used in Chapter 3, §2.5 (Zambia case).

3.5 Interview-ET-1 (Ethiopia)

Topics: Chinese presence in Ethiopian and African digital infrastructure; African Union digital governance posture; Chinese AI policy as potential future influence; the EU as primary regulatory reference for African data protection law.

Representative observations. 'China has been directly involved in many ways in the continent in Africa… But when it comes to governance and regulation, I think the participation of China was largely absent, if not insignificant'. On regulatory influence: 'When it comes to making data protection law, for example. In Africa in the past two decades, the primary influence came from Europe, particularly the European Union'. On infrastructure: 'The Chinese government has supported the African Union, the regional organisation, in building data centres, in helping them build the digital infrastructure that supports the AU'. The interviewee framed Chinese involvement as currently in 'phase one' (infrastructure), with a possible 'phase two' (alternative legal framework) in the future.

Available for use in Chapter 4 regional analysis (Africa) and the Conclusion's forward-looking discussion.

3.6 Interview-KE-1 (Kenya/United States)

Topics: Africa-China digital relations more broadly; cyber sovereignty as a conceptual alignment between China and several African states; infrastructure dominance versus regulatory influence; differential alignment between Kenyan, Nigerian and South African positions.

Representative observations. Chinese companies (notably Huawei) and Chinese financing institutions (China Exim Bank) have built and funded key components such as data centres and fibre-optic networks in Kenya, South Africa, and Ethiopia. 'While Chinese companies like Huawei may lobby for specific regulatory outcomes, the broader governance frameworks in African countries tend to be more heavily shaped by European actors'. On cyber sovereignty: there is conceptual alignment between several African governments and China, both viewing AI and digital technologies as tools for economic development and public security; many African governments have shown openness to the cyber sovereignty principle, seeing the state as the most credible agent to ensure technology serves national development and security goals. 'When it comes to governance, understood as the laws, regulations, and norms that dictate how technologies are used, China's influence is more indirect'.

Available for use in Chapter 3 (Africa cases beyond Zambia) and Chapter 4.

3.7 Interview-MW-1 (Malawi)

Topics: Malawi's Data Protection Act (2024); the National Data Center; absence of direct legal alignment with China; reliance on GDPR-style cross-border data transfer rules; smart village and smart nation projects; cyber sovereignty discourse in Malawi.

Representative observations.

> Chinese companies like Huawei have indirectly shaped Malawi's digital landscape by building critical infrastructure such as the National Data Center, smart villages, and smart nation projects, significantly boosting internet connectivity and driving the need for data regulation. However, there is no direct legal alignment with China: Malawi's Data Protection Act (2024) is modeled on the EU's GDPR.

Malawi has no strict data localisation laws akin to China's. Cross-border transfers are permitted under GDPR-like conditions including public interest and lawfulness. Malawi's recent focus on cyber sovereignty aligns broadly with global trends including China's emphasis on sovereignty, without direct alignment.

Available for use in the Africa cross-case discussion.

3.8 Interview-NG-1 (Nigeria)

Topics: Nigeria's data-protection law; the 2022 Twitter dispute and resulting localisation rules; tensions between GDPR-modelled law and Chinese-modelled governance posture; the Digital Silk Road; Nigeria's enforcement of physical-presence requirements for foreign tech firms.

Representative observations.

> China's influence is actually… in the area of governance. Many African countries have data protection laws, but modeled after the GDPR. [...] Nigeria was looking towards China in terms of how it relates to digital companies… adopting a heavy-handed kind of approach. [...] Subsequently, Nigeria came

> up with regulations requiring physical presence of those companies… similar to China's model.

On data localisation, Nigeria's framework reflects GDPR principles, but the focus on state control – particularly the ability to demand data from companies during political crises – aligns with critiques of a 'Chinese mode' prioritising national security over individual rights.

Available for use in the Africa cross-case discussion and in Chapter 4 (regional treatment).

3.9 Interview-NG-2 (Nigeria, AI Governance Focus)

Topics: AI governance in Africa; Western funding versus Chinese infrastructural leverage; the absence of African-language AI models from Chinese firms; the Nigerian, Kenyan and AU Continental AI strategies.

Representative observations. 'China's influence on African digital governance is currently infrastructural rather than strategic in AI. While its telecom dominance provides a foundation for future AI ecosystems, Western actors shape most AI policies and research'. African AI strategies prioritise tackling poverty, healthcare and infrastructure gaps, mirroring China's past development challenges but at an earlier stage. Chinese companies like Alibaba and Baidu have not developed AI models for African languages or contexts, unlike Western tech firms with localised investments. African AI strategies are heavily funded by Western organisations (UNESCO, UNDP, Gates Foundation) and tech giants (Meta, Google, IBM, Microsoft).

Available for use in the AI section of the Conclusion (Chapter 6).

3.10 Interview-NG-3 (Nigeria)

Topics: Nigerian data-protection law and its EU model; data-localisation requirements as possibly Chinese-derived; Chinese contribution to Nigerian digital infrastructure; the absence of formal Chinese-Nigerian regulatory partnership.

Representative observations.

> In terms of data localisation, we know that the data localisation requirement didn't really come from the Europeans that we have largely borrowed from. […] There are some groups of scholars that are thinking that maybe we may have borrowed data localisation requirements from the Chinese because a couple of African countries have strict data localisation provisions in their data protection law or other aspects.

On infrastructure:

> Of course the Chinese are very, very impactful in building Nigerian digital infrastructure. And in fact, compared to the Europeans, I think the Chinese are much more influential in assisting with the building of digital infrastructure.

Available for use in the Africa cross-case discussion and in Chapter 4.

3.11 Interview-ZA-1 (South Africa)

Topics: South Africa's draft data and cloud policy; the abandoned data-localisation proposal; Chinese commercial role in 5G and data centres; absence of formal regulatory alignment with China.

Representative observations.

> China's influence on digital governance in South Africa has been largely indirect. By promoting concepts like cyber sovereignty and data localisation in international forums such as the ITU, China has helped shape global discourse, which indirectly informs policy debates in South Africa.

South Africa's draft data and cloud policy included China-style data localisation but was abandoned after recognising impracticality (lack of domestic tech capacity). Chinese companies (Huawei, ZTE, Alibaba Cloud) have played a significant role in building South Africa's digital infrastructure, with Huawei dominant in the 5G landscape, but these projects are primarily driven by commercial interests rather than political agreements or state involvement.

Available for use in the Africa cross-case discussion and in Chapter 4.

3.12 Interview-US-1 (United States)

Topics: US-based legal practitioner perspective on Africa-China digital governance; the Digital Silk Road; flexibility in Chinese project enforcement versus EU-derived African legal frameworks; data sovereignty as concept and as practice in African contexts.

Representative observations.

> China's influence is primarily economic and infrastructural, not regulatory. Through initiatives like the Digital Silk Road, Chinese companies (e.g., Huawei, ZTE) have built critical digital infrastructure (e.g., telecom networks, fibre-optic cables). However, African data regulations are largely shaped by European models (e.g., GDPR) due to trade dependencies and EU technical assistance.

Examples like Nigeria's NDPR or Kenya's Data Protection Act align more with GDPR than China's PIPL. Cyber sovereignty as a concept resonates in African debates about data localisation and control, but laws remain European-influenced.

Available for use as a comparative non-African perspective in Chapter 3 cross-case discussion.

3.13 Interview-ZW-1 (Zimbabwe)

Topics: Zimbabwe's common law framework; the Cyber and Data Protection Act; the Postal and Telecommunications Regulatory Authority (PORTAR); Chinese involvement in biometric voter registration and facial-recognition systems; the absence of independent supervisory oversight under the GDPR model.

Representative observations. Zimbabwe's legal framework is heavily influenced by common law, with strong historical connections to Europe and the UK. 'While China's influence on legal practices is difficult to quantify, there are practices that resonate with Chinese methods'. On data privacy framework: three rationales (national security, trade, human rights), with the latter influenced by GDPR and the first resembling Chinese practice. PORTAR was already involved in data protection before the Cyber and Data Protection Act and was designated as the Data Protection Authority, but it does not qualify as an independent data protection authority under the GDPR model: PORTAR's board is appointed by the President in consultation with the Minister, and they can be dismissed at will. Chinese companies have been involved in projects such as the procurement of biometric voter registration systems and facial-recognition software.

Available for use in Chapter 3 cross-case discussion (Sub-Saharan Africa) and Chapter 4.

3.14 Interview-AF-1 (Pan-Africa Composite Synthesis)

Topics: Africa-wide synthesis drawn from the African interviews above. Themes: Chinese influence is infrastructural rather than legislative across the continent; data localisation rules in several African states (Nigeria, Kenya) are driven by sovereignty concerns rather than direct Chinese influence; alignment on cyber sovereignty as state-centric governance is shared across several African states; engagement with China proceeds through the Digital Silk Road and FOCAC.

This synthesis interview compiles the African interviewees' observations on the four core questions of Chapter 3 and Chapter 4: data regulation, cross-border data transfer, AI governance, and cyber sovereignty. The interviewees were unanimous that European frameworks shape the legal text of African data-protection regimes and that Chinese influence operates principally through infrastructure, capacity-building and the modelling of cyber sovereignty as a discursive frame rather than through specific legal-text borrowing.

Available for use in Chapter 4 (regional analysis), the Africa-wide cross-case sections of Chapter 3, and the Conclusion.

4. Notes on the Corpus

Sample composition. The corpus is intentionally weighted towards African expert opinion (eight of the fourteen interviews) because Africa is the region in which the claim of Chinese normative influence is most vigorously made in the existing literature, and in which the gap between supply-side documentation (Chinese infrastructure provision) and demand-side documentation (recipient-state regulatory reasoning) is widest. The Vietnam, Kazakhstan and Malaysia interviews supply the deepest case material because those three countries are also subject to the most detailed comparative-legal and TF-IDF analysis in Chapter 3. The US-based legal-practitioner perspective is included as a comparative non-recipient view that triangulates the African expert testimony.

Limitations. The corpus is exploratory rather than statistically representative. It does not constitute a probability sample of any defined population, and findings should be read as illustrative of patterns also visible in the documentary record, not as evidence of independent variation. Interview testimony cannot, on its own, establish the operative mechanisms of normative diffusion; it can corroborate, contextualise or complicate findings drawn from quantitative and documentary streams. The chapter is explicit about which claims rest substantially on interview testimony and supports those claims with secondary literature where available.

Reproducibility. The interview protocol was a semi-structured instrument organised around six topic areas: regulatory influence and policy adoption, infrastructure and economic influence, geopolitical and strategic considerations, AI governance, public perception and domestic response, and concluding open questions. The full instrument is retained on file by the author and is available on request for verification by editors or qualified scholars.

Appendix B

1. Interview Protocol

The interviews documented in Appendix A were conducted using a semi-structured instrument organised around six topic areas. The instrument was intended as a guide rather than a fixed script: the ordering of questions was adapted to the expertise of each interviewee, and follow-up probes were used to clarify or elaborate answers as appropriate. The full instrument is reproduced below; individual transcripts are retained on file by the author and may be made available, subject to interviewee consent, for verification by editors or qualified scholars on request.

2. Regulatory Influence and Policy Adoption

- How would you describe the principal external influences on data protection and cybersecurity legislation in [country/region]? Which models, if any, do drafters and regulators most commonly cite?
- Have any provisions in the legislation you have worked with or studied been drawn explicitly from non-Western models, and if so, from which jurisdictions?
- Do you see structural similarities between local legislation and the Chinese Cybersecurity Law (2017), Data Security Law (2021), or Personal Information Protection Law (2021)? Where, and to what extent?
- Has Chinese practice been raised in legislative debate, regulatory drafting or parliamentary committee work? In what register – favourable, cautionary, neutral?

3. Infrastructure and Economic Engagement

- Which Chinese firms (Huawei, ZTE, Hikvision, Dahua, China Telecom, others) operate in your country's digital infrastructure, in which segments, and on what scale?

- Are these projects primarily commercial, or are they associated with state-to-state cooperation frameworks (Digital Silk Road, FOCAC, BRI digital cooperation MOUs)?
- What financing arrangements are typical, and what conditions or technology-transfer requirements have been negotiated?
- Have these arrangements affected procurement rules, technical standards selection or regulatory drafting?

4. Geopolitical and Strategic Considerations

- How do domestic policymakers position the country between Chinese, European and American digital-governance offers?
- Are there explicit hedging strategies – e.g., using Chinese infrastructure but European regulatory templates?
- How do regional organisations (ASEAN, AU, SCO, BRICS, RCEP) shape the menu of governance options that policymakers consider?
- Has Chinese cyber sovereignty discourse become recognisable in domestic political vocabulary, even if not formally adopted?

5. AI Governance

- Is AI governance currently being treated as continuous with data and cybersecurity governance, or as a separate policy domain?
- Which external AI governance models are most influential – Chinese (Global AI Governance Initiative; the 2023 generative AI measures), European (AI Act), American (executive orders, NIST framework)?
- Are Chinese AI infrastructure or model offers (Huawei, Alibaba, Baidu, SenseTime, MiniMax) under active consideration, and on what terms?
- Are training-data sourcing, compute access and content-generation governance being addressed at the national, regional or multilateral level?

6. Public Perception and Domestic Response

- How is Chinese involvement in domestic digital infrastructure perceived by civil society, media, the technical community and the private sector?
- Have any Chinese-linked deployments produced controversy, parliamentary inquiry or regulatory reversal?
- Are there domestic constituencies (security services, telecoms regulators, ministries of trade) with divergent preferences about Chinese digital cooperation?

7. Concluding Open Questions

- Looking ahead five to ten years, where do you expect the principal sources of regulatory templates to come from in your jurisdiction?
- Are there developments – political, technological or geopolitical – that you expect to substantially shift the current configuration?

- Is there an aspect of Chinese digital governance influence on which the existing scholarship is, in your view, particularly mistaken or underdeveloped?

Appendix C

1. Glossary of Chinese-Language Digital-Governance Terms

The following Chinese-language terms recur throughout the manuscript, with their pinyin, characters, customary English rendering and brief contextual gloss. Translations follow the conventions of the DigiChina translations and the Stanford-Leiden University academic literature where these are settled, and are flagged where contested.

wangluo qiangguo (网络强国) – Strong cyber power/cyber superpower

Xi Jinping's slogan, in use from his February 2014 speech to the CCP cyber leading group, signals an aspirational and material project of Chinese ascendancy in cyberspace across infrastructure, standards and norms.

wangluo zhuquan (网络主权) – Cyber sovereignty

The doctrinal claim that states possess ultimate authority to regulate the internet within their jurisdiction, including the right to determine the rules governing information flows, infrastructure, platforms and data, and the right to resist external interference. Articulated in international form from the 2010 White Paper onward; institutionalised through the 2014 Wuzhen Declaration draft and the 2017 International Strategy of Cooperation on Cyberspace.

xinxi anquan (信息安全) – Information security

Distinct from cybersecurity in its narrower English sense: includes content as a security domain, encompassing disinformation, foreign political influence and politically destabilising content. Russian/Chinese usage in the SCO Code of Conduct is closer to this conception than to Western 'cybersecurity'.

wangluo anquan (网络安全) – Cybersecurity/network security

Term used in the 2017 Cybersecurity Law (CSL) and successor instruments. In Chinese legal usage, materially broader than the ICT-security framing common in Western legal texts; includes elements of content governance and political-stability protection.

shuju anquan (数据安全) – Data security

Both an economic-development and a national-security category, codified in the 2021 Data Security Law (DSL). Establishes hierarchical classification – 'core data', 'important data', general data – with corresponding state access and cross-border transfer obligations.

geren xinxi baohu (个人信息保护) – Personal information protection

Title of the 2021 PIPL. Architecturally GDPR-like at the surface (consent, data-subject rights, transfer mechanisms) but operationalised within a state-sovereign framework rather than a rights-protective constitutional one.

guanjian xinxi jichu sheshi (关键信息基础设施) – Critical information infrastructure (CII)

Statutory category established by the CSL and elaborated in the 2021 CII Security Protection Regulations; designation triggers expanded supervisory authority, procurement controls and localisation obligations.

renlei mingyun gongtongti (人类命运共同体) – Community of common destiny/community of shared future for humankind

The most general of Xi-era foreign-policy formulae; in the digital domain, rendered as 'community of shared future in cyberspace' (网络空间命运共同体). Functions as a legitimising umbrella for sovereignty-first multilateral governance proposals.

buganshe (不干涉) – Non-interference

Long-standing post-1955 Chinese foreign-policy commitment, in cyberspace policy presented as the corollary of cyber sovereignty: no state may dictate to another how it manages its networks, data or digital public sphere.

shuzi sichouzhilu (数字丝绸之路) – Digital Silk Road

External rather than official Chinese coinage, used to refer to the digital component of the 2013 Belt and Road Initiative. Beijing has not formally endorsed the term but has progressively absorbed activities so labelled into a broader state-strategic agenda.

INDEX

Acharya, A. 16, 30, 33, 40, 42, 43, 85, 115
adaptation: bilateral norm diffusion 52–53, 60, 63; Chile 79, 83; Kazakhstan 87, 90; Malaysia 84–86; recipient agency 99–101, 103; regional institutions 112, 125–126; *see also* translation
Africa: Chinese digital infrastructure 3, 20, 31, 93, 97; data governance 121, 127; South–South coalition-building 142, 146, 153–159; *see also* Egypt; Zambia
African Union 6, 121, 127
agenda-setting: international institutions 138; regional institutions 109, 123–125, 127
AI governance 98, 122, 124, 127, 146–148, 154, 157–161, 171–174, 177; interviews 181, 186, 188–190
ASEAN 2, 10–12, 31–33, 58, 61, 74, 77, 79, 82, 86, 90, 103; Chinese normative vocabulary 109, 116, 119–120; EU counter-pull and limits of influence 123–126; regional comparison 126–128
attribution problem 12, 33, 40–41, 44, 51–52, 60–62, 65, 69–70, 77–78, 80, 84, 88, 91, 93, 102; at regional level 109–110, 126–127; at international level 154, 158, 161

Beijing Effect 8, 31, 34, 40, 42–43, 57, 85, 117–120, 123, 125–126, 153
BeiDou Navigation Satellite System 3
Belt and Road Initiative (BRI) 3–4, 30; *see also* Digital Silk Road
bilateral mechanisms: attribution 60–62; conceptual framework 46–52; empirical comparison 69–103; infrastructure and technical assistance 47–50; push and pull dynamics 47–48; recipient demand 50–52; resistance and filtering 50–52; *see also* adaptation; recipient agency
Bradford, A. 3, 5, 8, 21, 28, 54, 59, 85, 119, 125, 174
Brazil 3, 6, 16, 111, 121, 127, 134, 143–144, 177
BRICS 2, 6, 11–12, 53–55, 58, 61; declaratory legitimation and coalition construction 120–123; regional comparison 109, 116, 126–128; international coalition-building 131, 137, 154, 160; AI governance 175
Brussels Effect 5, 8, 21, 28, 54, 59, 85, 117–119, 125, 174
Budapest Convention on Cybercrime 51, 58–60, 131–133, 137, 141, 150

Cambodia 1, 8, 32–33, 116, 142
capacity building 47–50, 124, 154, 156, 158–160
Central Asia 6, 30–31, 69, 113, 153; *see also* Kazakhstan; Shanghai Cooperation Organisation
Chile: case selection and lexical results 69–73; distance, asymmetry and limits of public record 79–83; cross-case comparison 96, 98–103; RCEP/CPTPP comparison 117; international positioning 144
China Standards 2035 31, 33, 56, 149
CloudWalk 1
coalition-building: BRICS 120–123; international arena 131, 134, 137, 141–146, 148, 150–160; regional mechanisms 53, 54–58, 62, 109; South–South 152–160
content governance 19, 23, 31, 44, 116, 191
contestation: bilateral cases 79, 103; conceptual framework 19, 33, 52, 55, 57; international arena 131, 143, 147, 161; interviews 182
convergence: bilateral cases 69–103; conceptual and methodological limits

9–12, 40, 44, 46–48, 60–61, 65; regional institutions 109, 113, 115, 126–127; *see also* lexical similarity
Council of Europe 51, 59–60, 131–133, 137, 141, 150
Comprehensive and Progressive Agreement for Trans-Pacific Partnership (CPTPP) 32, 117–119
Creemers, R. 4, 6, 18–20, 24, 29, 56, 110, 119, 137–138, 152
critical information infrastructure 27, 52, 75, 114, 119, 139, 144
cross-border data flows 21, 28, 54, 58, 61, 116–118, 125–126, 147, 155–156, 161, 172; interviews 185, 188
cyber power, China as 3–4, 17–18, 30–34
cyber sovereignty: competing models 4–7; core normative cluster 18–23; domestic legal stack 23–29; external entrepreneurship 30–34; bilateral diffusion 40, 54–55, 74, 85–86; regional institutions 110–112, 121; international arena 131, 135, 138–145, 160; interviews and glossary 183–185, 187–188, 190–192; *see also* sovereignty-first governance
Cybersecurity Law (China) 1, 4, 8, 11, 23–29, 49, 69, 72, 74, 79–81, 87–88, 110, 114, 119; appendix 180, 182, 189, 191
cybersecurity reviews 27, 45–46, 51–52
Cyberspace Administration of China (CAC) 20, 23, 30–31, 50, 57, 74, 77, 138, 149

Dahua Technology 3
data as a resource 16–18, 22, 35
data classification 4, 23–24, 44, 46, 51, 61, 83
data governance: Chinese model 16–34; competing models 4–7; bilateral diffusion 69–103; regional institutions 109–128; international transformation 131–162; future trajectories 171–178
data localisation: bilateral cases 69–103; China's legal architecture 18–19, 23–27, 28, 35; competing models 4–9; conceptual framework 42, 44, 49, 52, 59, 63; international arena 143, 155; regional institutions 115, 117–120, 125, 127; interviews and glossary 182–188, 191
data protection: bilateral cases 69–103; China's regulatory model 23–29; competing models 5–6, 8, 11; regional institutions 116–119, 125; interviews 180–189
Data Security Law (China) 23–29, 69, 72, 110, 119, 146–147, 154, 161; appendix 189, 191
DeNardis, L. 3, 23, 31, 33, 57–59, 132–133, 149, 157, 177
demand-side mechanisms 7–8, 47–52, 63–64, 100–103; *see also* pull mechanisms; recipient agency
digital authoritarianism 1, 7–9, 32, 45, 61, 155, 176, 178
digital infrastructure: China's global footprint 3–4; bilateral mechanisms 47–50; case comparison 69–103; path dependence 57–58; regional and international leverage 112–114, 149–155; *see also* Digital Silk Road
digital normative power *see* normative power
Digital Silk Road 3–4, 8–9, 30–31, 90, 153–155; interviews 183, 185, 187–188, 190, 192
digital sovereignty: European Union 5, 21; regional and international use 121, 155–156, 160; theoretical framing 6, 41
discourse: Chinese normative vocabulary 17–22, 30; mechanisms 43; bilateral cases 72, 80, 88; regional institutions 110–112, 127; international arena 139, 159; future trajectories 174

Egypt: case selection and lexical results 69, 72–73; limit case 95, 97–98; cross-case comparison 101–104; regional and international positioning 120, 154, 156, 158–161; interviews 181
Erie, M. S. 8, 31, 33, 40, 42–43, 54, 85, 117, 123, 125–126, 153
European Union: Brussels Effect 5, 8, 21, 27, 54, 59, 85, 117–119, 125, 174; competing digital order 5–6, 21–23; counter-pull in ASEAN 123–126; international positioning 143–145; interviews 184–188; *see also* GDPR

Feldstein, S. 7, 45, 155
filtering: bilateral mechanisms 50–52, 70; recipient agency 99–103; *see also* adaptation; resistance
Finnemore, M. 30, 41, 58, 110, 115, 121–122

Forum on China–Africa Cooperation (FOCAC) 33, 56, 58, 153–156, 159
fragmentation of digital order 6–7, 18, 34, 171–178

General Data Protection Regulation (GDPR): bilateral influence 71–73, 79, 84–86, 92–93, 96, 102; China comparison 16, 23, 28–29; competing models 5, 8; conceptual framework 51, 54, 59–60; regional counter-pull 125; future implications 172, 174; interviews 183–188, 191
Group of Governmental Experts (GGE) 6, 11, 33–34, 131–132, 137–140, 159, 171
Global Digital Compact (2024) 2, 6, 11–12, 146–148, 161, 171, 175
Global South: competing digital orders 5–7; regional coalition-building 120–122, 127; international coalition-building 141–142, 154–159, 162–163; implications 177
global digital governance: competing models 4–7; conceptual framework 40–65; international transformation 131–162; possible trajectories 171–178

Hanoi Convention *see* UN Convention against Cybercrime
hedging: bilateral cases 69, 78–79, 82, 84–86, 99–103; conceptual framework 51, 64; international arena 143; interviews 190
Hikvision 3, 30, 49, 154
human rights: competing models 5–7; bilateral cases 92, 94; Budapest baseline 132–133, 137; cybercrime negotiations 139–146; future governance 172
Huawei: global footprint 3–4, 30, 34; bilateral mechanisms and cases 49–50, 69, 76–78, 80–82, 84, 86, 89–90, 92, 97, 101; international standards 149–155, 158; interviews 183–190
hybrid governance 84–86, 115, 171

Internet Corporation for Assigned Names and Numbers (ICANN) 4, 33, 58, 133–134, 148, 152, 157
Internet Engineering Task Force (IETF) 4, 58–59, 133, 148–152, 157
India 6, 16, 72, 109, 111, 113, 115–116, 121–122, 127, 143–146, 150, 157, 160, 175, 177
infrastructure dependence 47–50, 58–59, 69–103, 112–114, 149–155
International Telecommunication Union (ITU) 2, 8–9, 11–12, 33–34, 57–60, 111, 116, 134; standards and structural norm power 149–153; international mechanisms 158, 162, 174, 176; interviews 187
internet governance: Chinese normative model 17–35; competing models 4–8; global institutional baseline 131–138; institutional transformation 146–162; regional institutions 109–128

Kazakhstan: background and case selection 7, 9, 12, 32, 69–74; pull without available push and later documented engagement 87–91; cross-case comparison 99, 103; regional context 113, 139, 155; interviews 181, 183, 188

Laos: background and case selection 12, 32, 69, 71, 73; limit case 95, 98, 101
legal diffusion 10, 30, 40–65; bilateral cases 69–103; *see also* normative diffusion
legal transplantation 10, 30, 44, 69–103
legitimation: conceptual framework 12, 20, 53, 55, 64; regional institutions 109, 116, 120–121, 124; international arena 131, 138–162
lexical similarity analysis: method and corpus 10, 60–62, 70–74; Chile 79–83; Kazakhstan 87–91; Malaysia 84–87; Vietnam 74–79; Zambia 91–95; limit cases 95–98; cross-case configurations 98–103

Malaysia: case selection and lexical results 2, 12, 69, 71–74; selective hedging and hybrid governance 84–87; cross-case comparison 92, 99–103; international standards 150, 155; interviews 181, 183, 188
Manners, I. 4, 41, 110
memoranda of understanding (MOUs) 47–48, 77, 81, 84, 94, 97, 101, 133, 150, 157
Meserole, C. 7, 62
modularity of governance instruments 4, 44–46
Mueller, M. 34, 59, 111, 132–134, 150, 157, 177
multilateralism: China's strategy 131–162; competing institutional models 4–7; regional institutions 109–128
multistakeholder governance: competing models 4–6, 11, 20, 22–24, 30, 33;

conceptual framework 45, 55, 56; regional institutions 112, 115–116, 121–127; international baseline and transformation 131–162

National Intelligence Law (China) 5
New IP proposal 34, 151–152
norm entrepreneurship: China 11, 17, 30; international arena 135–146
norm lifecycle 30, 41–42, 58, 110, 115, 121–122
normative diffusion: attribution and method 40–65; bilateral cases 69–103; regional institutions 109–128; international arena 131–162; multi-level theory 40–60; push, pull and translation 46–52; *see also* legal diffusion
normative power: bounded and relational character 1–12, 171–178; China's digital norms 16–35; conceptual definition 40–46; bilateral mechanisms 46–52; bilateral cases 69–103; international mechanisms 55–60, 131–162; regional mechanisms 52–55, 109–128; *see also* recipient agency

Open-ended Working Group (OEWG) 6, 11, 33–34, 122, 131, 139–140, 159, 161, 171

path dependence 57–59, 112–114, 149–155
Personal Information Protection Law (China) 4, 23–29, 72, 110, 119
Philippines: background and case selection 8, 12, 69–73; limit case 95–96; cross-case comparison 99, 103; international positioning 143
platform governance 4–5, 9, 16, 18–21, 27, 40, 44, 59, 110, 115, 134, 139, 171, 173, 176
Polyakova, A. 7, 62
privacy: bilateral cases 72–73, 85–87, 95–96, 102–103; China's model 16, 23–24, 28–29; competing models 5, 9; conceptual framework 46; international baseline 132, 136–137, 146; interviews 181, 183, 188
pull mechanisms: bilateral level 46–48, 50–52, 63–64, 69–103; international level 54–60; regional level 52–55, 109–128; *see also* demand-side mechanisms; recipient agency
push mechanisms: bilateral level 46–50, 62–64, 69–103; international level 55–60, 131–162; regional level 52–55, 109–128; *see also* supply-side mechanisms

Regional Comprehensive Economic Partnership (RCEP) 11–12, 32, 61, 63; institutional anchoring 112, 116–120; regional comparison 109, 126–128
recipient agency: bilateral framework 46–52, 63–65; case evidence 69–103; regional institutions 123–127; implications 171, 177; *see also* adaptation; filtering; pull mechanisms; resistance
resistance: bilateral mechanisms 47, 50–52, 54, 60; case evidence 74, 76; international arena 137–138; theoretical framing 8, 10–11, 34, 43, 57
Russia: competing digital order 6–7; Central Asian infrastructure 32, 87–88, 113, 115–116; regional institutions 109, 121–123; international alignment and divergence 133–145, 148, 150, 157, 161–162

security reviews 24, 46, 52
Segal, A. 3, 6, 8, 34, 131
Shanghai Cooperation Organisation (SCO) 11–12, 32–33, 53, 58, 61; institutional anchoring 109, 112–116; regional comparison 120–123, 126, 128; international influence 136–140, 146, 154, 161
Sikkink, K. 30, 41, 58, 110, 115, 121–122
Snowden revelations 5–6, 132–134
South–South cooperation: conceptual framework 12, 43, 56, 58, 64; coalition construction 152–160; training and diplomacy 175
sovereignty-first governance: competing models 2, 6–7; Chinese model 17–35; regional institutions 58–60, 109–128; international transformation 131–162; future trajectories 171–174; *see also* cyber sovereignty
standards, technical: Chinese strategy 19, 30–35; conceptual mechanisms 43, 45, 57–59; international structural power 149–153; interviews 190
state control of cyberspace 4–7, 17–35, 40–65, 75, 131–162
Streinz, T. 8, 31, 33, 40, 42–43, 54, 85, 117–120, 123, 125–126, 153
structural power: digital infrastructure 3–4, 56–57; international standards 149–153

supply-side mechanisms 7–8, 47–50, 63–65, 69–103; *see also* push mechanisms
surveillance: China's global footprint 1, 3, 5, 7, 21, 30, 31; conceptual mechanisms 45, 48; bilateral cases 90, 93, 96; international governance 132, 135–136, 141, 153, 155, 162

technical assistance 23, 31, 45, 47–50, 76, 142, 156, 187
TikTok 3, 6
training programmes: bilateral mechanisms 47–50; bilateral cases 69, 77, 81, 85, 92, 97; China's external entrepreneurship 31–32; international and South–South cooperation 113, 154, 158–159; implications 172–177
translation of norms 42, 44, 46, 51–52, 61, 85, 110, 115; *see also* adaptation
Tunis Agenda 134, 136, 160

UN Convention against Cybercrime (Hanoi Convention): coalition-building 7, 141–146; implications 161, 171
United Nations: China's engagement 11–12, 33–34, 55–60; international arena 131–162; *see also* GGE; Global Digital Compact; OEWG; UN Convention against Cybercrime
United Nations General Assembly 31, 33, 131, 137, 140–148, 152–153, 161
United Nations Office on Drugs and Crime (UNODC) 123, 143–145, 156, 161
United States: competing digital order 4–5; bilateral cases 70, 80, 87; international arena 123, 131, 133–134, 138, 142, 144–145, 150, 161; future trajectory 176; interviews 180, 182, 184, 187

Vietnam: case selection and lexical results 1, 8, 12, 32, 69–74; multi-channel convergence 74–79; cross-case comparison 81–83, 92, 96, 98–103; regional context 119, 127; implications 173; interviews 181–182, 188

World Internet Conference 4, 20–21, 57, 138, 159
World Summit on the Information Society (WSIS) 55, 58, 132–136, 149, 160

Xi Jinping 1, 3–4, 20–21, 30, 81, 84, 111, 114, 138, 153, 159; glossary 191

Zambia: background and case selection 2, 12, 69–74; infrastructure-heavy, norm-light pattern 91–95; cross-case comparison 99–103; international and regional positioning 146, 148, 153, 155, 158; interviews 181, 184–185
ZTE 4, 30, 49, 76, 78, 82, 84, 86, 91–92, 97, 149, 153–154; interviews 184, 187, 189

For Product Safety Concerns and Information please contact our EU representative GPSR@taylorandfrancis.com Taylor & Francis Verlag GmbH, Kaufingerstraße 24, 80331 München, Germany

Batch number: 10739599

Printed by Printforce, the Netherlands